COMMUNAL SOCIETIES IN AMERICA
AN AMS REPRINT SERIES

Moravian Journals

RELATING TO

CENTRAL NEW YORK

1745-66

AMS PRESS

NEW YORK

Moravian Journals

RELATING TO

CENTRAL NEW YORK
1745-66

Arranged and Edited by

REV. WM. M. BEAUCHAMP, S. T. D.,

FOR THE

Onondaga Historical Association

1916

THE DEHLER PRESS
SYRACUSE, N. Y.

Library of Congress Cataloging in Publication Data

Beauchamp, William Martin, 1830-1925.
    Moravian journals relating to central New York.

    (Communal societies in America)
    Reprint of the 1916 ed. published by the Dehler Press,
Syracuse, N. Y.
    1. Indians of North America—New York (State)—
Missions. 2. Iroquois Indians—Missions. 3. Moravians
in New York (State)—History—Sources. 4. Morovian
Church—Missions. I. Onondaga Historical Association,
Syracuse, N. Y. II. Title.
E78.N7B37   1976   266'.4'09747   72-8246
ISBN 0-404-11000-2

Reprinted from the edition of 1916, Syracuse
First AMS edition published in 1976
Manufactured in the United States of America

AMS PRESS INC.
NEW YORK, N. Y.

MORAVIAN JOURNALS RELATING TO CENTRAL NEW YORK.

In this volume are given all the Moravian journals relating to Central New York, beginning with 1745, when the first visit was made to Onondaga. This concerned the removal of the Shekomeko converts from Dutchess County. The mission there, commenced in 1740, was legally closed in 1745, and the converts went first to Bethlehem, Pa., and then to Gnadenhutten. As most of Pennsylvania was subject to the Five Nations, their consent was necessary and this was obtained. In October, 1859, the Moravian Historical Society erected monuments at Shekomeko (town of Pine Plains) and at an adjoining missionary site in the town of North East, N. Y.

Meantime Count Zinzendorf was thinking of the Five Nations, with many odd conceits. In an address in London, March 7, 1743, he said: "The Second Nation, and which properly governs the rest, is the Nation of the Onondagoes. Those are Philosophers and such as among us are called Deists. They are brave honest People who keep their word; and their general weakness is that they delight in Heroick Deeds; and this will be the main Difficulty in the way of their Conversion, to make them forget these their heroick Notions; for they have the Principles of the old Romans, that they look upon every one as a miserable Creature, scarce worth a Thought, who will not submit himself to them. . . . The Two other Nations which are stiled *Children,* are the Cajugas and Oneydoes, who regulate themselves after these Two Nations."

Caxhayen, an Onondaga chief, lodged with him in Philadelphia in 1742, for two weeks, and at a subsequent conference the Count received a fathom of wampum (186 white beads), which became Bishop Spangenberg's credentials at Onondaga in 1745. Meantime several attempts to reach that place from Albany failed. Coming by a different route Spangenberg was successful. David Zeisberger was in every party. A great favorite, he became a member of an Onondaga family. Hachsitagechte and Tiozihostote were two of his Indian brothers. The former died at Bethlehem, and was buried at Nain. Though De Schweinitz states this in his life of Zeisberger, there is no intimation of it in the journals, as will appear. Other records at Bethlehem, however, preserve many facts.

Practically the Moravians did no missionary work in this part of New York. They neither preached nor baptized. Religious conversation depended on the Indians. The whole work was one of preparation, a study of the language and habits of life. The results were few. With one or two exceptions, Zeisberger's Iroquois linguistic work has not reached the public, and is somewhat disappointing. The work was so quiet that it made little impression on the Onondagas. In his history (1849) J. V. H. Clark said they had no tradition of such visits. Schoolcraft (1845) said: " I called Le Fort's attention to the residence of the Moravian missionary, Zeisberger. He said there was no tradition of such residence — that the oldest man remembered no such mission; that they were ever strongly opposed to all missionaries after the expulsion of the Jesuits, and he felt confident no such person, or any person in the character of a preacher, had lived at Onondaga Castle; that there must be some mistake in the matter."

Many interesting papers stored in the Moravian Archives in Bethlehem have been published, some of which relate to the western part of New York, but more to Pennsylvania. The latter may be passed over, with slight mention of the former. Thus in American Notes and Queries, 4th series, 1:259, Zeisberger's two trips to Goschgoschkin, 1767-67,via Chemung River, led Gen. J. S. Clark to publish notes on the Chemung towns. Mack's Onondaga Journal of 1752 is in the 3d series, 2:50, but I had my copy from the Moravian. The latter journal has also appeared in the Pennsylvania Magazine of History and Biography. In the same magazine (2:424) is Spangenberg's Journal, edited by Mr. John W. Jordan. Mr. Clark said of this: " My copy (originally furnished by Mr. Jordan) contains quite a little of matter omitted in the magazine article, but nothing of any great importance." Gen. Clark was a tireless annotator, and wrote me a very full account of what he had done on Moravian matters. The Cammerhoff

Journal was translated for him by Miss Clara Frueauff, as were those of Zeisberger and Rundt in 1752, and Zeisberger and Frey in 1753. Hon. George S. Conover, of Geneva, definitely located many of Cammerhoff's sites. The journal of 1754-5 was translated for me by Robert Rau, and also those of 1766 by Augustus H. Leibert. In the Magazine of American History, 1897, I published articles on the Moravians at Onondaga. Loskiel's history is an excellent compendium, and there is much of interest in Reichel's Memorials of the Moravian Church. De Schweinitz's Life of David Zeisberger is very useful, and the journal of Post and Zeisberger (1745) to Canajoharie, has appeared in part. Some things are in the Documentary History of New York.

Linguistic works are many. Zeisberger's Indian Dictionary — English, German, Onondaga and Delaware, was published in 1870, by Prof. E. N. Horsford, the original being at Harvard College with others. In Philadelphia are several of his works on the Onondaga language, perhaps of importance. One of his essays on an Onondaga grammar has appeared in the Pennsylvania Magazine (11:442), but he called it the "Onondaga al. Maqua Tongue," disregarding his Indian friends' advice on mixing dialects. His unpublished lexicon of the German and Onondaga languages is in seven volumes. There are manuscripts of interest by others, and the Moravian Diary teems with little incidents.

BISHOP A. G. SPANGENBERG'S JOURNAL OF A JOURNEY TO ONONDAGA IN 1745.

May 24. We set out from Bethlehem. Brother Huber accompanied us to our first night's encampment, which was in the woods under a tree.

May 25. Arrived in Heidelberg, where we spent the day.

May 26. Reached Tulpehocken. As Conrad Weiser was not yet prepared for the journey, we called on friends. We lodged at Michael Schaeffer's.

May 27. Bro. Spangenberg having determined to advise the Governor of his journey, wrote him a letter, to which Conrad Weiser added a few lines, and dispatched it by John Joseph.

May 28. Bro. Spangenberg called on Pastor Wagner, who is in charge of the Lutherans. Spent the night with George Loesch. His wife assisted us in completing our tent.

May 30. At Michael Schaeffer's Bro. Spangenberg found Bro. John Joseph, who had returned with letters from Philadelphia and Fredericktown; he had traveled one hundred and forty miles in three days. Gov. Thomas sent greetings through Bro. Brockden, and that he approved of my journey to the Six Nations. Our company met at Christopher Weiser's, Conrad's brother. In the afternoon we set out from Tulpehocken with Conrad Weiser and his two sons. Michael Schaeffer accompanied us for a few miles, and Philip Meurer and Bro. Nieke to our first night's encampment. After traveling ten miles we came to Kittatiny Hills, which are high and rocky, and difficult for horses to climb. On reaching the top we came to " Pilger Ruh," where we dismounted and rested. After descending we entered Anton's Wilderness, where we pitched our first tent, built a fire, pastured our horses, partook of a light supper and retired to rest. Our course to-day was N. W. *Observations:* Noticed certain plants and roots, *e. g.* 1. A certain plant which, with its root, is used for snake bites — has blossoms like " geese flowers." 2. Steer's root, as the English call it, good for colic. 3. Hypocacooana, good for vomiting. 4. Mountain tea.

May 31. Arose early, looked up our horses, took a little breakfast, and then continued our journey in the Name of God Our Saviour. Bro. Meurer and Nieke returned to Tulpehocken, with letters to Mary Spangenberg at Bethlehem. After passing the Great Swatara, we climbed the Thurnstein, a high mountain, rocky, and almost impassable for horses. On the summit we refreshed ourselves at Erdmuth's Spring, which flows through the valleys until it empties into the Susquehanna. We were four hours in crossing the mountain. At " Ludwig's Ruh," at the foot of the mountain, we nooned. Here Laurel Creek flows past. After dinner our course was N. W. We passed through Anna's Valley, beautiful and pleasing to the eyes, which lies in among the hills. At the Double Eagle, on Benigna's Creek, we passed the night.

June 1. We set out early, crossed the Leimback, and came to Jacob's Heights, the place where Bro. Jacob Kohn lost Bro. Ludwig's Hebrew Bible, and subsequently found it. At noon we reached " Cool Bank," on the Susquehanna, where we dined on a mess of fish caught by Bro. Zeisberger. Hence we passed through Joseph's Valley. Here four large snakes, stretched on a fallen tree, opposed the brethren who were leading the horses, and for a long time would not budge. At " Marienborn " we rested, and afterward reached the " Spangenberg." The descent was perilous to limb and life; came to Eva Creek, and thence to Shamokin to Shikellmy's house. We found neither him nor Andrew Montour at home. The former had gone to the mill, a ride of forty miles, and the latter was out hunting. We were told that two ministers and an Indian had been lately here — probably it was the Presbyterian Brainerd, and his interpreter Tatami. He had assembled the Delawares in Shikellmy's house, and (as Shikellmy's people told us) informed them that on Sundays they should assemble as the whites do, and pray as they do. Hence he would build a house for that purpose, and stay with them two years. That the Governor had given him orders to that effect, and he would be glad to see the Indians hearken to him. To this Shikellmy said: " We are Indians, and don't wish to be transformed into white men. The English are our Brethren, but we never promised to become what they are. As little as we desire the preacher to become Indian, so little ought he to desire the Indians to become preachers. He should not build a house here, they don't want one." They departed for Philadelphia the next day.

June 2. This morning Conrad Weiser dispatched a messenger per horse to Shikellmy, for him to return without delay, as we were waiting for him to guide us to Onondaga. Bro. Spangenberg called to see Shikellmy's daughter's child, a girl of fifteen years, who has had the fever and ague over two weeks. He gave her some fever powders, and soon the fever left her. They are fine people. Bro. Joseph also went over to the island, to visit Madam Montour from Canada, who lately with her family had become Indianized. Sattelihu's sister had a boil on her neck, on which Spangenberg laid a plaster to soften it. Bro. Joseph wrote to his wife. In a conversation with Conrad Weiser, he proposed that the Moravians should send a good blacksmith to live in Shamokin, to serve the Indians. "These," said he, "would be glad, and agree to all reasonable conditions; the Governor, also, would not object." We will take the matter into consideration. In regard to Wyoming — Weiser yesterday expressed himself thus: "That he deemed the exile of the Indian converts from Shecomeko necessary for the salvation of the other Indians from their misery." We must await developments at Onondaga.

June 3. Joseph and Conrad crossed the river to visit the Indian King who lives there, and had the honor to smoke a pipe with him. Spangenberg also visited Andrew Sattelihu's sister, and bled her, and bound up the boil which had discharged freely. Shikellmy's grandchild has had a relapse, having eaten bear's meat and fish. The Indians have no regard for advice as to diet. A runner was sent after Andrew Sattelihu, who is hunting on the West Branch, to return at once, to go with us to Onondaga. Philip and Frederick Weiser returned home to-day, and took our letters to Michael Schaeffer for delivery. Visited John Hickman, an intelligent Indian, and also his neighbor Daniel, who formerly lived in Tulpehocken. A number of the Indians who reside here, had removed from Tulpehocken when their lands were sold. Conrad Weiser stated that the proprietor had recently written to him, that he should associate some one with him who was conversant with Indian affairs, who would in time be competent to succeed him. *Query.* Whether not some of the Moravians — say David Zeisberger — to go and spend some time in the Six Nations to acquire the language, with also the recommendation of Governor Thomas?

June 4. Andrew Sattelihu returned this morning, and at once came to see us. Bro. Spangerberg and Zeisberger were over to the Island to visit his sister, and found her better. The runner who had been sent after Shikellmy returned at noon, and brought us word that he would return to-morrow. We also visited Allummapees, the hereditary King of the Indians. His sister's sons are either dead or worthless, hence it is not known on whom the Kingdom will descend. He is very old, almost blind, and very poor; but withal has still power over and is beloved by his people; and is a friend of the English. *Observations:* A certain plant which has leaves like hyssop, and a very aromatic odor. Another root, which has a very pleasant taste, blossoms with violet flowers, has two leaves above, four in the middle, and two below.

June 5. Shikellmy returned to-day. We made the acquaintance of one Patrick, an Indian Doctor.

June 6. Prepared for our journey. Bro. John Joseph and Andrew Sattelihu went to hunt horses on the other side of the Susquehanna, and were successful.

June 7. Began our journey to Onondaga. Our company is composed of Spangenberg, Conrad Weiser, John Joseph, David Zeisberger, Shikellmy, Andrew, his son, and Andrew Sattelihu; seven in all. Crossed the river, and traveled up the West Branch. Passed Shawane Creek, and the site of the town that formerly stood there. Next came to the place where Shikellmy formerly lived — it is now deserted. The land is excellent in this vicinity, the equal of which is seldom found. Our course has been several miles W., and then N. W., until we reached Warrior's Camp, where we passed the night. Two Indian warriors overtook us, one belonging to Otstonwaken, and the other to Onondaga. The latter had neither shoes, stockings, blanket, gun, hatchet, steel, or knife, and was almost naked; yet was determined in this condition to undertake a journey of 300 miles through the wilderness. Conrad asked him how he expected to continue his journey in his present condition. He replied: " God, who was in the Heavens, had created the earth and all the creatures; he kept so many creatures alive in the wilderness, that he was able and would provide for him." Both warriors had returned from a maraud against the Flatheads, and had lost all save their lives.

June 8. Our course was N. W. We crossed a creek near the Susquehanna, Canachrirage. On the way we found half a deer, which an Indian from Otstonwaken had shot, and being unable to carry all of it home, had hung the rest up in a tree, so that whoever needed it might take it — which we did. At noon we reached Otstonwaken. The Indians here treated us very well; boiled meat, and placed it before us in a large kettle. In the afternoon we proceeded on our journey, and at dusk came to the "Limping Messenger," or Diadachton Creek, and encamped for the night. *Observations:* On our way we passed the Shawanese town, and the place where two years ago, when Conrad was traveling to Onondaga, he was met by twenty Shawanese, each with a rifle ,two pistols, and a sabre.

June 9. Conrad Weiser sent the Onondaga warrior, who had been traveling with us thus far, ahead to inform the Council of our coming. We gave him flint, steel, knife, and provisions for the journey. Last night our horses strayed back to Otstonwaken, hence we were compelled to lay by until noon. After dinner we resumed our journey, and entered the wilderness. Our course was N. Our path lay through the valley between the " Ant Hills," one hill resembling another side by side, and so high that we could scarcely see to the summit. They are all peaked and resemble Ant Hills. In the evening we lodged at the "Coffee House," on Diadachton Creek.

June 10. It rained hard all day. Our course was N. for ten miles, then we turned, N. E. We are still between the Ant Hills, and follow the Diadachton. The forest is so dense that for a day the sun could not be seen, and so thick that you could not see twenty feet before. The path, too, is so bad that the horses were often stuck, and had to be extricated from the bogs; and, at other points, it lay full of trees, that had been blown down by the wind, and heaped so high that we were at a loss whether to turn to the right or to the left. In the evening we came to a salt-lick, where elks frequent, and camped for the night. At this place once three Indians lost their lives. Two of the Six Nations had two Flatheads prisoners, whom they were taking to Onondaga. As their prisoners had deported themselves quietly, they were no longer bound. While the Naguas were preparing their meal, their prisoners seized their guns and killed one on the spot. The other was chased among the trees and killed, not, however, before he had mortally wounded one of his prisoners with his tomahawk. The other escaped. The mark of the tomahawk cuts are still to be seen on the trees.

Our guides, Shikellmy, and his son, and Andrew Sattellihu saw fit to give us Magua names, as they said ours were too difficult for them to pronounce. Bro. Spangenberg they named *T'gerhitonti* (i. e., *a row of trees*) ; John Joseph, *Hajingonis* (i. e., *one who twists tobacco*) ; and David Zeisberger, *Ganousseracheri* (i. e., *on the pumpkin*). *Observations:* At the salt-lick we found the tracks of Elks, who came there to lick the salt. The Elk is a species of deer, like horses without a mane.

June 11. Set off from the salt-lick and traveled N. E.; reached the end of the Diadachton, and left the Ant Hills behind us. The path was very bad, so that one of our horses almost broke his leg, by getting into a hole between the roots of a tree. In the afternoon we found a cold roast of bear, which Indians had left on the hunt. As the meat was good we prepared it for dinner. In the evening we came to the " Bear's Claws " and camped. The Indians took the claws from the bear, and nailed them to a tree, hence the name. Here an Indian from Tioga lodged with us. From him we learned that our messenger was already one day ahead of us.

June 12. Our course was N. E. During the afternoon we left the wilderness, in which we were four days, and had scarce seen the sun. Even our horses were quite inspirited once again to leave the woods. We crossed a creek called Osgochgo, and then came to the North Branch of the Susquehanna. Here we found the trees curiously painted by the Indians, representing their wars, the number that had fallen in battle, and the number they had killed. From this point our course was N. W. We went up the Susquehanna to Tioga, by the narrow path on the mountain by the river. Crossed the branch that is called Tioga, and here empties into the Susquehanna. Here we found a Mohican town. We proposed to pitch our tent near by, but the Indians came and urged us to lodge with them, as they had prepared a house and beds for us. We accepted their invitation with many thanks. This spot is about 180 miles from Shamokin, and in a charming region of country.

June 13. Our course was again N. E. We kept up along the Susquehanna, and nooned about fifteen miles above Tioga, on the river bank. We hobbled our horses and led them to pasture. One of them got into the river beyond his depth, and being hobbled could not swim, consequently was drowned. We hurried to his rescue, but could not find a canoe in time to save him. Hence this place was called " Gashnecariorum," i. e., *"the dear spring."*

June 14. Set off from the "Dear Spring," and passed three islands, which we called John Penn, Thomas Penn, and Richard Penn. In the afternoon we came to a stream called Owego, which empties into the Suequehanna. There is an old Indian settlement here, which was deserted last spring. We left the river to our right, and proceeded up the stream. Here and there in the woods, we found posts set up, painted red, around which the Indians had danced; and others, at the feet of which there were holes, where they tie their prisoners when they return from a maraud — fixing their feet into the holes so they cannot escape. We encamped to-night on the banks of a creek called *Tiatach-schiunge,* which empties into the Owego. In the forenoon our course was N. E., and in the afternoon N. W.

June 15. Followed the Tiatachschiunge Creek. Our course was N. W. After dinner we left the creek, and passed another called Ganowtachgerage. Hence we crossed Prospect Hill. At the foot of the hill we crossed a creek which runs into the St. Lawrence. Camped in the " Dry Wilderness," where we had but little water.

June 16. To-day our course was E. N. E. Early in the morning we passed the first lake, which is called Ganiatara-gachrachat, and also five others, which empty into the Susquehanna. Nooned at Lake Ganneratareske. Journeyed further, and came at night to the large lake, Oserigooch, where we encamped.

June 17. Our horses strayed back in pasture to Lake Ganneratareske, hence we were compelled to lay by until near noon. The road was worse to-day than we have had before on the whole trip. Soon after starting we got the first Onondaga water to drink, which tastes salty. Our course was N. W. After dinner we reached Onondaga, where we were heartily and courteously received, and invited into the King's house, which we accepted.

June 19. In the evening, the Indians paraded through the town to the music of violins, flutes, and a drum; and also around the house where we lodged.

June 20. Bro. Spangenberg bled our host. There came, also, many sick, and asked for medicine, which he gave them, and the use of which the Lord blessed. Conrad Weiser informed the Council of the object of his visit, and laid his propositions before them. Having done this, the Indians placed a kettle of boiled corn before him and his companions, and what was left they ate. The Council then retired into another house, where they counseled until in the evening. Then the Black Prince came and informed Conrad, that as it was so late, the reply of the Council would be given to-morrow. The Indians to-night had a dance in our house. One beat a drum, and about twenty danced around the fire. The leader was distinguished by having rattles hanging to his legs. All yelled savagely, and, after having danced a quarter of an hour, the sweat ran down as if water had been poured over them. The dance lasted three hours, and it appeared impossible for them to hold out so long. The men dance abreast, and the women follow, and whoever can appear the most grotesque and leap the highest, receives the most praise. *Observations:* Our new host's name is Aschanchtioni; the chief men are Cannassatego, the Black Prince, and Caxhayn.

June 21. Bro. Spangenberg bled two Indians. The Council again met, but owing to the absence of some of the chiefs, Conrad's propositions were only partly acted upon. They suggested that they be deferred until Spring, when all the chiefs will meet in Philadelphia at the Treaty. Their warriors, nevertheless, would be instructed to discontinue hostilities, and the Governor of Canada informed that the Shawanese had been unfaithful to Brother Onas, and that he had, therefore, struck them on the head with a hatchet. After this a kettle of food was placed before Conrad and his companions. The Black Prince invited the whole Council and us to a feast. On this occasion they returned the strings of wampum to Conrad Weiser which he had sent from the " Limping Messenger " to announce our advent. In the evening the Indians again had a dance of three hours.

June 22. Bro. Spangenberg bled an Indian, and then with Conrad Weiser, Shikellmy, and Andrew Sattelihu set out for Oswego. Bro. John Joseph accompanied them to the lake (Onondaga), to bring back the horses. Six bark canoe loads of Indians went along.

June 27. Bro. Spangenberg returned from Oswego. While yet far out upon the lake, Canassatego spied them,

built a fire, and prepared food. When Bro. Spangenberg
landed, he requested him to bleed him.

June 28. Made preparations for our return journey
to-day.

June 29. Began our return journey. Our first halt
was made at Tiatachtont, where Bro. Spangenberg bled
Cannassatego's brother, and conversed with the young
Indian Bro. Zinzendorf found sick at Wyoming, and recommended to our notice. Here, also, we parted with Conrad
Weiser and Andrew Sattelihu, who traveled by the path to
the left, while we, with Shikellmy and his son, go to the
right. At noon it began to rain in torrents, and we were
soon wet to the skin. We left the large Lake Oserigooch
to the right, and by night reached Lake Gannerataraske,
where we encamped. Our course was S.

June 30. The rain continuing, we kept our tent until
noon. Then our course was S. W. for twelve miles, and
then E. until near night. Passed Lake Ganiateragachrae-
tont, and came to the Dry Wilderness, where we encamped.

July 1. Set out early to-day. Our course for one hour
was S. E., and then S. until noon. Crossed the creek that
flows into Canada, and came to Prospect Hill, at the base
of which runs the Ganontachorage, which we crossed. At
noon we reached the Tiatachtschiunge Creek, where we
rested. Bro. Joseph, who has been sick all day, took drops
to sweat. After dinner we traveled S. S. E., and at evening
encamped on the last named creek. While Bro. Joseph and
a Catawba were cutting down a rotten tree, with which to
make a smoke to protect ourselves against the gnats, Shikellmy came on the other side, and narrowly escaped receiving Bro. Joseph's axe in his body.

July 2. Our course was S. S. E. until 3 o'clock, and
S. W. until evening. At noon we reached Owego, the site
of the old Indian town. Passed the three islands in the
North Branch, and came to the " Dear Spring," where we
lost our horse, and encamped for the night. In the evening, two canoes filled with Indian women from Tioga, came
up to hunt for wild beans. Bro. Spangenberg cut his foot
while gathering brush.

July 3. To Tioga, which we reached at noon, our
course was S. W. Here the Indians supplied us with some
provisions, but not sufficient for our journey — they had

but little to spare. Below Tioga we took the narrow path
along the Susquehanna. Towards evening we left the river
to our left, and at night camped on the Osgochgo. It rained
hard all night.

July 4. Our course was S. until noon. Passed the
" Bear's Claws," and encamped at the " Cold Roast."

July 5. At noon we came to the salt-lick whence the
Diadachton Creek issues. Toward night we found two old
Indian lodges, which we entered, as it was raining hard.
Our course until 10 o'clock was S. W., then W. until 12
o'clock, and afterwards S. W. We are now between the
Ant Hills.

July 6. Our course from 4 to 7 A. M. was S., then
S. W. till 9, then W. till noon. The Lord preserved us to-
day from two accidents. Early this morning, while riding
along the Diadachton Creek, Bro. Zeisberger fell with his
horse into the water, and struck his cheek on a stick he had
in his hand. For some time he lay unconscious. A little
farther lay a snake (a blower) as thick as the arm, in the
middle of the path. Bro. Spangenberg, Shikellmy, and his
son rode over it, and Bro. Zeisberger, who was leading his
horse, walked over it without seeing it. Last came Bro.
John Joseph — on him the snake turned, and attempted to
bite him and his horse twice. After our noon halt our
course was S., when we passed the " Coffee House," and left
the hill country. Three hours before night we reached the
" Limping Messenger," and the end of the wilderness, and
thence S. W. to Otstonwaken, where we lodged. As it had
rained all day we were wet to the skin, and as the Indians
had neither fire nor wood, we went to bed wet, and arose
next morning wet. For supper we had some fish, which
had been caught during the afternoon, for the Indians had
nothing to give us. We traveled 50 miles to-day.

July 7. Leaving Otstonwaken, we came again to the
West Branch; passed the Ganachrirage, and rested at noon
by the river. Our provisions were nearly exhausted. In
this strait an old Indian joined us, undid his pack, and took
out a smoked turkey, and told us to boil it — when we ate
and were satisfied. In the afternoon passed the "Streiter
Lage" (Warrior's Camp) and encamped by the river. For
supper we cooked a handful of rice for seven persons, which

the old Indian seeing, he got out some pieces of venison and put them in the kettle, and we had plenty.

July 8. This morning passed the place where Shikellmy formerly lived, next the Shawanese town and creek, and at noon reached Shamokin. Bro. Spangenberg and Zeisberger immediately crossed over to the island to visit Andrew Sattelihu's family, to deliver a message to his wife. On returning we found an Indian trader, from whom we purchased some flour. Continued on our journey, and at night reached " Marienborn."

July 9. Rested part of the day at " Marienborn," as the horses were much fatigued. Later in the day, when in " Joseph's Valley," we were overtaken by a fearful hailstorm. Hurried on, and when on the mountain the sun broke forth, and a beautiful rainbow spanned the valley back of us. Possed " Cool Bank," on the Susquehanna, and encamped on the Mechana Creek.

July 10. During the morning passed " Jacob's Height's," and came to the " Double Eagle." Here we found encamped a family of Indians, who on learning whence we had come, said we must be tired; and the man said to his wife, " Give them some spits full of venison." In return Bro. Spangenberg gave them knives and thimbles. Nooned at "Benigna's Creek," and at nightfall came to the " Thurnstein." As we were leading our horses down, Bro. Spangenberg, who was in advance, heard the rattle of a rattlesnake, and called to us to come kill it, but it could not be found. Encamped at the base of the " Thurnstein," on the Swatara.

July 11. Our course was S. E. We early entered " Anton's Wilderness," thence over the Kittatiny Mountain, and nooned on the Little Swatara. From thence we proceeded to Christopher Weiser's.

NOTES BY JOHN W. JORDAN, ON SPANGENBERG'S JOURNAL.

The Journal of Bishop Spangenberg was published in Vols. 2 and 3 of the Pennsylvania Magazine of History and Biography, (Hist. Soc. of Pennsylvania), contributed by Mr. John W. Jordan, with ample notes. He has generously placed the whole at my disposal, but his notes are necessarily shortened here and in a later journal.

"In 1745 it became evident that the Moravia Mission among the Mohegans of Shecomeko, in Duchess Co., N. Y., would have to be abandoned, unless its members could be induced to migrate to some locality in the then Indian country, where they would suffer no molestation from the whites. Bishop A. G. Spangenberg, David Zeisberger, and John Jacob Schebosch, on behalf of the Mission Board, set out from Bethlehem in May, for Onondaga, to treat with the Six Nations for permission for the Moravian Indians to remove to Wyoming." Consent was given, but they went to Bethlehem first, and in 1746 to Gnadenhutten.

Shebosch was born in Skippack, Pa., May 27, 1721, and died in Ohio, Sept. 4, 1788. His English name was Joseph Bull, but the Indians called him Shebosch (running water).

May 24. John Michael Huber came from the Tyrol in 1742.

May 25. Heidelberg in Berks Co., Pa.

May 25. Tulpehocken from the Delaware, Tulpewihacki, land of turtles. Conrad Weiser, the noted interpreter. Spangenberg first met him in 1736. Michael Schaeffer and wife came from Schoharie County, in 1725.

May 28. Loesch (now Lash), was a Schoharie Palatine, and went to Tulpehocken in 1723.

May 30. Charles Brockden, well-known resident, 1715-67. Weiser's sons were Philip J. and Frederick. John Philip Meurer came from Alsace in 1742, and George Nieke, from Herrnhut, in 1743. Kittatiny, "written also *Kechkachtamy, Kittochtinny,* (Delaware) signifying *endless hills.*" Pilger Ruh, (Pilgrim's Rest), a plain on the top of the mountain. Anton's Wilderness, from Anton Seyffert, and on Evans' map of 1759. Plants supposed to be Cohosh, colic root, Ipecacuanha and Gaultheria.

May 31. Great Swatara, in Pine Grove township. Thurnstein, Peter's Mountain, in honor of Count Zinzendorf in 1742. Erdmuth's Spring, headwaters of Wiconisco Creek, after Erdmuth, Zinzendorf's first wife. Ludwig's Ruh, Lewis's Rest, after Zinzendorf, in Wiconisco township. Laurel Creek, branch of Mahantango. Anna's Valley, after Anna Nitschman, in 1742; probably Lykens Valley now. Double Eagle or Spread Eagle of Scull's map of 1759. Benigna's Creek, after Zinzendorf's daughter, now Mahantango or King Creek.

June 1. Leimback, or Mahanoy Creek, in Jackson township. Jacob's Heights, spur of Line Mountain, Northumberland Co. Joseph's Valley, after Spangenberg, who was often termed Bro. Joseph. Marienborn, after castle of that name. Spangenberg, after Bishop S. Eva Creek, after Eva May, Spangenberg's wife, now Shamokin Creek, in Upper Augusta. "The Delawares called it the *Schachamekhau*, i. e., *eel-stream*." Shamokin, "Written *Schahamoki* or *Schahamokink* by the Delawares; by the Iroquois *Otzinachse*. Sunbury occupies the site of the old Indian town. "Andrew Montour, alias *Sattelihu*, son of Madame Montour, was for many years in the service of the proprietaries as assistant interpreter." Zinzendorf described him in 1742. . "His cast of countenance is decidedly European, and had not his face been encircled with a broad band of paint, applied with bear's fat, I would certainly have taken him for one. He wore a brown broadcloth coat, a scarlet damasken lappel waistcoat, breeches, over which his shirt hung, a black Cordovan neckerchief decked with silver bugles, shoes and stockings, and a hat. His ears were hung with pendants of brass and other wires plaited together like the handle of a basket. He was very cordial, but on addressing him in French, he, to my surprise, replied in English." The mill, Chambers's Mill, mouth of Fishing Creek, built 1730-35. Brainerd, the Rev. David, Moses Fonda Tatemy, his interpreter, baptized by him, July 21, 1745. *Shikellimy*, alias *Swatane*, Oneida chief, represented the Five Nations in Pennsylvania affairs in 1728, and in 1745 was their viceroy in Shamokin. His oldest son, Tachnachdoarus (spreading oak), or John Shikellimy, succeeded him.

June 2. Shamokin, 1749, "lies partly on the east and the west shore of the river, and partly on an island. It contains upwards of 50 houses and 300 inhabitants. About one-half are Delawares, the others Senecas and Tutelars."

June 3. "Allummapees, or Sassoonan, was King of the Delawares as early as 1718, and in that year headed the deputation of Indian chieftains at Philadelphia." The Conoys lived at Tulpehocken, 1705-33.

June 4. Allummapees, in 1731, killed his nephew, Shakatawein, in a drunken brawl.

June 7. Shawane Creek, the Chillisquaque, flowing into the Susquehanna from the northeast. Scull's map places an Indian town at its mouth. Shikellimy's former home, near borough of Milton. Warrior's Camp, from warriors, in Delaware township.

June 8. Canachrirage is Muncy Creek. Ocochpocheny on Scull's map. Ostonwaken, or French Town, from Madame Montour. Weiser also called it Olstuago, Otsnehage and Otstuacky. He was first there in 1737, and then said, "It is so called from a high rock which lies opposite." The village was on both sides of the mouth of the Loyalsock. Diadachton is Lycoming Creek.

June 9. Valley and Ant Hills are Dismal Vale (1749) and Burnet's Hills.

June 10. Salt lick in Lewis township.

June 11. Left Ant Hills in McIntire township. "Bear's Claws," probably Leroy township.

June 12. Osgochgo, called by Weiser, Oscahu, i. e., *the fierce,* now Sugar Creek, above Towanda. Path by river, now Break Neck Narrows. Tioga Branch, now Chemung. Heckewelder says: "Tioga is corrupted from Tiaoga, an Iroquois word, signifying *a gate.* This name was given by the Six Nations to the wedge of land lying within the forks of the Tioga (or Chemung) and North Branch — in passing which streams the traveller entered their territory *as through a gate.*" (Error, W. M. B.)

June 13. Dear Spring, in Tioga, N. Y.

June 14. Deserted village near Owego. Tiatachschiunge, now Cattatong Creek, probably in Candor.

June 15. Left creek a few miles above Candor. Ganowtachgerage, now West Creek in Richford. Prospect Hill in town of Harford. Creek is Virgil Creek in Virgil, tributary to Fall Creek, flowing into Cayuga Lake. Dry Wilderness in Virgil and Cortland.

June 16. Ganiataraghrachat, probably Crandall's Pond, Cortland township. Five other ponds, two of them Swain's and Chatterden's. Ganneratareske, Big Lake in Preble. Oserigooch, large lake in Tully.

June 17. Onondaga, then on both sides of the creek. Others had the same fancy about salt water. King, "Probably Canassatego, alias 'The Word,' sachem of the Onondagas. His name figures in all the principal transactions of the Six Nations from 1734 to 1750. Died Sept. 6, 1750."

June 20. Loskiel states, " that Tocanontie, an Iroquois sachem, was called the 'Black Prince,' because his chest was literally black with a network of devices and designs, tatooed into the skin with gunpowder." Zinzendorf, in his narrative of a " Journey from Bethlehem to Shamokin," in September, 1742, also states: "The Black Prince of Onondaga is a terrible savage. On one occasion he broke into the stockaded castle of the enemy, scalped the inhabitants, and escaped unhurt. He died in the jail at Montreal." Caxhayn or Caxhayton, Canassatego's counsellor, was in Philadelphia as a messenger in February, 1742, and remained two weeks, lodging with his family in the Moravian parsonage, and meeting Zinzendorf there. Died in the autumn of 1749.

June 29. Tiatachtont, near northwest line of La Fayette, N. Y.

July 11. Little Swatara in Bethel township, Pa.

NOTES ON SPANGENBERG'S JOURNAL, BY REV. W. M. BEAUCHAMP, S. T. D.

In the Moravian journals Indian names are of two classes. Algonquin, commonly having labials; Iroquois, always without them. In the Moravian dialect, in all Indian names CH has the sound of GH, unless followed by a vowel; J has the Y sound, and G and K are interchangeable. Thus words which look very unlike may sound the same.

David Zeisberger shared in every journey to Onondaga, wrote an incomplete Onondaga lexicon and an essay on Onondaga grammar, as well as a complete grammar of that dialect. Later, he did more in the Delaware and cognate languages. He was born in Moravia on Good Friday, April 11, 1721. When nearly seventeen he went to Georgia and a little later to Pennsylvania. In February, 1745, he and Frederick Post tried to reach Onondaga via Albany, were brought back and imprisoned, but released soon enough for David to join Spangenberg's party. Most of his real missionary work was done in Pennsylvania and Ohio, and he died in Goshen, Ohio, Nov. 17, 1808.

Bishop Augustus Gottlieb Spangenberg was born in Prussia, July 15, 1704, and died in Saxony, Sept. 18, 1792. He was one of the greatest of the Moravians, and was known among them as Brother Joseph. For nearly eighteen years he presided over the United Brethren in America.

June 10. Magua or Maqua was a frequent Algonquin name for the Mohawks. The names of the three Moravians were given informally, as was often the case. Sometimes the ceremonies are quite elaborate.

June 12. Heckewelder was in error. Tioga is a frequent Iroquois local name, either alone or in combination, always referring to the meeting of two large streams. This Tioga was a gateway, but the name did not show this. The Mohican town there was of Delawares.

June 13. The estimate of 15 miles from Tioga to the Dear Spring is evidently too much. The latter seems just south of the New York line.

June 14. The three islands may be the group just north of the line and in Tioga County, close together and of considerable size. About a 15 miles' ride would bring the party to Owego in the afternoon, and they may have lodged eight miles north of this, on the Cattatonk in Candor, their afternoon route being northwest. When Weiser was at Owego in 1737, there was a Cayuga town east of the creek.

June 15. Ten miles N. N. W., this day, would have brought them to the head of an affluent of the Cattatonk (Wilseyville Creek) in Caroline, before noon, or by a much longer route along the main stream, more to the northwest, near the same place. Thence they crossed, after dinner, to a creek called Ganowtachgerage, which I now think Six Mile Creek, though at first following Mr. Jordan. Fall Creek, which they crossed later in the day, is a tributary of Cayuga Lake. Where they crossed, Six Mile Creek flows southwest and they may have thought it tributary to the Owego. Nothing is said of the outlet. I see no reason to suppose West Creek was crossed, but a slight divergence would bring the party to either Virgil or Fall Creek, practically one stream.

June 16. On the U. S. topographical chart but three

ponds now appear in the town of Cortland. Some may have been drained, but in the five mentioned Ganneratareske and Oserigooch should be included. Ganiataragachrachat is the *end lake,* the first of a long group. Lake Ganneratareske is Big Lake in Preble, and the meaning given me was *on the way to the long lake,* or Oserigooch. Morgan's name for the west branch of the Tioughnioga is O-nan-no-gi-is-ka, *shagbark hickory,* and the sound is suggestive. Oserigooch is Big Lake in Tully. The other Tully lakes they did not see. The whole group is called by the Onondagas T-ka-ne-a-da-her-neuh, *many lakes on a hill.*

June 17. Their course was now nearly due north, but the mention of northwest implies that they followed Onondaga Creek from Tully and through Cardiff, the land being low, and thus they had the worst road of the whole trip. Mr. Jordan thought that Canassatego's was "the King's house," but if so they took lodgings at once across the creek. Canassatego's name meant *upsetting a house placed in good order.* That it meant *the word* is an error derived from an allegorical song after his death, it being a breach of etiquette to use the name of the dead for a while. Weiesr was told that " The town I was going to was no more inhabited by such good Friends as formerly, and now more especially since the *Word* died, meaning Canassatego, the evil Spirits would reign." In 1744 he was described as "a tall, well made man; had a very full chest and brawny limbs. He had a manly countenance, mixed with a good natured smile. He was about 60 years of age; very active, strong, and had a surprising liveliness in his speech." At his death Weiser held a partial condolence to clear the way for business, and a fuller one at Albany in 1751.

June 19. Violins seem strange at Onondaga at that day. The New Religion now prohibits their use.

June 20. Indians were then fond of being bled, even more than white people. Aschanchtiono, (Kaghswughtiooni or Red Head of Johnson)', *wampum belt lying down,* lived with others on the east side of Onondaga Creek, but in 1750 was there alone. At that time he was a noted French partisan, but became Johnson's strong supporter and friend. That year Cammerhoff " called on the old chief Gaschwehtioni, and found him very polite and sensible, a man of great decision of character." He became Speaker in 1755, and died the next year.

Caxhayton or Caxhayen was another chief, prominent as early as 1736 in Pennsylvania affairs. Weiser wrote his name Caxhayion.

Tochanuntie, or the Black Prince, from his dark complexion, was another chief, prominent in the same affairs, but hardly recognizable in New York reports. Two reasons are given for his complexion: That he was tattooed and that one of his parents was a negro. An account in 1744 said he was "a tall, thin man; old, and not as well featured as Canassatego. I believe he may be near the same age with him. He is one of the greatest warriors that ever the Five Nations produced." In 1749 he died at Tueyah-dasso, on his way home from Philadelphia.

June 21. Onas, a *feather* or *pen*, was the Iroquois name for Governor Penn. Conrad Weiser, interpreter and Moravian, was often at Onondaga, 1737-50. He was born in Wurtemberg in 1696, coming to New York in 1710. In 1729 he went to Berks County and became interpreter for Pennsylvania in 1732. He died July 13, 1760, and was buried in the family graveyard near Womelsdorf. Beside the road there has been erected a granite marker with this inscription: "200 yards|south from|This Spot is the|Home and Grave|of|Conrad Weiser|Indian Interpreter|Berks Co. Historical Society, 1914.|"

June 22. Weiser alone kept an account of the Oswego trip, with O. S. dates. (Clark's Onondaga, i. 301.) As his report was official he nowhere mentions his Moravian friends, and gives no details of the journey to Onondaga. On the Oswego trip, beside chiefs, there were "about one hundred persons, men, women and children, going to Canada at an invitation of the French Governor."

June 29. Tiatachtont was Tue-yah-das-so (hemlock knots in the water), in La Fayette. The hill was crossed to reach it, but it was little below the top. This seems an odd name for a village on a hill, but it also belonged to Green Lake on the Clark reservation, two miles north, where it is very appropriate. Bartram said the apple trees were protected by stakes, adding: "All the Indians, men, women and children, came to gaze at us and our horses; the little boys and girls climbed on the roofs of their cabins, about ten in number, to enjoy a fuller view." It is now known as Indian Orchard. In Bartram's trip in 1743 the party separated here, and he also took the right hand trail. In returning local names vary in spelling.

June 30. The direction should evidently be W. after S. W., as they went E. N. E. over the same road, going to Onondaga. The day's journey was but 16 miles, as they started late.

July 1. They went 12 miles to Catatonk Creek at noon. Then 10 miles to camp.

July 2. They went 10 miles to Owego, and then 15 miles to Dear Spring. Distances are approximate.

July 3. At noon they reached Tioga.

DIARY OF THE JOURNEY OF BR. CAMMERHOFF AND DAVID ZEISBERGER TO THE FIVE NATIONS FROM MAY 3-14 TO AUGUST 6-17, 1750.

Thursday, 3-14 May. Br. Cammerhoff left Bethlehem for Gnadenhutten this morning at 8 o'clock in order to proceed from there to Wajomick. He was accompanied to Gnadenhutten by his wife and the Brethren Pezold and Horsefield. They arrived there toward evening, much to the joy of all the white and brown Brethren and Sisters. His traveling companion, David Zeisberger, had left Bethlehem on Monday for Shomoko, to meet us in Wajomick with our traveling companion, Hahotschaunquas.

Sunday, 6-17 May. Br. Cammerhoff left Gnadenhutten for Wajomick, after having taken an affectionate leave of the white and brown Brothers and Sisters. The Brethren Martin Mack, Gottlieb Pezold and Horsefield accompanied him to Wajomick. Br. Schebosch and Cammerhoff's wife went with him as far as the first night's lodging, John's Rest, and returned the next morning to Gnadenhutten.

Wednesday, 9-20 May. We arrived at Wajomick, and at once went to the Nanticoke Town. We were very kindly welcomed, but as our David had not come yet, and we had received no tidings of him, we walked down to the Susquehanna, and encamped on a hill opposite the great plain.

Thursday, 10-21 May. Our David came from Shomoko,

but alone, as the Gajuka was not able to come yet.   He had, however, promised to join us in two or three days.

Thursday, 17-28 May.   We made the necessary preparations to start on our journey.   Our traveling companion, the Gajuka, had not arrived; we determined, however, that if he did not come to-day we would start.   We felt very sad at the separation from our pleasant companions, and would have liked to have them travel with us to Onondaga. We heard of Indians at the Falls on the Susquehanna, and we supposed that our Gajuka was among them.   We breakfasted all together, and then some of our party went down to the Susquehanna to load the canoe that we have bought here for our journey, and which we found very convenient. Whilst they were thus engaged, our traveling companion, the Gajuka Hahotschaunquas, arrived in his bark canoe, with his wife, Gajehne, his son, a boy of about 14, named Tagita, and his daughter, a child of 4, named Gahoea. They came up to our fire with their luggage.   The Gajuka was exceedingly friendly, and glad to find us here.   He had been six days on the way from Shomoko, had been greatly delayed by heavy rains and storms.   The high waves had dashed into his canoe and filled it so completely that everything in it, powder included, had been perfectly wet.   He at once made all preparations for drying his goods, so that we might be able to start to-day.

We were all very grateful to the Lord for His gracious leading in this matter, for if the Indian had delayed one hour more in coming, he would not have found us, and it is doubtful whether he would have overtaken us on the whole way, and had he arrived sooner he might in some respects have proved a hindrance to us, so that we felt that all was for the best.

The Gajuka was very glad to become acquainted with Br. Gannachragejat, or Martin (Mack), and immediately made him a present of an otter.   Martin gave him his Indian shoes, and the Brethren who were going to return, made some little presents to his family, which pleased them greatly.   The three brethren, who had accompanied me hither, could now return feeling better satisfied concerning us.

I then wrote to Bethlehem.   Martin, Gottlieb and Horsefield got ready and started at 10 o'clock in the morning

from our Hill of Peace, (the name we had given to our
quarters). They took an affectionate leave of David, the
Gajuka and his family, and I accompanied them as far as
the Nanticokes Town, took leave of all there, and in parting
they said they would be very glad to see us return again.
They were all exceedingly friendly. They are indeed a
dear people, and we cherish a very hopeful feeling toward
them.

I left the Town with my three friends, and went on
with them for about a half mile, to a hill on their way to
Wombhallobank. There we commended each other to the
Lord's gracious protection until we should again be re-
united, and parted with many sad feelings, I returning to
the Hill of Peace. I arrived again at our quarters, and now
David and I felt that we were indeed alone, trusting in
the Lord to guide us. We took our first meal together, and
afterward conversed much about our intended journey. I
then wrote. David and the Gajuka made preparations to
load the canoe. When we had loaded it we saw that it
was too small to contain all our things; the Gajuka therefore concluded to take along the bark canoe, which he had
brought with him from Shomoko.

We left our beautiful Hill of Peace about 2 o'clock in
the afternoon. David and I, with the boy and girl, set out
in our canoe, and the Gajuka and his wife in their hunting
skiff. It was very pleasant, and I should have liked some
of our friends to have seen us glide smoothly over the
water. We sailed by several islands on the west side of
the Susquehanna, and passed a dismal looking region, very
dreadful to behold, because of the high rocks, which tow-
ered above us like a wall. The Susquehanna was very deep
everywhere. We saw much coal. At last we reached
several falls. We could only proceed with much difficulty,
and were obliged to drag the canoes up over the rocks.

On the opposite bank of the Susquehanna there is a
large plain, at the end of which we met a few Tutelars.
Farther up we again saw three huts. The father, or rather
father's brother of our Justine, the wife of Nicodemus,
whose house is in Gnadenhutten, lives there. His name
is Peskucha. We heard a great noise, and afterward
learned that there was a crazy Indian there, for whom the
old man was to cure, being considered a great doctor.

In the evening we reached some dangerous falls, over
which we passed, and then encamped just above them. We
built ourselves a hut out of the bark from the walnut trees,
which grew there in great abundance, and then we laid
down to rest, David and I on one side of the fire and the
Gajuka and his family on the other. We called our quarters the Gajuka's Post House. [For some days unim-
portant matter will be omitted.]

Friday, 18-29 May. We broke camp early. . . .
After we had gone some distance we again saw three Indian
huts, inhabited by Delawares. . . . At noon, as we
disembarked, a very heavy rain-storm came up. On the
heights on this side of the Susquehanna, close to the shore,
passes the great path to Tiaogu. On account of the high
wind and rain we were obliged to lie by for several hours,
during which David fished and a Delaware visited us. . .
. . We started again and crossed the large creek which
the Delawares call Gachanai and the Maquais, Hazirok. It
is generally considered as the boundary line of the plain
Skehantowa.

We landed at the point where it empties into the Susquehanna, and visited two Delaware huts. . . We then
went on and pushed into the mountains, which here hedge
in the Susquehanna very closely. We called the one on this
side the Mountain of Joy. The other, on the opposite shore
of the river, rises back of the great plain. As evening had
come on we encamped on this side of the water, at the foot
of the high mountains. . . . We built a hut of bark
and named this spot the Skehantowa Pass. The Susquehanna from this place, where it flows into the mountains,
we called David's Strait, because David is the first Moravian Brother who has steered his little bark through it. In
the evening the Gajuka related much of the Aquanoschioni.
He told us, amongst the rest, that the nearest counsellor of
Ganassateco, who had been with us in Philadelphia, and
whose name was Tohekechnati, had died.

Saturday, 19-30 May. We left our quarters early, proceeding through the mountains, where the Susquehanna
makes great curves, and the current is very rapid. We
met several canoes, with Indians going down the stream.
. . . One of them proved to be Anton's own brother, the
one next to him in age. They at once turned their canoes

and sailed with us to the nearest house, occupied by Nathanael and his three brothers, his mother, and besides the brother of Rebecca, Nathanael's wife, named Masnaront, and several other Indians.

The Indians call this place Pehendametuckquannuk. We sailed to the shore, and found many Indians standing there. I at once discovered our Nathanael among them. . . . Nathanael was very glad to see us. He looked very bright and lively. . . . Having heard that Anton lived several miles farther up the river, and that his son was very sick, I resolved to rest here to-day with my Brethren. David went to the Gajuka to speak to him about it. He at once consented, and said that I was a great man and could make whatever arrangements I pleased. . . . I started with Nathanael and his brother Christian to visit Anton. . . . At last we reached the place and found seven or eight huts, in a very fertile tract of land, beyond which rise very high rocks. I could notice by the peach trees growing there that this was a very old Indian settlement. The Indians were all out of doors except Anton. I went to his hut and found his wife Johanna there with his sick son. . . . I then went into another hut, and there I met Anton, who jumped up, embraced and kissed me, and scarcely knew how to express his joy. . . . I spent a very happy hour with these three friends. . . . Tochtapassen came in, an Indian who had frequently visited in Gnadenhutten. . . . Soon after eight or nine Indians entered, and several of them sat down near me. [A long talk followed.]

Sunday, 20-31 May. Nathanael brought us some nut milk as a token of his regard. . . . Whilst we halted at noon, in order to partake of some food, David fished and was very successful. To-day we passed through many curves; the current began to be very rapid, and . . . we found rowing very difficult. We did not pass any huts to-day. . . . We named the mountains on this side of the Susquehanna *Snake Mountain,* because we saw snakes in great numbers, lying on the stones and rocks near the shore, basking in the sun. To the opposite mountains we gave the name of *Dragon's Head.* . . We passed many islands. Toward evening we put up a tent of bark. The Indian boy fished, and caught more than we could eat. We named our quarters Sunfish, and rested well and undisturbed.

Monday, 21 May-1 June. We started early. Our course lay over dangerous rapids and rocks, which made our passage a very difficult one. . . . We crossed a creek as wide as the Lehigh at Gnadenhutten. It empties here into the Susquenhanna, and is called Sto-ke creek. Above it we saw two Indian huts. . . . Tenkhanneck begins here. . . . We sailed on and crossed the creek Tenkhanneck, from which this beautiful region, so pleasant and fertile, receives its name. Farther on we saw several huts. . . In the curves, where the mountains strike the river, there are generally high falls, and the current is very swift. Our Gajuka found quarters for us on this side of the Susquehanna, near some high, steep rocks. We encamped there and built ourselves a hut.

Tuesday, 22 May-2 June. The Gajuka started out early with his gun this morning. He wounded a deer and brought home a young one, not more than two days old. Afterward he, and David and I, went to look after the the wounded deer, and succeeded in bringing it home after a tramp of several miles. It began to rain very hard. . . We enlarged our hut and made it more secure.

Wednesday, 23 May-3 June. There arose a severe storm, followed by a very heavy rain, so that we were obliged to spend the day here. The deer came to the opposite shore continually, and we named it the Deer Pasture. During the afternoon we had built quite a town, having in haste erected four huts, in order to bring our goods under cover. The hut we occupied was quite large, and we called it David's Castle. The town we named Gajuka's Town, because he had chosen this point.

Thursday, 24 May-4 June. To-day, being *Ascension Day*, according to old style, we thought of it as a mission festival. . . . At noon we resolved to break camp, though the wind and rain continued. . . . We again passed over very steep falls, the ascent of which cost us much hard work, especially as the wind was against us, and the rain began to pour in torrents. . . . In the afternoon we came to an Indian farm. An Indian from the shore called to us to come over to him. He was a Delaware, had a plantation and a strange looking lodge. The Maquais call him Otcongoe, i. e., a great sorcerer. . . . He offered us food. . . . We continued on our way, and toward evening came to three Delaware huts, or rather . . . to a very old Indian town, named Onochsae. It is so called because immediately opposite a mountain rises from the river that is hollow inside, like an arched cellar. From this the creek . . and the whole neighborhood receive their name. . . .

Friday, 25 May-5 June. The weather cleared, but . . we were obliged to spend the whole morning mending our canoe. . . . When our canoe had been thoroughly repaired we started. . . . In the evening we built a hut. . . We called our quarters the Horned Tree, because near to our tent there stood a tree, in which the antlers of a deer had been laid, and now appeared to have grown into it.

Saturday, 26 May-6 June. Early this morning the Gajuka started out before in his canoe. . . He wanted to hunt along the shore. . . . Overtook our Gajuka. He had seen only a wolf, and shot a few ducks. We again had to pass over a dangerous cataract. . . . The water falls down as from a mountain, and makes the current very rapid. . . . With much difficulty we passed over another cataract. . . . On proceeding we came to a place called Gahontoto [Wyalusing] by the Indians. It is said to be the site of an ancient Indian city, where a peculiar nation lived. The inhabitants were neither Delawares nor Aquanoschioni, but had a language of their own, and were called Tehotitachse. We could still notice a few traces of this place in the old ruined corn-pits, etc. The Five Nations went to war against them, and finally completely exterminated them. The Gajukas had many prisoners, who remained among them, but there exists nothing more of their nation and language. The Gajuka told us that these things had taken place before the Indians had any guns, and still went to war with bows and arrows. He related to us that the Nanticokes were considered as brothers by the Five Nations, as they had never gone to war against them. They had, however, warred with the Tuscaroras, Tutelars, and Shawanese, and they had only been adopted as brothers at a later date. It is plain to be seen that although the Tuscaroras are counted as belonging to the

Five Nations, yet they are not as highly esteemed as the
other nations, and bear a bad character among them. He
told us that the Shawanese had lived beyond the Catawbas
and the Cherokees, which must have been in Spain. They
had gone to war against the Cherokees and the Five Nations
at the same time, had surrendered to the latter, and had thus
come into this country. . . . In the evening we pitched
our tents in a very beautiful cleared spot. Gallichwio was
so delighted with it that he called it *Mon Plaisir in the
Wilderness.*

Sunday, 27 May-7 June. We were obliged to contend
with a very wild and strong current during the whole day,
and with much difficulty succeeded in passing many falls.
. . The Susquehanna was frequently so blocked up
by islands that we could with difficulty find an opening
through which to pass. . . . David went on to shoot
pigeons, of which we saw great numbers. He was very
successful. . . . We encamped in the high grass, so
tall that we could not see over the top of it, and named the
place Rose Meadow, because of the quantity of roses growing there.

Monday, 28 May-8 June. Very early this morning a
Delaware Indian came to us in his canoe, with his children.
They came from Tiaogu, and are going to the chase. He
stayed a little while with us, and was very friendly and
unassuming. He told the Gajuka that all up in their neighborhood were preparing to war against the French Indians,
and Zisagechrohne in particular would raise the hatchet
against the Five Nations, and this would occur before the
corn was knee high, which means three weeks hence. .
. . Having gone some distance we met with several
Indian families who were engaged in hunting and had
encamped. We landed and went to them. They immediately regaled us with some roasted bear meat. It tasted
very good. They were very friendly and modest, were Delawares, but could speak the Maquai tongue, and lived in
Tiaogu. From them we learned that it was a four days'
journey from Tiaogu to Anohochquage, the city of the Tuscaroras, therefore about 200 miles distant, as they usually
reckon 50 miles a day's journey. . . . Continued on our
way, crossing a creek named Oskoehka (Towanor Creek)
here flowing into the Susquehanna. David remembered to

have passed over it with Br. Spangenberg, seven or eight
miles from the Susquehanna, in the great wilderness.
. . Afterward we came to a very old Indian plantation,
near which the Gajuka told us that the trail through the
great wilderness strikes the Susquehanna. David and I
went on shore and succeeded in finding it. It was a very
pleasing thing to remember that our Brethren had been
here five years ago. The mountain over which the trail
passes we named Joseph's Heights. We then went on
through the region called the narrow path, where the trail
passes for some distance along a very steep and high preci-
pice. It is very dangerous, especially for horses. . . .
We encamped just at that point where the trail touches the
Susquehanna, and we could see Tiaogu before us. We built
a hut and spent a happy evening.

Tuesday, 29 May-9 June. It stormed and rained hard
during the whole morning, so we kept on quietly in our
Caravansary (thus we called our quarters) where we were
dry and comfortable. Our Indians began to paint and deco-
rate themselves, as they expected soon to reach their people,
and especially their own Gajukas. When the rain had
ceased a little we continued and came to a branch named
Tiaogu. Here the Susquehanna proper makes a bend to
the right, N. E., and the other branch to the left, N. W.
and W. N. W. We entered this, leaving the river and passing several huts without landing. We were obliged to pass
several deep falls, where the water rushes as through flood-
gates. . . . Upon the whole this branch appears to be
a succession of falls and rapids. A little farther on we
came to three huts inhabited by Delawares. They invited
us to come to them, which we did and they at once offered
us food. We found a great number of women and children.
The men were all absent on a bear hunt. After leaving
there we passed several huts and had to ascend some very
dangerous falls, were forced to get out of our canoe and
drag it up. At last we came to a beautiful plain, on which
stands an Indian town inhabited by Gajukas, named Ganatocheracht. This was the port for which we were bound,
and from whence we were to continue our journey by land
to Onondago. We gave it the name of the Haven of
Peace. According to our reckoning we had traveled 200
miles from Wajomik to this place. No doubt the distance

would be greater by exact measurement, and by land I should estimate it to be at least 160 miles. . . . A crowd of men, women and children gathered to see us, and gazed at us with much surprise. Among them were many fine looking people, who made an agreeable impression on us. We were then solemnly invited by a man named Haetwe, to lodge in the house of Tianoge. As we afterward found, Haetwe is a man in authority among the Gajukas. Tianoge, whom David knew, was not at home, but had gone to Owego, a half day's journey from here. We accepted this invitation gratefully, and all immediately offered their services, and were so active in bringing our goods to shore, that we looked on in amazement. A truly fraternal welcome awaited us in the hut. . . . Haetwe had met David before in Shomoko, and said to him, " I salute you, my brother Ganousseracheri." They had already spread out a bear-skin for us, and assigned a place for our goods. Haetwe's brother, Haetehook, who lives on Long Island and who also knew David, was there. The women and children were particularly friendly, and made preparations to regale us with venison.

The evening was spent in conversation with our host. He described very circumstantially our way to Onondago. . . . We made inquiries about the land of the Sennekas, and especially concerning the three chiefs with whom we had become acquainted in Philadelphia last year, and whose names we mentioned. Our host knew them, and said we must be important people to know the great chiefs of the Five Nations. He told us that they had lodged with him on their return. He described the road very minutely, and said that Indians lived all the way up along the river, and that it was about four days' journey from here to Zonesschio, i. e., at least 200 miles. We, in turn, told him of our journey, and acquaintance with Ganassateco, Ganhajen, and the others of Onondago, subjects of great interest to him. It is a certain thing that great men enjoy more respect and authority among the Indians than is commonly supposed. They look upon an acquaintance with them as a great honor. We went to bed in a happy frame of mind.

Wednesday, 30 May-10 June. To-day we rested considerably, especially my dear David after his hard work on

the water.   Many Indians visited us during the morning,
who were very modest and friendly.   One came from Tute-
lar, whom the Maquais called Gachwae.   He had spent
much time in Shomoko, and knew David well.   He had just
come from Anajot and Anahochquage, and related much of
that neighborhood.   This Indian was now on his way down
to Shomoko, and we sent word to our Brother Anton
Schmidt, that we had arrived here safely after a journey ot
12 days from the Wajomick. . . . Our Gajuka now
went to look for his horse, which he had left in the woods,
and which we were to make use of in our journey to Onondago.   We conversed much with our host, who is a very
polite and sensible Indian.   We made a few small presents
to him, his wife and brother, with which they appeared
much pleased.   As we are now going to Onondago, and can
take but little with us, we spoke to him about our baggage,
and asked him where we could store it until our return.
He immediately offered us his storehouse, and assured us
that he would take good care of everything, and would also
secure our canoe. . . . He and his brother showed more
affection toward each other than I have ever seen among
Indians, and we were very much edified by their behaviour.

David and I then went out and took a general survey of
the neighborhood.   We saw that there were eight or nine
huts across the river, all filled with people.   The Tutelars,
who have moved up here from down the Susquehanna, have
begun to build a town on that side, and expect soon to have
some more of their nation here.   We then went on through
the woods toward the Susquehanna for some miles.   We
came across the road on which Br. Spangenberg and his
company had traveled five years ago, from Tiaogu, via
Owego, an old Indian town, to Onondago, and afterward
reached the Susquehanna.   We found a pleasant spot on
the banks, enjoyed some refreshments, and talked of our
plans. . . .

Thursday, 31 May-11 June.   It had rained hard during
the night, and the river had risen very much.   Early in the
morning we heard that our canoe had been driven away.
David found it some distance down the river, whither it
had been taken by some Indians; he brought it back and
fastened it.   The weather cleared; we wanted to start and
talked the matter over with our Gajuka.   He did not seem

inclined to go, but promised, however, to look for our horses. He did not return until late at night, and had not found them. Our stay was agreeable, but yet we would have liked soon to reach Onondago. Many Indians visited us and were very friendly. Some thought we were traders, and inquired about this one and that one. It was not necessary for us to make many explanations, as our host enlightened them. The children in the house began to feel at home with us, and liked to be where we were, which impressed us pleasantly for the future. In the evening the women in the town held a festival, but we remained undisturbed in our house, and went to sleep comfortably.

Friday, 1-12 June. The Gajuka started out early to look for the horses. In the meantime we had an opportunity of talking over much with our host. David related to him about our Brethren, told him all our Indian names, where we lived, described the road from Skehantowa, and also told him what kind of a people we were. He also mentioned our connection with the Five Nations and the great men among them, to all of which our host listened with much attention and astonishment. We were truly grateful to the Lord for having given us this opportunity of becoming better acquainted with the Gajuka Nation, for they are one of the strongest nations, and not as weak as is commonly supposed. My Indian name being Gallichwio in the Gajuka language, I sometimes felt like saying to myself: I am dwelling among my own people, and when I shall be able to say that in its true meaning, my heart will rejoice.

At noon our Gajuka at last arrived with the horses. To our great astonishment we discovered that our host, without having said a word, had decided to give us his horse to Onondago, as he no doubt saw that we could not proceed with that of the Gajuka. . . . Our host also gave us a saddle and bridle, which David was able to mend for our use. While doing this we conversed with him. He told us that Onondago lay N. of us, and the land of the Sennekas W. N. W. We took an affectionate leave of our host and started off together, David and I, the Gajuka and his wife, but the boy and girl remained. We went on till toward evening, when we came into a wilderness, and entered a wood so dark that we could not see farther than where we

stood.   We quickly built a hut near a creek named Ganhotak, and rested comfortably in it.

Saturday, 2-13 June.   David rose early and went fishing in the creek, and caught some trout.   The Gajuka told
us that, long ago, Tutelars had lived in the neighborhood.
We started off again, but were obliged to cross the creek
twice.   We tried to ford it on our horses, but might have
had a dreadful accident, for they were wild and untrained,
and had scarcely been used, so that we were in great danger.
The road we had to take was a very strange one, such as I
had never yet seen anywhere in this country, and difficult
to describe to anyone unacquainted in this wilderness.   The
underbrush was so dense that we could scarcely see day-
light; many thousand immense trees lay on the road, which
the horses had either to go around or jump over.   We were
obliged to cross the creek about thirty times, and generally
waded through it.   Beside all this there were many marshy,
muddy places.   Notwithstanding these difficulties we felt
encouraged to go on, being sure of the Lord's presence.
After we had continued for some time in the valley, we
ascended a wild and rocky clift, and when we had reached
the mountain, which was very high, the Gajuka prepared
our dinner.   Though at a great height yet we had no view
at all, because of the dense forest around us, so wild and
dark that we might have supposed ourselves in a deep
valley.   We refreshed ourselves with some Indian corn,
which we had boiled in the morning, and which the Gajuka
had carried here on his back.   We had no water, as there
was none to be found here.   We thought specially of our
friends in Bethlehem and Gnadenhutten to-day.   We named
our quarters the Indian Sabbath Lodgings, and again
started off on our way.   As the road was very bad and
dangerous here, the Gajuka led us for some time through
the forest, over the fallen trees and through the bushes, so
that sometimes we could scarcely find our way out.   We
crept along as well as we could, and after having gone on
a few miles more we came to the road, and again found
water.   It was, however, all a wilderness, and we passed
through swamps, marshes and bushes.   As the weather
was very cloudy it increased the darkness, so that at times
we might have supposed that night was coming on.   We
passed through a neighborhood which the Indians called

Kassickahe, because of the tall trees there. It is true that there are a great many there, and of such a height as can hardly be imagined. There were three posts painted red, on which the Indians had fastened by their feet, according to their usual custom, the three Gatabes whom they had taken prisoners.

We built ourselves a good, secure hut, and the Gajuka did the same, for we expected rain. We named our quarters the Tabernacle in the War Camp. David and I remembered how wonderfully we had been led over strange and difficult paths, and then retired to rest. It rained very hard all night.

Sunday, 3-14 June. To-day, being Whitsunday, according to the old style of reckoning, I thought specifically of all our congregations in this country. It was very wet in the morning. It never gets very dry in this wilderness, as the sun cannot penetrate the thick forest. We started, notwithstanding the dampness. Our way led us, like yesterday, over the mountains, through swamps and valleys, and finally to a lake, which was not very large, but yet several miles in circumference. Toward the south it empties into the Owego creek. The Indians have named it Ganiatarenge. Here we rested, and the Gajuka gave us some geographical information, telling us that from here, W. and W. N. W., we were not far from the land of the Sennekas. He said it was four days' journey from Gajuka N. W. to the French, five days' journey to a large river named Gatarochqui, wider than the Delaware at Philadelphia. This river flowed from Lake Niagara, famous for its large falls. He described the falls as being as high as if we were to place four or five pine trees one upon the other, (we saw some here which were certainly more than 100 feet high), and said that he had been there four times.

White people, Frenchmen, were living there and had a fort; there were also some Indians scattered about in the neighborhood. You could travel there in eight days from Gajuka, taking a course about W. N. W. The journey might also be made by water, and that way was shorter but more dangerous, because of having to pass through many lakes, where strong winds prevailed, which made a canoe passage dangerous. Then he told us of Quebec in Canada, called by the Indians Tiochtiage, situated on a river of the

same name, which is the St. Lawrence. He described it
as a large city, surrounded by a wall requiring half a day
to pass around it. It is built very irregularly, for the
stables and the farmers are in the center of the city, and
the French Governor lives there also. Quebec lies N. N. E.
from Gajuka and is about nine days' journey from there
on foot. He said it was possible to drive there from Gatarochqui; but the road was very bad. It was a ten days'
journey from Schenectady to Quebec. There was a lake
about half a day's journey from Quebec, so that the Ohio
could be reached by water. The Ohio, he said, was as wide
as the Susquehanna at Harris's Ferry. The Mississippi,
called by the Indians Zinotarista, he described as lying S. W.
from here. He said that the three Indians with whom we
are acquainted, in Zonesschio, lived about half-way between
here and the Ohio.

After we had rested for some time, we continued on our
way and reached the foot of a mountain, where the Gajuka
said his child was born. As we ascended the mountain he
pointed out a cross to us, which marked the spot where the
Gajukas had fought with the Tehotitachies. In going up
the mountain we found a fruit that the Indians call Esta-
chioni. It is as large as a plum, but not of that form, has
no kernel, is only pulp, has a sour sweetish taste, is very
juicy, and quenches the thirst; we ate freely of it.

This is the first warm day we have had since leaving
Wajomik, and we perspired freely, going down the mountain into the country called by the Indians Tianontinaou.
We were overtaken by a very heavy shower and thunder-
storm, but went on notwithstanding, and came to a beautiful spring, to which we gave the name of Pentecostal
Spring. We took our dinner there. Then we traveled on,
and were again overtaken by a heavy shower and thunder-
storm. As night was coming on we built ourselves a hut
near a creek named Sto-ke, at a place where much sugar
has been boiled. We succeeded in getting our things under
roof before the rain. We spent a happy evening together.

Monday, 4-15 June. It rained during the whole night,
and continued as hard this morning, with a heavy wind-
storm, so that it seemed at times as if we would be obliged
to remian here, and we had no desire to do this. A few
Indian women from Ganatocheracht came to us; they had

left there shortly after we did. We then resolved to start on our way, although the shower had not ceased, and everything was very wet. Our road was very bad; it lay through swamps and marshes, and was made almost impassable at times by the fallen trees, so that at times we scarcely knew how to proceed. At last we reached the foot of a high mountain, called by the Indians Untagechiat, and came out of the forest, (where we had traveled for three days, and in which we had not had any view at all) into an open plain. We called the forest Edom, and the mountain which traversed it Seir. We came to a lovely plain, overgrown with fine tall grass. It differs from Wajomik in having bushes here and there, but otherwise it is equally beautiful.

The plain is several miles wide. It extends S. S. W. and N. N. E. On both sides of it are mountains extending in the same direction; they form, as we discovered later, the boundaries of the dense forests lying behind them. We also saw that Indians had formerly dwelt here, and found traces of them.

We went in the plain through the high grass, and crossed a creek. There I saw a beech tree, more than six feet in diameter and eighty feet high. The creek is named Nochwaio. We crossed two other creeks; the first named Notantakto, and the second Nogaene. All these creeks flow into one lake. We saw the last creek, after rushing on wildly, fall perpendicularly from a height of ninety feet. It was indeed an interesting and thrilling sight.

We then passed through the plain over several hills, and at last came to a lake, which the Indians called Ganiataragechiat. We reached it at the point where the before mentioned creeks empty into it. At first it flows from E. S. E. to N. N. W., and then, as we saw on the morrow, it inclines to the N. and at Gajuka to the N. by E. In the beginning it is from three to four miles wide, continues thus for a time, then widens from five to six miles, until at Gajuka it is from seven to eight miles wide. It is a very long stream, for we traveled 50 miles along it, and saw it later from ten to fifteen miles farther on, so that it must be at least seventy miles long before it flows out. Its water is as clear as crystal, and the Indians say deeper than they can tell. There are many fish in it, especially eels. Hills and mountains bound the lake on both sides. Many large and small creeks rush down from them and empty into the lake, often falling down over the rocks from a height of ten, twelve to twenty feet. Beyond the lake there is a particularly large creek, named Tschochnioke, which, as the Gajuka and another Indian told us, falls over the rocks from a height of 150 feet, and empties into the lake.

We camped on the shore near the head of the lake, and intended to partake of some refreshments, but as we saw smoke rising on the other side, the Gajuka went around and found Indians living in a cave in the rocks, near the mouth of the creeks, close by the lake, just as we had seen some living near the banks of the Susquehanna. The Indians named the place Onochsoe. As the Gajuka was so slow in returning and it was growing late, we determined to remain and put up a hut. The Gajuka brought us turtle's eggs and dried eels.

In the evening the Indian who lives on the opposite shore, whose name is Hakoento, came over and was very friendly and modest. He told us that to-day or to-morrow the chiefs, of whom 4 are from Gajuka, would start for Onondago, and that several chiefs from the other Nations would also meet there. This was pleasant news for us, as we could now be certain of meeting them all assembled together in Onondago, a very rare occurrence. Afterward we had a long conversation with the Gajuka and the other Indian, concerning the lakes in this neighborhood. The Gajuka, who has traveled much through this region, drew a map on a piece of dry bark, and showed how one could go by water from Gajuka into the St. Lawrence, and in like manner to Niagara Falls. He also told us that the Susquehanna did not rise from the lakes, but that it gradually grew very small and almost disappeared, and that soon after branches from small lakes, of which they pointed out several to us, flowed into it and formed it. We conversed until late on this subject, and went to bed in a comfortable frame of mind.

Tuesday, 5-16 June. We rose early to start for Gajuka, as we had a long journey before us. Our way appeared much longer than we had supposed by the Gajuka's description. The Gajuka's wife, with two other women, went down the lake in a canoe, which they had borrowed from the Indians. We again had a visit from the Indian who came to see us yesterday. He brought with him another young man, who was very modest and friendly. After they had breakfasted with us we set off. Today we crossed at least 200 creeks which enter into the lake. The latter broke in great waves when a little wind arose, and we could easily imagine that it might be very rough, and roar like the ocean during a storm. We named our quarters Land's End, because from here a long trip can be made by water, and in this neighborhood most of the streams flow into the country of the French. The Indians told us that down at the end of the lake, there lived French Indians from Canada.

After we had continued on our way we reached a creek, called by the Indians Gientachne, where their warriors usually encamped. Here we saw the whole chancery court or archives of the Gajukas, painted or hanging in the trees. Our Gajuka gave us a lengthy explanation of it all. When the great warriors go to war against the Gatabes, they make a painting of themselves. We saw several of these fine works of art, done in Indian style. On their return they add their deeds in a painting, showing what scalps they have taken, what they bring with them in the shape of treasures, bracelets, wampum and the like. The Gajuka pointed out to us, with much importance, what he had himself painted, as he had been to war twice. The one time he had brought back 8 prisoners and 2 scalps, and on the other occasion 3 prisoners.

As we journeyed on I thought much about our Indians, and David and I wished that we might live to see them brought to the true God. We continued on, passing over a beautiful plain, watered by many creeks, all of which empty into the lake, and at last reached a spot called Tschochniees, inhabited by Gajukas. There were two huts there, but we found only one woman, with several children. Everything looked very miserable and deserted. We heard yesterday that provisions were growing very scarce in this neighborhood. A few miles farther on we met an Indian woman with two large girls, of whom one was a Cherokee, who had been brought here as a prisoner 7 or 8 years ago.

The woman was the wife of the Gajuka chief Onechsagerat, and her name was Tiungue. She told us that her husband had today left Gajuka for Onondago. She was much surprised at our company, and asked the Gajuka what our business was. He said he did not know, only this he knew, that I was a great man, who was traveling to be present at the great council in Onondago, and having given her this information he left her. This was the explanation which he gave everywhere. The Indians were very modest and did not examine us, and were quite satisfied to know that we are not traders, and are going to Onondago. From this they infer that we have business of great importance there. Onondago is a greater place in their eyes than is commonly supposed.

We went on for some distance and then rested a little, refreshing ourselves with some dried eels. Our course lay N. and sometimes N. by E. Toward evening we reached the first farms of Gajuka, which are still at some distance from the towns. It had already grown dark when we arrived in the town. It is situated on the lake, and on a creek by the name of Gaheskao. We had gone to-day, as we saw on our return, fully fifty miles, making altogether 180 miles from Ganatocheracht, rather more than less. We felt tired, as we had walked very fast all day in order to reach here. A great crowd at once assembled around us, in which were many fine, brave looking fellows. They were, however, very modest, and only looked at us with astonishment. The Gajuka led us to the last house at the end of the town, where his grandmother and several of his friends lived. Here we were very kindly received, a deer skin bed was immediately prepared for us, and we were shown a place for our luggage. The Gajuka then told them our names, which greatly astonished them, as also some information which he gave them concerning us. They offered us eels and Indian corn, and then we retired thankful and happy, glad to be able to rest on our long and fatiguing journey.

Wednesday, 6-17 June. We slept late and rested a little, for although we wanted to leave here to-day, yet we did not intend to travel very far. As soon as we were up we received many visits from Indians, among the rest from an old chief named Gechsagoat, who lives here. He was very modest and friendly, inquired where we came from, and our Gajuka told him our names, and that we were traveling to Onondago; he appeared fully satisfied. Our Gajuka's brother, Tschochahaese, also came and was very friendly. Indeed all who saw us here did so with pleasure,

and we could feel that we were welcome, and were gladly
seen. The Gajuka's old grandmother, who is probably 90
years old, was very industrious and busy, preparing us
food. She spent the whole morning baking bread for us
to take along on our journey; she also gave us some very
fine salt, which is made here. All her actions seemed to
indicate that she has a secret intimation of our mission.
May the Lord reward her for all her kindness! The man
of the house, named Hanuntschistaa, went out on the lake
on purpose to spear eels for us; he brought home a very
large one, which he presented to us with much pleasure.

We then took a stroll around the town. There are about
20 huts altogether, most or them large and roomy, with
three or four fireplaces; they are well built and waterproof.
They have small entrance buildings on both sides, and four
or five families can lodge in every cabin. The chiefs of the
Gajuka Nation live here, and many other people also; fine,
large, strong looking Indians, and many young people. We
felt comfortable at this place, and could easily have enjoyed
a half year here. The Indians, to whom we were perfect
strangers, showed us such confidence as white people seldom
have a right to expect from Indians. They received us in
as kind and brotherly a manner as we could possibly desire.
I wish that Brethren could be stationed at all these places;
such whose hearts burn with love toward the Indian, willing
to learn their language and adopt the Indian mode of life,
an easy thing to do when prompted by love to them. We
thought the Daily Word for to-day particularly appropriate
to be read in this place, and David and I commended this
people specially to our Father's keeping.

The Gajuka received a large quantity of belts and
fathoms of wampum from a war captain, who was keeping
them to take them to the chiefs at Onondago, but as he
was sick, he was afraid that if he should die they might
die with him, i. e., be lost. We left here a few hours before
sundown, our host accompanying us, as the Gajuka had
different matters to attend to, and he promised to overtake
us shortly. Our course lay N. N. E. We saw several huts
along the lake. We had a pleasant road, light woods, and
very good land. After proceeding about 10 miles, just as
it was growing dark, we reached Ganiatarage, another
Gajuka town, where a chief by the name of Sakokechiata

lives.   Our Gajuka has also lived at this place, and we put
up at his house, where lives his old mother named Ganechs-
cheta.   She received us most kindly.   She at once gave us
something to eat, and our guide told her where we came
from and where we were going.   Not far from here, farther down the lake, which flows N. at the other end, and is
called Tiuchheo where it empties, there is another Gajuka
town named Sannio.   David and I spent a happy evening,
talking much about the heathen and our plans for their
welfare.

Thursday, 7-18 June.   To-day we directed our course
toward the heights of Onondago; we approached very nearly
but did not quite reach them.   Our Gajuka came to us very
early from Gajuka.   After we had eaten something, and
left such baggage for safe keeping as we would not need,
we started on our way.   It led us at once into a wilderness,
which continues from here to Onondago.   We named it the
Salt Desert, because of the many salt marshes and salt
springs we found there.   Then we passed through a very
dense forest, so dark that we could hardly see our way, and
with many marshes and swampy places, into which the
horses often sank and could scarcely proceed.   Our course
is N. E.; this is the direction of Onondago from Gajuka.
We passed a large creek named Garontanechqui, and after
we had continued for 12 or 13 miles we reached a lake
named Achsgo.   Where we saw it it was about three miles
wide.   We could also see nine to ten miles of its length,
but we could not see the end of it.   At the lower end, where
it is about one mile wide, we were obliged to ride through
it; we saw some Indians wading across.   The bottom was
clear, bright sand, and the water very fresh and cold.   We
found the two Indians on the other side; they were going
on the chase.   One of them was the chief of Ganiataraga,
named Sagogechiata, a tall man, who really showed by the
expression of his face that he was a man of distinction.
He was very friendly; our Gajuka told him about us.   After
we had smoked a pipe with him, we went on again into
the wilderness, where there was nothing but swamps and
marshes.   We came to a lake named Sganiatarees.   It flows
S. E. and N. W. and empties toward the N. W., is about two
or two and one-half miles broad, but we could not see the
end of it.   We crossed at the lower end, where it empties

into a rapid creek with a swift current, and then pursued our journey in the wilderness. As we journeyed I thought much about our expedition to Onondago, and prayed that the Lord might direct all matters according to His will.

Friday, 8-19 June. I wrote our Diary in the morning, and then we conversed with the Gajuka, who told us much. He said that on the day of our arrival at Gajuka, a messenger from the land of the Sennekas had passed through to Onondago, and had brought the news that it was actually true that the French Indians, and particularly the Zisagechrohne, (those who live above Niagara on Lake Ontario) wished to go to war against the Five Nations. The war was to begin as soon as the corn was in the ear, so that they might have something to eat, and for this reason the Sennekas were gathering together and fortifying themselves. He said this was the news they had received, and must be true, because, among Indians, if the same message were received twice, it must be correct. He also said that these Indians lived from six to seven days' journey from the land of the Sennekas. They were strong in numbers, but were miserable warriors, who, when they had fired, ran away, and five Schwanos were equal to thirty of their men, for they stood firm to the end.

The cause of the war was because the French, who are the instigators of it all, wanted Ohio and all the land there belonging to the Five Nations. Thereupon he began to talk of the whites in general, who, as he said, coveted so much the possessions of the Indians, and were greatly increasing in numbers in this region. In the beginning they would bring only a calf, and in a few years they would have a whole herd of cattle, and this was the same case with the white people. Besides, they used many arts and much cunning, to talk the Indians and their chiefs out of their lands, and then gave them nothing worth talking about in return. When they were talking over matters in making a treaty with the Indians, they spoke English, and thought the Indians did not understand it, but last year some were there who understood it very well.

We then gave him some information about our Brethren, and told him how we had bought land for Indians from New York State, who had lost theirs, and that they now lived on it, planted, and had built quite a pretty town. This was news to him, and he was greatly astonished. We told him the names of the Brethren's settlements, which pleased him.

Afterward he explained to us that the War Archives, which we had found on the trees, had been painted by French Indians, (their paintings can be recognized by the crosses which they paint on them), when they made war upon the Cherokees and brought back prisoners from them. We named our quarters the "French Camp," and then went on toward the Onondago hills, which we were to reach to-day. After having advanced considerably we descended a very high, steep hill and immediately after ascended another of the same height. We named these two peaks the Princes' Heights. The latter continues, with several breaks and very bad roads, until Onondago and the foot of the mountain is only reached when the place is in sight. We arrived here after having traveled 70 good miles from Gajuka, therefore 250 from Ganatocheracht, 450 from Wajomik, and at least 550 from Bethlehem. I cannot describe my feelings at the sight of Onondago, and I prayed earnestly for the Lord's guidance.

As we descended the mountain the Gajuka asked us where we would lodge. We directed him to lead us to Ganassateco; this astonished him greatly, and he could not understand how we should want to go to such a man first of all. We felt, however, that it was proper to announce ourselves at the right door at once. Our Gajuka did not know his house, and was obliged to make inquiry in the first houses we came to. There were seven large cabins close together. The chiefs were all assembled in one of them ,but we did not know it. Our guide did not seem to have understood the directions given him, and led us around for some time in Onondago, until David inquired himself, and the Indians told him exactly where to go. On the way, in the beautiful lowlands where they were planting, we found a large company of 33 women, who were hoeing corn, a laudable occupation here. At last we reached the house of Ganassateco. There is a large pole before it with an English flag on it. The house is very large and roomy, and well built.

We inquired for the chief, but did not find him in, as he was at the Grand Council. His wife met us very kindly, and said that she had sent word to him, to let him know that we had come. In the meantime the house was being swept, and after an apartment had been prepared for us, we were invited into it, and the one side, which had been covered with beautiful mats, was assigned to us. It was large enough for six Brethren to have lodged there comfortably, and was on the same side of the house as Ganassateco's own apartment. A room opposite to us was shown to our Gajuka, and we were received with as much cordiality, affection and distinction, as if we were persons of the greatest importance. I cannot express our feelings of gratitude to the Lord, for we saw plainly that He had gone before us and prepared our way.

They soon gave us something to eat, and more was being prepared, when a deputy from Ganassateco arrived, inviting us to his Council. This was an unexpected and important message to us. We at once followed our messenger to the house, and he introduced us. When we entered we saw a goodly assembly of important people sitting around their fire, Ganassateco in the midst of them. We immediately went toward him, and he came to meet us. We shook hands with him, as well as with all the others, and greeted them. He knew at once who we were, called us by name, and seemed very much pleased to see us. He began to laugh for joy, in his peculiar manner, and one felt and saw that we were welcome guests. Thereupon they made room for us in their midst, but the Gajuka, who, much astonished, had followed us at a distance, sat down near the door in order to listen.

We sat down, and all looked at us very kindly, particularly those two who had been in Philadelphia, Ganatschiagaje and Ganechwatikhe, (Totegechnati and Ganhajen, and another had died). There was another Indian there, by name of Gashecoa, whom David had known in Shomoko. Not one in the whole Council gave us a grum or suspicious look, but all were cordial and brotherly, and acted as if we were old friends and men to be trusted. I wished my friends, Tgarihontie (John de Watteville's Indian name), and Tgirhitontie (Bishop Spangenberg's Indian name), could have been with me to see this sight, quite worth a journey to Onondago. The assembly consisted of from 24 to 34 persons. Beside the Onondagos were the chief of the

Oneidas from Anajot, named Garistagona, and another old Oneida, and the then chief from Gajuka, named Onechsagerat.

After we had been silent for a little while, I began to speak as follows: Brethren, we have come here to visit you, as we promised in Philadelphia, and gave you a fathom of wampum as a pledge that we would come. We have been sent by our Brethren in Bethlehem to bring you a message, and have arrived safe and well at your fire in Onondago. We are glad to meet you here all together. We wish, first of all, to rest one or two days from our journey, which, as you know, has been long and dangerous, and then we will meet with you again, and tell you the object of our coming. David then translated this message into the Maquai language. My words were received with great applause, accompanied by the usual exclamations of affirmation, in which the voice of Ganassateco was particularly loud, and he showed by his appearance how pleased he was.

We told them that the Gajuka, Hahotschaunquas, was here in the house with us, that he had acted as our traveling companion from Wajomik, as Schickellimy's sons, Thachnechtoris and Sojechtowa, could not come with us for want of time. We told them what route we had taken on our companion's account. They were much interested. Many old men, some very venerable in appearance, who saw us for the first time, smiled to us very kindly. We presented them with a pipe of tobacco, a valuable gift.

Thereupon, to our astonishment, an old Oneida began to sing the message which he had for the Council, in a very high tenor voice. He continued for more than half an hour. It was a message from Sganiotaratichrohni, or from the Nanticokes in Wajomik; firstly, concerning the renewal of their covenant, and their gratitude for permission to remain and plant on their land at Wajomik. Secondly, it referred to the land which they still own in Maryland among the whites. The belts were only white, and very poor compared to ours. The Oneida repeated his message and handed over the belts to Ganassateco, who made some remarks and then delivered them to the Council. Afterward Ganassateco told them our names, and mentioned particularly Tgarihontie and Tgirhitontie, whom he had seen and heard in Philadelphia. He told them that they were now across the great waters, and then related his experiences in Philadelphia. A servant was told to bring us something to eat. While we were enjoying it they conversed much with us. We then took leave of them and went to our quarters. David and I were filled with gratitude to the Lord for having thus prepared our way, and brought us at once into the Grand Council, where we and our cause were known.

The news of our arrival soon spread through the whole town. It is a very unusual occurrence for white people to visit Onondago, but no one asked us whether we were traders, or what our business was. All seemed to know us and greeted us kindly. When we arrived at our lodgings we found that they had prepared a meal for us, and our hosts were unremitting in their attentions. An Indian woman, a relative of Ganassateco, who was very tidy and industrious, attended to our wants most carefully. The Indian bread they gave us was better than any I have yet seen. They had a larger provision of Indian corn than is common among Indians at this season. I felt inexpressibly grateful to the Lord for having brought us here in safety.

In a short time the Gajuka chief, who had been in the Council, came to see us. He was very friendly, shook hands with us and said: I am very glad to see you, Brethren. He told us that he would return to Gajuka to-morrow, described his house, and invited us to visit him if we came there, and seemed to regret his having been absent when we passed through. He then inquired about different persons in Shomoko, and took a very affectionate leave of us. Soon after our good friend, Ganassateco, came home. He came to our fire, and appeared so pleased to be able to entertain us, that he scarcely knew how to express his joy. He seemed to feel perfectly at home with us, and treated us like our old friend, Swatane, in Shomoko. He inquired much about Tgarihontie, and said that Tgirhitontie had told him, in Philadelphia, that three of us would come. We said that Anuntschi (Nathaniel Seidel's Indian name) was to have come with us, but because Tgirhitontie had gone he was obliged to remain at home. We perceived that our old friend had remembered very carefully all he had heard, and that he had certainly expected us in Onondago. Therefore if we had not undertaken our journey this year, the Five Nations would have lost confidence in us, for they depended fully on our word, and expected us to come. We were thankful to lodge with our good friend Ganassateco. He told us that he had much to do, and many matters to arrange. We might, indeed, imagine ourselves at a great court, where all the affairs of state are concentrated. It is plain to be seen that the Onondagos are the greatest lords among all the nations, and that the others are quite willing to say "Yea and Amen" to all that they decide upon. We had many proofs of the fact.

Ganassateco asked whether we had recent news from Philadelphia. I told him that I had not been there in a long time, but that I had notified the Onas or Governor, of my journey hither. He asked much about our journey; said we might have come by a shorter route through Owege. We told him that we had been on the way for 35 days from Bethlehem, had stopped a week in Wajomik, and stayed a short time in Ganatocherati and Gajuka. Then he wanted to know why Thachnechtoris and Sojechtowa had not traveled with us. We told him that they had excused themselves for want of time, and because they had heard that war was pending in this neighborhood. He said they knew nothing with certainty, but were daily expecting chiefs from the Zisagechrone (French Indians) and then it would be decided. He then said he would retire, and left us with kind expressions, going to his bed-chamber, which was next to ours. We also went to bed and slept well this first night with our brethren in Onondago.

Saturday, 9-20 June. To-day we observed as a day of rest in Onondago. We felt that the Lord is with us. We slept late, and when we arose our hosts soon brought us refreshments, and attended most carefully to our wants. Several chiefs visited us; they were very friendly and liked to converse. Ganechwatikhe, who lives next door to Ganassateco, related to us of Totegechnati, Ganassateco's counsellor. He told us that he had been very sick on the whole journey from Philadelphia; finally he had a hemorrhage and had died at Tiachton, an Onondaga town, four or five miles from here. He also mentioned another who had been in Philadelphia, and had died last winter.

We were very glad to have arrived here safely, and be able to become personally acquainted with the Indians, a matter of great importance. Ganechwatikhe said their journey here had been a very slow one; they had been more than 30 days on their way from Shomoko to their home. They had traveled by water until two days' journey from here, to a creek where Delawares live, and had then come here on foot. Afterward Ganassateco went to the Council, which is again in session to-day. I took a little walk, and asked the Lord to direct and counsel us in all our affairs. After much conversation on the subject, David and I concluded it would be best to make known our errand first to Ganassateco alone, and explain it to him, so that he could understand it fully and be able to propose it to his Council, which would probably then consider it of more importance. This would facilitate matters for us, as we have not quite mastered their language, and are not at home in their manners and modes of expression. Their language is much richer and more complete than the one spoken in Shomoko, which numbers many less words. Here the Indians have a much greater choice of words and phrases, and we can easily hear that their language is a more cultivated one. We thought we could first explain our matters to Ganassateco, with whom we conversed much, and repeat them to him until he had fully understood them.

In the afternoon David and I crossed the creek Zinschoe, and passed through the rich corn fields, going up the creek to the house where Br. Joseph had lodged with his company, when he was here. At that time there were a number of huts, of which we could still distinguish the sites and ruins, but only 2 houses remained standing. From here we went directly toward the creek, into the thicket, and found a pleasant spot to rest. We sat down, and remembered in grateful words the Lord's goodness, in having watched over us so graciously thus far. Then we prostrated ourselves before God, and offered up fervent intercessions in behalf of the Six Nations, praying the Lord to grant us to see many from among them, hungering for the Bread of Life.

Then, resting on the promise of the Lord's presence, where two or three are gathered together in His name, we celebrated the Holy Communion, and we fully experienced the blessings of the promise. We named the spot the Brethren's Chapel in Onondaga.

Several Indians visited us; all were very kindly disposed. The chief living in the house nearby, came and conversed with us. He said that when Tgirhitontie and his company had lodged in his house, he had been out hunting. He had returned shortly after, but they had left, and he had not been able to make their acquaintance. He is a very sensible and steady man, who feels friendly toward us.

On our return home in the evening we again found a meal prepared. Ganassateco came in soon after and talked very freely with us. The man who served as our messenger to the Council also came. He explained to us that he held the office of assistant to the Council. He then asked us many questions about our Brethren, where we lived, and how far we were from Philadelphia. We answered him at length, told him how far we lived from Wajomik, and that the nearest road from there to Philadelphia passed through Bethlehem. He was much astonished to hear this, and said that last summer, when he was in Philadelphia, he had intended visiting us, but Conrad Weisser, however, had dissuaded him from doing so, telling him that it would be a round about way. He felt provoked at this, and said he had told him untruths. Upon this occasion we invited him, if he should ever come there again, to come from Wajomik to Bethlehem, promising to help him on his journey with horses to Philadelphia. He might then convince himself that this is the nearest route. He was much pleased, and asked, with great interest, whether we had good horses. We told him we had. We had an opportunity of relating to him of the Brethren; we described their towns, and our whole conversation with him was such as we were wont to have with Swatane.

There was another old chief there, named Gajagaja, to whom Ganassateco afterward related and explained much about ourselves. He was also a very pleasant and polite man, who enjoyed our society and visited us frequently. Ganassateco asked us how long we intended remaining here. We told him we could not tell. He said that we should remain in his house as long as we pleased. Afterward an old chief came in and sat down with us. He told us that he was an Oneida from Anajot, and that his name was Garistagona. He was very affable, and immediately began to talk to us. He said he was no great man in Onondaga, and but a small man here. Ganassateco was the great man here and of much importance. In his own city, however, and among his own nation he was also a great man. By what we could understand from his conversation, and from what we learned afterward, he is the head chief of the Oneidas, and lives between this place and Anajot, a good day's journey from here, but spends much of his time in Onondaga. He had been in Philadelphia last summer, but not in the house in which we lodged. He was very anxious to make our acquaintance, and visited us frequently, conversing much with us. Genassateco then retired for the night, and the others went home. David and I spent some time talking over our plans, and asked the Lord to make it clear to us, whether this would be a suitable time to renew our former proposition, viz., of asking their permission for several Brethren to live 2 or more years among them, and learn their language thoroughly.

Sunday, 10-21 June. This morning, soon after we arose, we were served with a bountiful meal. On the whole they were very particular, in Onondaga, that we should not feel the need, of anything, and were anxious for us to relish their fare. Ganassateco's manner was very kind and cheerful; he considered it an honor to entertain us in his house. Later I took a walk, and thought prayerfully of all our matters, asking the Lord to show us His will clearly in perplexities. Upon my return the Council had begun to assemble in our hut. Soon after Ganassateco brought in a scalp of a Gataber; it was skilfully painted and tied to a stick, and had been taken by some warriors who had recently returned from war. It was the subject of a long discourse. David then told Ganassateco that, first of all, we would like to talk over our matters with him alone, so that we might give him a clear idea of our wishes, and that he might then propose them to the Council for us, as we were not perfectly familiar with their language and customs. He consented and immediately arose and left the Council with us.

We seated ourselves on a tree, not far from his house, and made this our Council chamber. We then spoke as follows: Brother, I, Gallichwio and Ganousseracheri, have been sent to you by our Brethren, Johanan, (Zinzendorf's Indian name). Tgarihontie, (Watteville's), Tgirhitontie, (Spangenberg's), who live across the seas, and our Brethren Ganechragijat, (Mack), Anuntschi, (Seidel), and all

who live in our settlements, as messengers to you and your
Council, and to our Brothers, to Aquanoschioni, (Iroquois),
to bring you kind greetings, and, as a token of their feelings
towards you, they send you this fathom of wampum. He
examined the string closely, and asked whether the message
we brought came also from our Brethren across the seas;
and when we said that it did, and that we had received letters from Tgarihontie and the other Brethren, our words
seemed doubly important, and he seemed much astonished.

Thereupon I brought forward the belt of wampum, took
it in my hand, and first told David its signification, saying:
Brethren! Our Brethren on both sides of the sea send this
belt of wampum to our Brethren, the Aquanoschioni, to renew, strengthen and prolong our bond of fellowship with
them. Then I related, very circumstantially, how 8 years
ago, Johanan had spoken with the great men of the nations,
who had been in Philadelphia, when he met them in Conrad
Weisser's house in Tulpehocken. He had made a covenant
with them, and had also received a fathom of wampum
from them. I set forth the conditions of the covenant, viz.,
that we were no traders, and did not come to them from
love of gain, or desire to seize or buy their lands, neither
had we come to the Indians like the priests in the land of
the Maquais. I explained briefly what Johanan had then
said to the nations, and told them that in consequence we
had traveled to their Brethren on the Susquehanna at Wajomik, Shomoko and Long Island, and had been received by
them as Brethren. A result of this covenant was that 5
years ago Tgirhitontie had come here to Onondago and had
visited them, but as none of our Brethren were familiar
with their language, they could not speak to them. In accordance with this covenant we had, with their knowledge
and consent and the desire of Shikellimy and other Indians,
sent one of our Brethren to Shomoko as blacksmith, in order
to work for the Indians. He was still living there and
would remain longer. All this was to be confirmed by the
belt of wampum, while it declared, at the same time, that
we asked permission for several of our Brethren to dwell
among them for a number of years, in order to learn their
language thoroughly, and thus make known to them our
intentions. Thereupon I handed over the belt to David,
who translated all my words into the Maquai language, and

he then presented it to Ganassateco. He accepted it and examined it very carefully, and we could perceive that he considered it of great value.

I then brought forward a fathom of wampum and said: Brethren, on our journey here we halted for 8 days in Wajomik. Several of your Brethren from among the Sganiataratichrohne, or Nanticokes, visited us, and said they would like one of our Brethren, a blacksmith, to dwell among them, to make their guns and axes, and whatever work of that kind was to be done. We answered them, saying: that the land on which they lived belonged to the 5 Nations, and that they had authority to decide in cases of this nature. We were unable to take any steps in this matter, for we were a people who did not wish to gain an entrance to the Indians in any underhanded manner, and therefore, if they wished a blacksmith, they must ask permission of our Brethren, the Aquanoschioni. They granted the justice of our remarks, and expressed themselves unwilling to do anything without the consent of the 5 Nations, and commissioned us to mention their wishes to the Council here in Onondaga, and hear their opinion on the subject. I said: For this reason, Brethren, we give you this fathom of wampum, in order that you may deliberate on this subject, with your brethren, and give us an answer. David translated all this, and gave them the fathom of wampum.

I then took another fathom of wampum and said: Brethren, last summer, when you were in Philadelphia, we made the acquaintance of our Brethren, the Sennekas, and especially of the 3 chiefs, Achsochqua, Hagastaes and Garontianechqui, who live in Zonesschio. They invited us to visit their land and city on our journey hither, and therefore we give you this fathom of wampum. We then said that these were the words and message we had been charged to bring from our Brethren to the Aquanoschioni. All these propositions we wished him to lay before the Council, in order that they might discuss them and give us an answer. We also told him that we had brought with us some gifts from our Brethren to the Council, and that we desired them to make known to us when they were assembled, so that we might present them.

Thereupon he took the wampum, string by string, into his hand, and began to repeat what we had said, in order to see whether he had fully understood us. When he came to the belt he clasped his hands, and asked whether such wewre not our wishes, viz., that we and the Aquanoschioni should be united. We said, yes, and that we should continue to be more closely united and never be separated. We were astonished to see how well he had comprehended all, especially what concerned our mission to the Indians, and the reason of our coming to them.

After he had said that he would make known our propositions to the Council we went home to his house. Many of the chiefs were still there. He told them that we had spoken with him alone, because David was not perfectly familiar with their language, and that we had therefore explained our message to him, so that he might announce it to them. He at once showed them the fathom of wampum and belt and intoned, in the usual Indian fashion, the signification of each, and we saw and heard that he had well understood our words. He laid special emphasis on our not being traders, who come to the Indians to trade with them for furs, or to gain their lands. Neither were we like the priests in Schenectady, (of whom the Indians appear to have a very poor opinion) ; he said that we had priests among us; indeed he believed that most of our Brethren were priests, but quite a different class of people. In order to express this he made use of a word intended to convey the idea that we were good and true Christians. All present were attentive to this explanation, and afterward held a meeting in another house.

David and I took a walk together, and conversed much on the subject of the Lord's gracious guidance thus far, believing that He would continue to be with us in the future. When we came home we found a beautiful repast provided by our hosts. We gave them some needles, some ribbons and scissors, gifts which appeared to afford them much pleasure. After a few hours had elapsed Ganassateco came home, and told us that he could do nothing with his people, as they had become intoxicated; he hoped to be able to speak to them to-morrow. He then talked to us about his family, telling us that he had a son, who was not at home at present, and a daughter who was in the house. His wife was taken sick to-day with fever and pleurisy. Toward evening we had many visits from the drunken Indians; they were, however, not malicious, but very cordial. The old Oneida chief, Garistagona, remained a long time with us. He knew that to-day was Sunday, and sang and preached to us, showing how the priests in the land of the Maquais and Anochquage performed. After he had continued in this way for some time, he wanted to know whether he imitated them correctly. We, however, told him that we did not at all understand their customs, as we were not people like the priests, and had no intercourse at all with them. At last he left us, having told us much about the priests. I could not sleep much during the night, because of the drunken Indians. David, however, who is more accustomed to it, was not disturbed thereby.

Monday, 11-22 June. The Daily Word for to-day: " The Lord bringeth the counsel of the heathen to naught," gave us much food for reflection. To-day we spoke to our Gajuka, Hahotschaunquas, telling him that, as we could not tell when our matters here would come to a close, it would be advisable for him to return to Gajuka to-morrow, with the horses, they being a source of annoyance to us here, and might even be the cause of trouble. We would follow on foot as soon as possible. He was ready at once, and decided to leave to-day. Time had seemed long to him here in Onondaga. He had not found any congenial companions. The people whom he met, and with whom we associated, were too far above him in position. We were glad to be rid of the care of our horses. We have found, here and elsewhere, that traveling on foot is the only way to journey among the Indians, because, with horses, it is frequently impossible to pass over the rough and swampy roads, sometimes covered by fallen trees, making it difficult to lead horses over them, while pedestrians can proceed much more easily; besides, when we reached an Indian settlement, we were harassed day and night by the care of our horses, and were in constant dread of their being shot or injured by drunken Indians, from which danger no one, not even the greatest chief could protect them.

We packed all the luggage we could not carry, and sent the Gajuka away with it. The Indians were very glad that we sent off the horses. We were anxious to see how matters would progress. After noon several chiefs assembled here, to whom Ganassateco intoned our message, and explained at length the signification of the belt and fathom of wampum. He could not tell them Johanan's name, but described him as a very good and important man, who had a European name that he could not remember. By this we saw it was of great importance that so many of our Brethren bore Indian names, and are known to them. He described Tgarihontie and Tgirhitontie to them. We presented them with a piece of tobacco, and placed it in their circle. They were much pleased and divided it among themselves.

Ganassateco then delivered the fathom and belt of wampum to another chief, probably for safe keeping until the Council could deliberate concerning them, which he professed that they would do on the morrow. Afterward they were again invited to a feast and left us, to begin anew their drunken carousals. Ganassateco remained at home, and we had an opportunity of explaining to him the nature of the position which Johanan occupies among us. We did it in language adapted to his comprehension. He had not, thus far, been able to form a clear idea of him. I then spent some time writing. Many drunken Indians came into our house, but were kindly disposed. In the morning David went to the creek to fish; on his return he conversed with Ganassateco on many subjects. He was very lively and intelligent.

Tuesday   12-23 June.   During the morning several chiefs visited us, to whom Ganassateco explained our plans and the message we had brought. He did it openly, in our presence, and we saw how fully he appreciated our wishes in every respect. Afterward he came and talked to us on various subjects. He told us that there was in his house a Gatabe boy, whom the warriors had brought along in the spring, with a woman and girl of the same nation. He then went to the Council, which was to assemble in another house. In a few hours he returned, saying that he made every effort to present our case to the Council, in order to procure an answer for us, but was obliged to abandon the hope of doing so for the present; for we could see for ourselves, the Indians had been drinking freely during these days, and were continuing in their drunken revels, so that we would perhaps be obliged to wait a week, and in the meantime be much annoyed by them. He suggested, therefore, that we should leave our case in his hands, and he would present it as soon as practicable, and then send us the answer by a special runner to Wajomik, Shomoko, Philadelphia, or whatever place we should designate. We told him that we preferred hearing the result of the negotiations from him personally, and in Onondago, and proposed to him that we should visit the land of the Sennekas, and then return to Onondago for our answer. We asked him whether he consented to this arrangement. He said that he did, and could see no objection to it. We told him that we would consider the matter, and then give him a final reply.

We seriously reflected on the subject, and went to Ganassateco and told him that we had considered the matter, and had come to the conclusion that we would now visit Zonesschio in the land of the Sennekas, and return to Onondago in about 20 days. We requested him to present our case to the Council during this time, and have our answer ready, as we should certainly return for it. He agreed perfectly to this plan, and promised to do his utmost in our behalf, saying that he thought the Indians would soon come home, (some of them had left since our arrival, because in a few days they expected their enemies, the Zisagechrohne, from Canada,) and would then at once bring forward our affairs. He thought we need scarcely be absent for 20 days, but might return sooner. He described very minutely our route to the land of the Sennekas through Gajuka. We perceived by this that he did not look upon us with the least mistrust or suspicion, and we accepted this information as a great mark of favor from the Indians, for it is not a matter of indifference to them that white people should know the various trails through their country. We told him that we would start from here tomorrow.

Afterward we ordered some provisions from our hosts for the journey. We were obliged to carry all on our backs, and provide ourselves with a large quantity, because Gajuka is in a very miserable condition, and it is impossible to procure any food there. They prepared some Cittamun, and baked Indian bread for our journey. We then deliberated as to what we had best do concerning the presents we had brought for the Council in Onondago. Seeing no possibility of being able to return them, as we had hoped to do, we resolved to hand them to Ganassateco, and request him to offer them in our name, whenever the negotiations with the Council in our behalf should take place. We called him, and in the presence of two other chiefs, Kagokaga and Gashekoa, told him that these were presents sent by our Brethren to the Council in Onondago, and we would request him to distribute them as soon as the Council had assembled. He asked us whether they were intended for all, and when we replied, " For all the chiefs." he accepted them. and after he and the others had examined them with much admiration, he again packed them up. He then gave an account of us and our Brethren to the two others, and told them how he had seen Tgarihontie and Tgirhitontie in Philadelphia, and had been in our house, all the Onondago chiefs having dined with us. He described everything so minutely that we saw plainly how nothing had escaped his notice. Afterward he spoke to us concerning Johanan, his appearance, and his being the son-in-law of Tgarihontie, also with regard to the acquaintance of Johanan with Gashajen, 8 years ago, in Philadelphia.

In the afternoon David and I went out to see something of Onondago. We went down along the creek Zinochsoe, and found a few huts. Onondago is very much scattered, but the population is greater than one would at first be led to suppose. It consists of 5 small towns, beside the single scattered huts. The whole country is very beautiful and fertile, and Indian corn grows there to perfection. As they keep no cattle, no fences are needed.

When we came home we prepared our packs for the journey, and had some conversation with Ganassateco, who, we were sure, had done all in his power to expedite our affairs. When he was able to gather together only a few chiefs, he had immediately intoned the objects of our mission to them, and begged them to meditate on the subject, so that when the Council should meet they might be able to express their opinion, but all to no effect. Ganassateco's wife was very sick to-day, and therefore 9 to 14 old women came this evening to the house, and offered a sacrifice. They drank to excess, and then danced around the fire as well as they could. At last Ganassateco chased them out of the house, so that from midnight on David and I were able to sleep. We committed our case into the hands of the Lord, and were grateful for all His past mercies.

Wednesday, 13-24 June. It rained very hard this morning, but still we resolved to make a start, and made various preparations for it. We had no straps for carrying. ...David went out and procured some inside bark, and with it manufactured a pair, as well as he could. Thus we were able to carry our burdens, even if not very conveniently, for they were very heavy, as we had provisions to last us for 200 miles. We recommended our matters most earnestly to Ganassateco, bidding him put them in order until our return. I gave my coat to Ganassateco for safe keeping, as it was too heavy. We then packed up our things, took leave of him, and began our journey from Onondago, where we had this time spent 5 days and 5 nights, and had received many blessings. We then ascended the first Prince's Peak, and as it was very warm we perspired freely. We rested a little in the French Camp, and then went on, arriving in the evening at the Lake Sganiatarees, where we built a hut, for which we proceured the bark at a great distance. To-day was St. John's Day, so we named our quarters The Pilgrims' Hut at St. John's Beach. We spent a very happy evening, and were especially glad to be alone and not to have any Indians with us. We had traveled more than 30 miles to-day, in Indian shoes, because ours were torn. This cost me many painful steps and my feet hurt me very much, but I managed to get along. We spent the evening in singing hymns together, and then slept well.

Thursday, 14-25 June. After a very delightful morning we started on our way. We were immediately obliged to cross the lake. On our journey hither we had ridden through it and found it very deep. Now we went to the outlet of the lake, along the creek, trying to find some trees where we could cross, and at last found a place where much timber and many trees had drifted, and we succeeded. We marched on, and after noon arrived at Achsgo and encamped at a spring, where, in the heat of the day, we refreshed ourselves with some Cittamun, (i. e., Indian corn, roasted in the ashes and pounded to flour,) and water. Afterward there was no other means of getting over but by wading, because that where the lake empties into the creek the current was too swift and the stream was too deep. We got ready, tied our baggage together and went into the lake, which it took us about an hour to cross. As it was quite deep and went up to David's arm-pits, we were obliged sometimes to stand still in the water and rest, because of the heavy bundles we carried. We, however, succeeded in crossing safely, and got ready to continue our journey.

Then two women came to us; they were on the chase (the hunt) with their husbands. They led us to a horse, which lay there almost dead. It had been shot in Gajuka by Indians, because it had committed depredations in the corn. This was a new proof to me that horses are very unsafe among the Indians, for this one had belongeed to her husband, who is a chief of the nation. The woman wished us to shoot the horse, but we would have nothing to do with it. Then one of the women began to question us, asking who we were and where we came from. We answered her, and she told us that she was originally from Anajot, and had been baptized by a preacher there, and her name was Margaret, and that the other woman, who was with her, had also been baptized and was named Christine. She said that there were many baptized Indians in Anajot, and there were always one or two preachers there. Her husband, she said, was chief Gajuka to Sagogachgatha, whom we had lately seen at the lake. He, however, was not baptized. She intended soon to travel again to Anajot, in order to have her child baptized. It was 5 or 6 months old, and she had it with her.

She then inquired about Shomoko and the relations of Shikellimi, of whom David could give her tidings, for which she was very glad, and told us that she was Shikellimi's sister. She looked very much like his family. Afterward she was very curious to know what our errand into Onondago had been, and asked whether we had been sent by the Governor in Philadelphia, and had delivered our message at Onondago. She asked us to be kind enough to tell her, so that she might have something to relate to her husband, on his return from the chase. Thereupon David answered her, saying that we had not exactly been sent by the Governor, but that I myself was a great man, and had traveled to Onondago in the interest of my own affairs. We had, it is true, delivered our message, but our affairs were not terminated, and therefore we were obliged to come to Onondago once more, and could not tell her anything before the time. Then she went away.

It was intensely hot, and the flies troubled us greatly. A very heavy thunder storm came directly toward us, and we made all possible haste, reaching Ganatarage just before the rain, stopping with the mother of our Gajuka. He himself was not at home, but had gone to Gajuka. The women of the town held a festival, at which we, too, were present. All went on very quietly. Each one had brought some provisions; one much, another little, and these were divided among all. As we were hungry they tasted very good.

Friday, 15-26 June. We rested long to-day. The great heat of yesterday had made us very weak and tired; afterward we prepared for our journey. We bought a pair of straps for carrying, from our Gajuka's mother, as ours of bark would not answer well, and our baggage had grown heavier. Then we started on our way. It was intensely hot, and David had a great load to carry, between 50 and 60 pounds, and besides, his gun, and powder and lead. However, we were happy together, and when we arrived at Gajuka we immediately met our Gajuka outside, and went with him to our old quarters, although we had intended to lodge with the old chief. We were particularly welcome to the old grandmother of the chief, who is really very much attached to us, and soon waited upon us with a dish of eels. Another Indian also presented us with some. They seem the only things to be had at Gajuka, for the Indian corn looks dry and miserable.

The Gajuka thought we had come from Onondago in order to go home. We told him, however, that we had not finished our affairs there, but would have to go there once more. In the mean time we wanted to go into the land of the Sennekas, to Zonesschio. We asked him, at the same time, whether he would accompany us, as we did not know the way. He stopped to consider a moment, and then resolved to go with us. Thereupon David and I visited the old chief, Onechsagerat. He was not at home but soon came, was very glad to see us, and welcomed us kindly.

He is a very sensible, serious and steady man, and at the same time very sociable. We saw, from his demeanor, that he really loved us, and that Ganassateco, on his late visit to Onondago, must have given a correct account, for the man dealt with us as if we had known him a long time. He immediately told his wife to get something to eat, and to bring along a pewter spoon, (probably the only one in the house) which she did. We discussed various matters with him, concerning our errand to Onondago, saying that we thought of making a journey into the land of the Sennekas, and would then return to Onondago to receive our answer. He said it would be well to visit their neighborhood, and become acquainted with the Indians there, and seemed to think that we ought to have a thorough knowledge of all Indians, their affairs and lands. He related to us that many years ago he had lived in Canastoge, probably on the Susquehanna, in the neighborhood of John Harris. We told him of the Brethren, and described to him where we lived, which seemed to please him very much. David told him of Shomoko and Shikellimi's relatives, with whom he was acquainted and in whom he was much interested. Then he invited us to come to his house to-morrow morning, before starting. He wanted to make us a warm drink.

We then returned to our quarters, and afterward took a little walk along the lake and held pleasant converse together. Our old mother had, in the mean time, cared for us and found a means of crossing the lake to-morrow, having spoken to a man who had a large canoe, and was willing to take us over for some tobacco. She was much troubled because she could not give us any Indian corn to take with us, as there was no more to be had here, but we comforted her, and told her that we had brought provisions for our journey from Onondago. During the evening we had many visits from Indians, who were all very modest; afterward we retired.

Saturday, 16-27 June. We were called very early to the old chief's, Onechsagerat's, who had yesterday invited us to breakfast. We went there and were curious to see what he would offer us, as he had said that he would make us a drink. When we got there he set out a tea table, consisting of two blocks used for crushing corn, and then he prepared some very good tea, to which he added Indian bread. The tea cups were a very large spoon and a wooden dish. The tea was boiled in a kettle which hung over the fire. The chief himself was our waiter, and was very attentive to our wants. It tasted very good. We looked on this as our Sabbath Love Feast.

We talked over with him our visit to Onondago, and many other matters. He was very bright, and we could see that we were welcome guests. He told us that he was on the point of accompanying another Indian to Onondago, who was going to Schochery, a distance from Gajuka of about 6 or 7 days journey, if you walked very fast, therefore at least 200 miles. He invited us to visit him again on our return from the land of the Sennekas, which we promised to do. He presented us with some salt for the journey, for he said there was none to be had there, as here and in Onondago were the only salt springs to be found. In Onondago, as well as here, they boil quite fine white salt. We took a very affectionate leave of the old chief, returned to our quarters and packed up our things.

Our ferryman had already arrived. He was a fine, modest Indian, named Gannekachtacheri (this is also the name Secretary Peters in Philadelphia bears). He is of importance among his nation, a great warrior, and said to be always very successful in war. We then took leave of our hosts in Indian fashion, and went with our Gajuka to the lake, which was pretty rough and broke in great waves, it being quite windy. We got into our bark canoe and set off. Some Indians in another canoe went with us to Nuquiage. Our bark vessel danced around bravely on the waves, and the water came in freely, as the lake was very wild. Near the shore the water was green, but in the middle it was blue as the ocean, and the Indians say it may be 20 to 30 fathoms deep. In the middle of the lake we saw in the east and northeast the Gajuka town of Sannio, about ten miles distant; in the west a town called Ondachoe, said to be larger than Gajuka, about 15 miles from us, but which we could not visit this time.

We crossed the lake in about two hours, landed, and then started on our way. It was again intensely hot. Our course lay west by north and west northwest. We soon entered a wilderness, which we called the Dry Desert, because we found no water, and were obliged to suffer from great thirst on account of the intense heat. At last, after we had walked about 20 miles, we came to the first running water, which Gallichwio named the Golden Brook, because, although the water was rather warm, it tasted so good to him. We continued our journey and walked very fast, from 14 to 15 miles, again without water. At last we came to a creek called Ganazioha, where we found an Indian, who had procured rum from a French trader living farther on, near Lake Nuquiage. We went on and arrived about an hour before sunset at Nuquiage, a Gajuka town. The Indians went directly toward the house of the French trader, who fills the whole neighborhood with his rum. Then we went into it also, and he bade us welcome. He immediately offered us roasted eels, and made us punch to drink, and inquired whence we came. We told him as much about ourselves as it was necessary for him to know.

He was entirely in Indian dress, could speak the language of the Sennekas very well, but, as he said, could neither understand English nor Low Dutch. His merchandise consisted chiefly of rum, of which he had but little remaining.

The Indians then began to drink in good earnest. An Indian also came for rum from Zonesschio, in the land of the Sennekas, a place at least 120 miles distant. We had much trouble to get our Gajuka away, and when we succeeded he was half intoxicated. The trader allowed us to use his boat to cross the river, which flows from the lake and is very rapid and deep. Generally it is necessary to wade there, where the river flows out of the lake. The current is so swift, and the river so deep, we must be very sure footed to be able to pass through it. We walked a short distance along the water's edge, toward the boat, and found that it was on the opposite shore. The Indian who was to row us over, swam across and brought the boat, in which we crossed. We passed over a beautiful plain, where the grass stood as high as a man, and then continued up the river to Lake Nuquiage, from which the village receives its name. The Indians say that the lake is very much larger than Gajuka Lake, and that both flow together, and then through Lake Tionctora into Lake Ontario. We constructed a hut for ourselves, as well as we could. In the evening we heard the intoxicated people in the town, making a great noise. We called our quarters the Pilgrim's Retreat, and were glad to have escaped the storm so safely. During the night there came up a thunder storm, with a pouring rain, and as our hut was not secure we could not keep dry; however, we felt ourselves safe in the Lord's keeping.

Sunday, 17-28 June. Early in the morning it was very wet and warm. We made an early start. Our course lay west southwest; we came into the land of the Sennekas, which borders on that of the Gajukas. About four miles from the lake we came into the neighborhood of the site of the old city of Ganechstage, which is said to have been very large. It was destroyed by the Onontio or Governor of Canada, according to what the Indians say, 60 or more years ago. Now we could discover where the farms must have been. It is a very beautiful tract of land, with good springs of fresh water. It lies so high that one could see from here to Gajuka, about 50 miles distant. From the road we could see that it must have been a very large city. A few isolated huts are still standing, from which led footpaths. We took one of them. It led us too far to the left, and we at last entered a beautiful, fruitful valley, where we encamped along a creek, and ate some of the pigeons David had shot on the way. The Gajuka told us that when the French had destroyed the city, they had killed only 7 Indians, but had taken the whole city, which was very large. The surrounding country is very pleasant, like a pleasure garden in the desert, to which I know no comparison in this country.

We saw clearly that we had gone too far south, and out of our course. The Gajuka therefore went to look for the way. He found the huts which constitute new Ganechstage, and asked directions. We started going directly to the right until we came to the footpath, and saw the city, consisting of only 8 or 9 huts. This time we did not enter it, but continued straight on and came into a terrible wilderness. Then we had a worse road than we had on the whole journey. The Gajuka told us, in starting, that we would have to pass over a bad road, and if he said the road was bad, it must certainly be *very* bad. Thus far we had at least been able to travel on the ground, but now we went through swamps and marshes, where the flies troubled us greatly. For miles we were obliged to walk on trees and branches, as on both sides were deep marshes, bushes and thorns, which make an inconvenient bridge, for we sometimes slipped from the trees and branches, and fell into the swamp, and could scarcely get up again with our heavy bundles. We called the road the Long Bridge. It would have been quite impassable with horses, and the Indians say that no one can travel this road except on foot. After we had continued in this swamp for about six miles we came to a creek, called Axoquenta or Firestone Creek. From thence the road was a little better. Toward evening we reached an old Indian settlement, where a city by the name of Onnachee is said to have stood, but which is now uninhabited. We were caught in a dreadful thunder and rain storm, and were thoroughly drenched, particularly in going through the tall grass. We went on a little farther and encamped along a creek called Otochshiaco. David built a hut as best he could, with the little bark to be found. We tried to dry ourselves at the fire, and called our quarters Senneka Mail Station, and went to sleep, feeling cold and wet.

Monday, 18-29 June. The day began very warm, and we felt rather tired, as we had been walking very steadily for some days. Our breakfast, according to the custom of the Indians, consisted of some Cittamun, boiled in water. This was our fare for breakfast, dinner and supper. We then started and soon reached a place called Otochtschiaco, from which the creek receives its name. Forty or fifty years ago, as the Gajuka told us, the 5 Nations fought a battle there with the Zisagechrohne, and defeated and took them prisoners. We continued on our way to Lake Onnachee, passing along its shores to its outlet, where it is crossed by an Indian bridge. This was the first of this kind that we had seen. It was constructed on stakes, driven into the ground and bound together by bark, and on these small trees and poles had been laid, over which we were obliged to walk; a very dangerous proceeding. The water was very deep and clear, and we saw many fish in it. We encamped on the opposite shore while David fished.

The lake flows N.E. and S.W., toward N.E., and empties

into Lake Tionctong, and fron thence into Lake Ontario. This is the last lake which takes this course, as from here all the water flows in a different direction toward the north, directly into Lake Ontario. The whole aspect of the country changes here, and becomes more mountainous than we have yet seen it. After resting a short time near the lake, an Indian crossed the bridge, carrying a deer which he had shot in this neighborhood. He was very friendly, inquired where we came from, and expressed great surprise when he heard that we were from Philadelphia, and had come from Onondago. He left us, but soon returned and talked to the Gajuka, who, as usual, informed him that I was a great man, and had brought a message to the Council in Onondago. Thereupon he invited us to dine at his house, which, as he described, was a few miles distant from here, in the Seneca town of Ganataqueh. We spent a short time fishing in the lake, and caught a peculiar kind of fish, unknown to us. Thence we proceeded to the town, which is situated on a hill. The huts were ornamented with red paintings of deer, turtles, bears, etc., designating to what clan the inmates belonged. We entered the house of the man by whom we had been invited. He welcomed us very kindly and offered us corn and beans. His name is Tanochtahe, a great warrior, as we could learn from the paintings in his house, and he bids fair to become an important personage among them. He invited us to stay with him to-day, as he wished to regale us with venison. We resolved to remain, as we needed the rest, and I did not feel very well. He at once assigned a couch to us, and then took 2 guns, went out and fired a salute of 4 shots, to announce to the whole town that a distinguished man had come under his roof. We then lay down to rest, and he made preparations to boil a kettle of venison and corn for us. An old chief, named Nenhogawe, and two others soon came. He wakened David and bade us welcome. He assumed an air of great importance, and inquired in a very authoritative way, who we were? whether we were envoys from Onas? whether the Nations would come down this year? etc.

To all this David replied as follows: We come from the vicinity of Philadelphia, are not envoys of Onas, but Gallichwio has traveled to Onondaga concerning his own affairs. He had made his propositions to the Council, but as yet had received no answer, and was, therefore, unable to say what feelings they entertained with regard to the propositions. It would, for this reason, be unadvisable to speak of matters before the time, which might never come to pass. The Indian then made many inquiries of the Gajuka, who could give him no other information than that we had been in communication with the great men in Onondaga. This was all he knew. At last this satisfied him, and he told us that he was well acquainted with Conrad Weisser, had enjoyed a good drink in his house. He had also been in Philadelphia, but not last summer.

During this afternoon many Indians visited us. I had an attack of chills and fever, accompanied by severe headache, with great exhaustion. In the evening a drinking bout was held in the old chief's house, to which our Gajuka was also invited. After they had been together for some time a message summoned us to come down to them. I excused myself on the plea of not being well, and David went alone. They saluted him, and said that because we had come into their town they wished to show us a mark of great respect, and therefore invited us to be present at this feast. David addressed them: We were not people who could tolerate drunkenness. We only used strong drink when needful for purposes of healing.; but to drink to excess was wicked and injurious, as they doubtless knew from experience. They urged him at least to drink their health, which he did. In the meantime the old chief explained to the others, in a long address, intoned and sung in the Indian manner, what David had said. Then they gave him something to bring to me, as I was sick. When he returned to them he said he would retire, as we intended to leave to-morrow. They again drank his health, and allowed him to depart in peace. We commended ourselves in prayer to the Lord.

Tuesday, 19-30 June. Our night was a very disturbed one and we could sleep but little, for all in the town were in a state of intoxication, and frequently rushed into our hut in this condition. There was every reason to think that fighting might ensue, as there were many warriors among those who were perfectly mad with drink. We did our utmost to prevail on our Gajuka to sleep, so that he might become sober, for he had completely lost his senses by drinking,. but all to no purpose. It was easy to see that it would not be well for us to remain here longer. From our hostess, who was still sober, we learned the way to Zonesschio. When they saw that we intended to start, our host and another Indian, each took a gun and fired a number of shots, after which they and a drunken old chief went with us. David begged the Indian woman to go with us, in order to show us the way, for all the others were drunk, but she did not come. As the Indians accompanied us they fired continually, right over our heads, but the Lord watched us so that no harm came to us. The Gajuka remained behind, and we went on our way alone. I was very weary, and all my limbs ached. We had left without having had anything to eat.

Our way led through swamps, and for a long distance we found no water. In the afternoon we reached a creek, where we encamped. David refreshed me with some tea and Indian bread, that our hostess had baked for our journey. We went on, generally taking a course to the west. There were many hills to be ascended, adding greatly to the fatigue of our journey. We were, however, strengthened to travel more than 30 miles to-day and at last reached a creek, near which, on a slight ascent, stood the Seneca town of Hachniage. In the first hut we entered there were only women at home. We then went to another, occupied by the chief of this town, named Tschokagaas. We entered and saluted him. He received us very kindly and bade us be seated. He was a venerable, unassuming old man. He expressed great surprise at seeing us, and asked whether we had traveled alone and had no Indian with us, and wanted to know how we had been able to find the way. We told him who we were and where we came from, and what had been the fate of our traveling companion. He showed great pity for us, and said that he was much pleased to entertain us. He had boiled trout and Indian corn, and wondered whether we could eat Indian fare, as not all the Asseroni were able to. We assured him that we could eat anything that Indians did, a fact which seemed to please him very much, and he set before us a large kettle full, that tasted very good. We conversed much, and gave him some information concerning ourselves and the Brethren. He told us that one chief whom we intended to visit was not at home, but had gone to Ohio, but that the two others were.

David and I walked out to see the lake, which is very near and is called Hachniage. It is not very large, but a large creek, with considerable falls, flows from it toward Lake Ontario. In a quiet spot, which we named Hall of Joy, we read the text for the day and lifted up our hearts in prayer to the Lord, in the land of the Sennekas. On our return we spent a happy evening with our host. He told us that from here to the great Falls of Niagara, which are 80 fathoms high, it was as far as to Onondago, i. e., about 170 miles. To Lake Ontario the distance was between 90 and 100 miles, and about 2 days' journey S. E. to the river Tiaogo, where we had left our canoe. We retired and slept very comfortably. Our Gajuka arrived late at night. He had slept off his intoxication, and had at once started to join us.

Wednesday, 20 June--1 July. We rose very early, as we wished, if possible, to reach Zonesschio to-day. Our host was very friendly and conversed much with us. He told us it was a 3 days' journey from here to the Ohio, where the Indians had lately made and launched their canoes. About a day's journey from Zonesschio to Ohio, across the mountains, there was an oil spring, from which the oil gushed from the earth with great force and permeated the whole neighborhood. He showed us some of this oil, which he had himself procured there last autumn and preserved in a · calabash. It was too sharp to take inwardly, he said, but was much used and very good for out ward applications in cases of pain in the limbs.

After having partaken of some food we started on our way with our Gajuka. A goodly number of boys and girls escorted us out of the town and pointed out our way. We were abliged to ascend a high and steep hill, which we named Turkey Hill, because of our having shot a turkey on it, a most acceptable gift at this time, our provisions being in a very low state. The heat was intense and we perspired freely. Our course lay W. We crossed a creek named Noehnta, flowing from a lake of the same name, surrounded by high mountains. After going on a little farther we crossed another creek, and rested because of the great heat. My heart was filled with many grateful thoughts to the Lord for His gracious leading.

Having been refreshed by our rest we made considerable progress on our way, and reached another lake, named Ohegechrage, going some distance along its shores. We were obliged to ford it at its outlet, where it is very deep. This exertion fatigued us very much, and I was feverish with much pain in my head and heaviness in my limbs. We came to a hunting lodge, and as I was very tired we halted. David roasted the turkey he had shot, and we ate it with much relish, but yet it was scarcely sufficient to appease our hunger. We spent a pleasant evening, talking over the way we had come.

Thursday, 21 June-2 July. I passed a sleepless night, partly because of the flies, and partly because I was very tired and suffering with dreadful pains in my head. David was much concerned about me, and said I looked very sick and miserable. I prayed to the Lord to help us in our trials. We prepared for our journey, and named our quarters Tgarihontie's Monument, because he is by name a Senneka. As we continued we saw many tracks of elks; they, as well as buffaloes, abound in this country. It was about 10 miles from our resting place to Zonesschio, where we arrived quite early in the morning. The village consisted of 40 or more large huts, and lies in a beautiful and pleasant region. A fine large plain, several miles in length and breadth, stretches out behind the village. The river Zonesschio, from which the town derives its name, flows through it from S.S.E. to N.N.W., and empties into Lake Ontario. The road from here to Ohio leads W.S.W., 70 or 80 miles from here. The Ohio River flows from N.E. and makes a curve of S.E. and then S., emptying into the Mississippi. It is a very rapid river, with many falls in the upper part, but afterward is said to flow on a fine smooth stream.

When we caught sight of the town we heard a great noise of shouting and quarreling there, from which we could infer that many of the inhabitants were intoxicated, and that we might expect to have an uncomfortable time. On entering the town we saw many drunken Indians, who all looked mad with drink. We inquired for the lodge of the chief Garontianechqui, and were obliged to pass through the whole village in order to reach it.   On our way we were everywhere surrounded by drunken savages.   The sachem was not at home, but his wife, an aged, good little woman, stood outside of the hut and gave us a kindly welcome, urging us, however, to enter, as a great drunken crowd surrounded the dwelling and wanted to approach us.   We went in and sat down, but were immediately followed by the drunken savages, some of whose faces wore an expression more dreadful than anything we had ever seen, showing that they had been in this frightful state of intoxication for some days.   Our Gajuka grew anxious and perplexed, and left very hastily, as he no doubt feared some trouble in store for us.   In the meantime the sachem's wife sent for her husband.   He came, after much delay, but was drunk like the rest.   He, however, recognized us and bade us welcome, expressing his pleasure at seeing us.   The house was soon filled with savages, who made a terrible noise, yelling frightfully.   Our lives being in danger we were led to a small hut near by, which they thought more secure.   It was quite a narrow place, with so little space that 6 or 7 men could scarcely stand within.   We sat down in a corner and waited to see how matters would proceed.   The old chief came to us and wanted to converse.   He said that his house was the largest in the town, and the meeting place for the Council as well as their fortress, so that he could not keep the drunken Indians out of it.   We told him to go away and sleep until he was sober, which he promised to do, for we wanted to talk over our affairs with him to-morrow.   His wife brought us some food, which was only half cooked because of the drunken Indians, but we had no opportunity or quiet time in which to eat it.

Although they gave us Garontianechqui's youngest brother as a protector, a man about 30 years old, yet his presence was of no avail; great crowds came in to us, men and women, who, with but few exceptions, were intoxicated and kept up a frightful noise.   A few of those who were partly sober, tormented us with all sorts of questions.   One in particular, who could speak a little broken English, was especially annoying.   He told us that he was the only one who understood English, and gave us to understand that we should use him as interpreter in our affairs.   David, however, told him to speak to us in Maquai, as we found that language more intelligible than his English, which was very imperfect. We told them that we had come from Onondago, where we had held a council with the Indians, and had merely come here to visit them. There were some Twightwees here, who had been present at the treaty in Lancaster two years ago. They live farther down the Ohio, and are very tall, fine looking Indians, but a very savage and rough people.

After we had spent several hours in this noise, and there seemed to be no means of keeping off or protecting ourselves against the drunken savages, the sachem's wife begged us to go up into their garret. She gave us her brother-in-law as guard to keep them off, (the drunkards). They all appeared to fear that we might be hurt. We climbed up into the loft, which was a veritable prison, only large enough for us to lie side by side. It was under a shingle roof, on which the sun shone, intensely hot. At the gable end there was a hole, barely large enough for David to creep out, and I could effect an exit only with great difficulty. David and I sat there together; I very tired and trying in vain to eat some of our half cooked beans and corn. David at last, after several attempts, succeeded in making me some tea. It was a difficult matter to conceal anything from the drunken savages. We comforted one another with the Daily Word, and felt assured of the Lord's presence with us in this distressing situation.

During the afternoon the second chief, who had been in Philadelphia, named Hagastaes, visited us. He was, however, so drunk that we could have no sensible conversation with him, and we only signified to him that on the morrow we would like to speak with him and Garontianech-qui, and therefore wished them to be sober. He then left us. We heard and saw more noise and confusion than we had yet witnessed anywhere. The sachem's wife did her utmost to keep off the drunken savages, and we were no longer much annoyed by them. Notwithstanding our miserable couch, we felt secure, believing that the Lord had led us here, and that we were safe under the shadow of His wings.

Friday, June 22-July 3. We spent a very noisy night; the confusion and noise never ceased, and the drinking was kept up all night long. There were about 200 drunken

people in the town.   They procure the rum in canoes from
Oswego, as the Zonesschio flows into Lake Ontario, which
is about one day's journey from here.   High falls in the
river make it impossible for them to descend in their
canoes, and they must carry them up and down.   Rum
causes them to lose all self-control, and when they have once
begun to drink, they cannot stop till they have consumed
all the liquor in the town.   David and I deliberated as to
what we had best do under these circumstances, for there
appeared no prospect of a change.   We finally decided to
remain to-day and start on our return to Onondago to-
morrow.

Soon after both chiefs, Garontianechqui and Hagastaes
came to us, as we had told them that we would converse
with them to-day.   They were, however, both, and one in
particular, still as much under the influence of liquor as
yesterday.   They put several questions, and always came
back to the same idea, that we had been sent with a message from the Governor or Conrad Weisser, and were commissioned to invite them to come to Philadelphia.   We assured them several times that such was not our errand,
and reminded them of our Brethren Tgarhontie and Tgirhitontie, Anuntschi, etc., and of what had been said to them
in Philadelphia by Tganiatarechoo or Pyrlaeus.   We told
them that we had been sent by our Brethren to renew and
confirm our covenant with them on various subjects.   At
the same time we related, as briefly as possible, the chief
points of our affairs in Onondago.

David repeated these several times in order to see
whether they had fully grasped the idea.   The task seemed
to be a hopeless one, and so we told them that we would
leave here to-morrow and return to Onondago, in order
there to await our answer from the Council.   Thereupon
they tried to persuade us to remain at least two days
longer.   By that time all the liquor would have been consumed, and they would then call the chiefs together, in
order to speak to us.   We told them, however, that we
could not postpone our leaving any longer than to-day, and
that we would start to-morrow at break of day, for we
had said that they should cease drinking, in order to be in
a condition to speak to us to-day.

They repeatedly urged us to remain and then left.   We,

however, were decided on carrying out our intention of leaving here on the morrow. We therefore asked the sachem's wife, who had cared for us so faithfully, to prepare some Indian meal for our journey. From the whole state of affairs we plainly saw that on this visit we could accomplish nothing here, but only keep the promise made in Philadelphia, to acquire a more correct knowledge of the land of the Sennekas and their people. In Philadelphia we and our people had formed an incorrect idea of the Sennekas, as they had there given quite a different impression of themselves, and had adopted French manners, whereas, in their own country they were perfectly natural, and showed themselves in their true colors. Although in Philadelphia we took all pains to explain to them our connection with Aquanoschioni, yet we saw clearly that they understood little or nothing, and were still in the dark as regarded our affairs. We did not feel as if they felt as kindly and affectionately toward us as did the Onondagos and Gajukas.

On the whole, the Sennekas are a much rougher and more savage nation than the Gajukas and Onondagos. I do not see how, at the present time, any one of our Brethren can possibly subsist and live among the Sennekas, while, on the contrary, among the Gajukas and Onondagos we felt that the Lord was opening a way for us, and that our mission and what we are trying to do is being made plain to them. From the very beginning of our entrance into the land of the Sennekas, David and I had both experienced a strange, unaccountable feeling of depression, as if Satan and all the heathen powers of darkness were seeking to resist us. We comforted each other with the Daily Word, and entreated the Lord to protect us against the snares of Satan.

I remained in our hut very tired. In the evening, when I left our prison for a short time, I could scarcely walk, as I had eaten very little for several days. During the afternoon my faithful David tried to make some tea for me. It was a great undertaking, for he was obliged to procure the water half a mile to and from, and had to pass all the houses, filled with drunken Indians. On his way back with the kettle of water, several of the drunken savages caught him and drew him into a house, took his kettle, drank the water, and it was only after many efforts that he succeeded in regaining the kettle. He returned to the spring and filled it a second time, but some drunken savages pursued him again. He, however, ran too quickly for them and gained the hut, but by a long circuit through long grass. David then boiled the water, with much trouble and fear, and we refreshed ourselves with some tea, the only nourishment I had taken in two days.

In the afternoon Garontianechqui's third brother, who was still sober, came to see us and conversed much with us. He was a fine looking man and resembled our Gottlieb in Gnadenhutten. We again told him of our intention to start early to-morrow morning, and gave him a piece of tobacco and several pipe-stems, to present to the chiefs when they were sober. We asked him to tell them that we deeply regretted having come such a long distance without being able to talk with them. For his wife we left some thread and needles, and desired her to bake some corn bread this evening for our journey. She was prevented from doing so, howver, by the drunken Indians, and we could procure none. Toward evening David went out once more, and on his return a troop of drunken women came rushing madly toward him. Some of them were naked, and others nearly so. In order to drive them away he was obliged to use his fists, and deal out blows to the right and left. He climbed up a ladder, but when he had scarecly reached the top they seized it and tore it from under his feet, but he regained our retreat in safety.

In the meantime the yelling and shrieking continued frightfully in the whole village. It is impossible to describe the confusion to any one who has not witnessed it. Late in the evening Garontianechqui's wife brought us the Indian meal she had prepared for our journey. It was most providential, for without it we could not have started. One of the chiefs, Hagastaes, visited us quite late, but he was still drunk, and we could have no conversation with him. He was not satisfied with our plan of leaving to-morrow. We went to sleep, sure of the Lord's protecting care, praying Him to have mercy on this miserable people and bring them into His fold.

Saturday, 23 June-4 July. During the whole night the orgies continued in the town, and I scarcely slept at all. Early, at first dawn of day, we both arose, packed up and prepared for our journey. At first we did not venture to leave without giving notice, and as we could not go down into the hut from within, David did his utmost to awake our protector by repeated calls. We also rapped vigorously to arouse him, but all to no purpose; and we looked upon it as a special providence of the Lord that the Indian did not awake. He might, perhaps, have made our departure known in the town, and thus we would have incurred the risk of being detained. As we had told them yesterday that we intended to leave early this morning, we resolved to depart quietly, asking the Lord to guide us. David was obliged to jump out of the opening and search for the ladder, which the savages had removed. We then wished to throw out our packs, but David's was so large that he found it necessary to open it, and cast down its contents singly. All this was done amid great fear of being seen by the drunken savages. The Lord watched over us in such a manner that all the drunken savages were in their huts, not a creature to be seen. Even the dogs, numbering nearly 100 in the whole village, were all quiet, wonderful to relate, and not a sound was heard. A dense fog covered the town, so that we could not see 20 steps before us. A squaw stood at the door of the last hut, but she was sober and returned our greeting quietly. In short we saw clearly that the Lord Himself had removed all obstacles from our path, so that we could depart unhindered. Our feelings on climbing the hill on which the town lies, can be more easily imagined than described. Our hearts were filled with gratitude for this signal deliverance, while at the same time they yearned with pity toward this people, for whom we entreated the Lord to open to them the gates leading to the way of life, now so doubly barred by His enemies and Satan. David and I will certainly never, as long as we live, forget our sojourn in Zonesschio.

We hastened with all possible speed, and though I had not taken any food for several days, I felt unusually bright, and was able to hurry on, much to my own and David's surprise. We passed Tgarhontie's Monument, reached Lake Ohegechrage, went through the creek, and made a fire to prepare some food, for we were very hungry. David boiled some Cittamun in water, as we had nothing else. With this we refreshed ourselves and rested after our trials. We feared the danger of pursuit, because of their unwillingness yesterday to have us go, but we remained unmolested. They were, doubtless, too deeply intoxicated to have any recollections of what had transpired.

It grew very warm as we proceeded, and owing to the hills we were obliged to climb our journey was very fatiguing, but we felt thankful and were in good spirits. At noon we reached Lake Noehnta, encamped there on account of the great heat, and refreshed ourselves with Cittamun and cold water from a brook. Afterward we ascended Turkey Hill, which is very high and steep, and we were strengthened beyond our expectation, so that we were able to reach Hachniage in the evening. We at once went to the house of the old chief Tschokagaas, who had lodged us before. The old man and his wife were at home. He at once received us very kindly, bade us sit down, and offered us some food, which we enjoyed very much. He was surprised to see us return so soon from Zonesschio. We gave him an account of the condition in which we had found Zonesschio, and at the same time told him the object of our mission, what we had lately done in Onondago, and what we had desired to tell the Senneka chiefs in Zonesschio, so that at some future time he might make it known to them. He appeared well satisfied with our communication, and said that they were in the habit of drinking very freely in Zonesschio, but that in his neighborhood very little rum was used. He was a very bright, intelligent man. We felt very comfortable with these people.

The chief told much of his journeys S.W. and S.S.W. He had been about 20 days' journey distant at the Ohio and Mississippi, therefore about 1,200 miles from here. A great many Indians lived there, and he says they have large towns. Where he had been, farther up, a great many white people lived in large cities, surrounded by high walls, with large houses and towers. He meant churches. He said, however, that they were not English. They spoke a different language from the English and French, but used silver coins, like the English. According to his description of their dress and manners they must be Spaniards. He told of the silver mine there, which is said to be a very rich one; that silver was found pure in the earth, and that formerly the whites had waged a long and bloody war with the

Indians, in order to gain possession of it. Thus he talked very interestingly about the nature of the country, the rivers, lakes, etc., and inquired about our circumstances and where we lived. Whereupon we told him of our Brethren and of our connection with the Indians, and gave him much information, which seemed to please him.

His son brought home a large trout, which he had killed with an arrow in the brook near the village. It was the largest and finest David and I had ever seen. It was at least ¾ of a yard long and very heavy. He made us a present of it, and we found it a most acceptable gift.

Sunday, 24 June-5 July. Early this morning, after having enjoyed our trout for breakfast, we took an affectionate leave of our host, and prayed sincerely that the Lord might reward him for all the kindness he had showed us. He is certainly a man inclined to listen to the preaching of the Gospel. We then started. It was intensely hot, and we knew that our journey lay through a region where we would find but little water. After having gone some distance we grew very thirsty, and quenched our thirst with some whortleberries that were tolerably ripe, and David shot a few pigeons. At noon we at last came to some stagnant water, all covered with a green scum. We were almost perishing with thirst, and were so worn out that we drank some of this water with Cittamun. Mosquitoes, the great plagues of the wilderness, troubled us dreadfully. While we rested, we conversed on the subject of our mission to the heathen, and our hearts warmed as we spoke of our calling and our work.

We then proceeded and met an Indian from Ganataqueh, who was going to the chase. David asked him how matters looked in the town, whether they were drinking? He answered, No. The heat was so dreadful that we almost fainted. Not a leaf moved throughout the dense forest. In the afternoon we again arrived at Ganataqueh. Only a few of the male inhabitants were at home; all had gone to the chase. The chief, Nenhogawe, who had entertained us on our former visit, was also absent. We therefore only rested in the shade before Tanochtahe's hut. A very friendly man came up and talked to us. He mentioned a chief living in Ganechsatage by the name of Gajinquechto. He said his house was large and we could put up there. He

also described the nearest route from there to Lake Nuquiage, where we had lately been. We soon continued on our
way to Lake Onachee, where we met several Indians. A
heavy thunder storm arose, and we made all possible speed
to reach our former quarters before the rain came on. We
succeeded in doing so, but the bark of the hut had been so
dried by the great heat that we found it useless; we then
set to work to peel some as quickly as possible. The rain
poured down upon us, but we did not allow ourselves to be
interrupted in our work, and completed our hut, built a
large fire at which we could dry ourselves, and afterward
we ate several pigeons that David had shot. We spent a
happy evening singing hymns together.

Monday, 25 June-6 July. To-day we rose early, before
break of day, and after we had breakfasted on our usual
dish of Cittamun we started on our way. During the morning we had a very heavy shower and our clothes were wet,
either from rain or perspiration, from morning till night.
We, however, went on quietly and in good spirits, notwithstanding our discomforts. We crossed the fourfold swamp,
the long bridge, and many marshes and bogs. Because it
was very wet and slippery I often sank deeply into them.
The mosquitoes worried us dreadfully, and in spite of all
the marshes we found no drinking water. In the afternoon we arrived at Ganechsatage, and repaired to the house
of the chief Gajinquechto. He and his wife were not at
home, but came after we had been there a short time,
received us very kindly, and at once offered us venison.
We made inquiries concerning the route we were to take.
The sachem's wife went with us and pointed it out, and so
we journeyed on, passing old Ganechsatage, and at noon
reached a spring. Here we halted because of the heat.
We met several Indians who had been hunting with bows
and arrows.

Thence we proceeded to Lake Nuquiage. A few miles
this side of the lake we met several Indians, of whom we
inquired whether the lake was deep. They assured us that
it was not. However, when we reached the lake and came
to the place where we were to wade across, we saw that it
was very deep and the current very swift, yet we had no
idea of its real depth. There appeared to be no other means
of crossing than to wade, because we were too far from the

town to make ourselves heard by shooting or calling. We made all needful preparations, and tried to arrange our things in such a manner as to keep them dry. David then ventured into the lake, but had scarcely advanced three steps from the shore when the water came up to his body, and the current was so strong that it carried him off his feet. When I saw in what great danger he was, I hastened to his aid, but he continued on until the water reached his arm-pits. He tried to stem the current and could scarcely keep up. He determined, however, to persevere. He turned with all his might against the stream and succeeded in reaching shallow water, and at last came to land. I followed him up, but when I got into the current I stumbled and fell, as I had been hurrying to assist him. The current threw me down. I groped, trying to touch ground, but could not, and was carried on, the water growing deeper and deeper. At last I came down on my feet and began to walk, when the rapid current threw me down once more. David called to me, and thought I had already become confused and did not know where to go. If he had jumped into the stream the current might have carried us both off. However, I rose again and from where the current was deepest, and at last gained the shore. Only a few steps further down I would have been driven into a deep hole, from which it would have been impossible to escape. We and all of our belongings had become thoroughly wet. I at once remembered my books and papers, and opened them with all our other things and laid them in the sun to dry. Our tinder box was also quite wet.

After all was partially dry we went to the French trader, who was still there. He welcomed us very kindly, and saw at once that we had passed through deep waters. He said that we ought to have waded across the lake. There the water was not so deep, nor the current so swift. He gave us some roasted eels, all that he had to offer, as his stock of provisions was very low, because Indian corn is already very scarce. The trader could only speak to us in the Maquai language. He told us that he intended shortly to go to Oswego. to purchase more goods, his supply being nearly exhausted. We would gladly have bought some powder from him, as we had scarcely any more, but he had none.

Though it was late in the day we continued on several

miles, passing through the Indian town. Then we got on
a wrong footpath and went too far to the left, but a girl
whom we met directed us aright. In the evening we
encamped along a creek, but we could not put up a tent, as
there was no bark in the neighborhood. We built a large
fire in order to dry all our wet clothing. To-day we had
come a long distance, much farther indeed than we had
expected, and we felt very tired, but very thankful to the
Lord for His gracious help.

Tuesday, 26 June-7 July. We again rose very early,
and after our usual breakfast of Cittamun, boiled in water,
we started on our journey. It soon began to rain and we
were thoroughly drenched, but we marched on bravely, and
at noon reached the creek where we had rested the last time,
but which was now almost dry. We quenched our thirst
with water and Cittamun, for we knew that we would find
no water between this and Gajuka Lake, a distance of about
15 miles from here. After a short rest we hastened on,
because we wished, if possible, to cross the lake to-day,
though we did not know how we would be able to do this,
there being no canoe on this side, and as the wind came
from the other side, a shot could scarcely be heard. It
rained very hard and grew cold, so that we did not tarry,
and arrived at the lake several hours before nightfall.

There was no canoe to be found on this side. We at
once built a very large fire, hoping that the smoke might be
seen on the opposite shore, and fired several loud shots.
These, however, were not heard, on account of the strong
wind blowing from that quarter. We thought we would be
obliged to spend the night here, and if there was no change
in the weather tomorrow, it would be necessary for us to
make a canoe. David made one more attempt, but he had
loaded his gun so heavily that he was almost stunned by its
discharge. The noise was deafening, but still it was not
heard on the other side. However, an Indian, who was
coming up the lake in a canoe, heard it and at once came
toward us and paddled us across. We still had a little
Cittamun, and as we were very hungry we ate it, and offered
some to the Indian. He saw that we had a scanty allow-
ance for ourselves, and declined taking any. He was a fine
looking, friendly man. He told us that 20 warriors,
returned from war, were over in the town. The canoe in

which we crossed was a very poor one. It was very small, and as the lake was rough the waves broke over it, and we were obliged to keep on bailing it, until we reached the other shore at dark. The man was much pleased to receive a gift as a token of our appreciation of his faithful labors.

We felt very thankful to have crossed, and repaired to our old quarters at the Gajuka's grandmother's, our faithful hostess. She was very glad to see us, had expected us, and had been very much concerned, not knowing how we could cross the lake. She asked whether we had not fired, as they had heard nothing. We gave her an account of our doings, and told her how we had crossed. Matters looked very distressing as regarded provisions, and there was scarcely any food to be had in the whole town. The corn had given out, and they had been compelled to procure much from Onondago, carrying it on their backs, a very troublesome mode of transportation. Our hostess gave us what she had: viz., a little meat soup, made of corn meal; not sufficient, however, to satisfy the cravings of our appetites. Many warriors visited us in the course of the evening. They were all very friendly and modest. David and I spent a very pleasant evening, and felt at home with our kind friends.

Wednesday, 27 June-8 July. We slept late, being weak and tired. We had scarcely arisen when the chief Onechsagerat sent an invitation for us to breakfast with him. No invitation could have been more acceptable, for we were very hungry. On our arrival we found that he had prepared tea for us, and had brought biscuit from Oswego, in order to show us a special mark of attention. The chief was a bright, intelligent man. He inquired about our visit to the land of the Sennekas, and we told how we found almost all the inhabitants of Zonesschio drunk, and unable to talk over our affairs. We were therefore obliged to return without effecting our purpose. He seemed to be much displeased that we had met with such a bad reception. We told him that to-morrow we intended to start from here for Onondago, and that as soon as our matters were dispatched there, we would return here and then journey home. We then took an affectionate farewell of our host, gave him a small token of remembrance, and retired to our quarters. He is a man who appears to feel true friendship for us, and we wished him the Lord's blessing.

They all seemed to be kindly disposed. Many of them knew David, having met several times in Shomoko, through which place they had passed. Our old hostess took much trouble to buy a little corn for our journey, but did not succeed in getting any, as there was great famine in the town. All that we had to eat was a dried eel; rather poor for a tedious and fatiguing journey. David mended our shoes for our journey, as they were much torn. In the evening we heard a dreadful lamentation for the dead. It was over the remains of one who had recently died.

Thursday, 28 June-9 July. We rose early and made all needful preparations for our journey. Our good old hostess had done her utmost to procure some food for us, but in vain. She felt mortified and sad at her want of success. We comforted ourselves together, as she herself had nothing either. There was at least one advantage in our trials; having no provisions to carry, our packs were not heavy and we could easily move on.

After we had journeyed some distance David shot a pheasant, and this served as food. We arrived at Ganatarage, and went to our former lodgings, in the home of the Gajuka's mother. There we met our Gajuka, who at once inquired how we had fared in Zonesschio. He said that so many drunken savages, perfectly mad with liquor, had come toward him, that he had been frightened and had at once left, for he knew that the Sennekas were very vicious and angry when drunk, and always ready to fight. We told him that in about 10 days we expected to be in Ganatocherat, and wished him to be there by that time, with the horses we had brought along and the luggage we left here. This he promised to do. Again we tried to purchase some Indian meal for our journey, but here also there was none to be had. We were, therefore, obliged to venture on our journey through the woods to Onondago without provisions.

Our trail led at once into the wilderness. We grew faint and weary, and waded through Lake Achsgo, which is broad and deep, with much difficulty because of our fatigue. David shot several squirrels, so that we might at least have food of some kind. We reached Lake Sganiatarees, John's Beach, early in the evening. David at once went to fish and was very successful, so that we had both squirrels and fish for our supper. We enjoyed our evening meal with grateful hearts, and remembered how mercifully the Lord had watched over us amid all dangers.

Friday, 29 June-10 July. In order to reach Onondago in good time we rose very early, and after a breakfast of the fish caught yesterday we set out, passing through the Salt Wilderness. Gnats troubled us greatly in the woods, and we scarcely knew how to keep them off. David shot two pheasants on the way, which we roasted by a fire, when at noon we reached a creek and had water to drink. We then went on, passing over the first and last Prince's Peak, and arrived at Onondago in the afternoon.

In going to Ganassateco's house, whither we at once directed our steps, we saw many Indians, who observed us very closely and seemed much surprised to see us so soon again. When we reached Ganassateco's house we learned that he was not at home. He had yesterday gone to Oswego, to be absent 5 or 6 days. There was no one at home except an old Indian, who usually lives next door, but who at present occupied the house with his wife, in order to keep it in order. They welcomed us very kindly and were very glad to see us again, and regaled us with food, for which we were truly thankful, as we were very hungry. The Indian Ganechwatikhe, who had been in Philadelphia, also visited us. We inquired whether our offers had been discussed in the Council, and wanted to know what had been the result. He said they had not been presented, and he knew nothing about them.

The old Oneida chief then came and was glad to see us. We at once inquired whether they had already considered our offers. He said they had not. Yesterday Ganassateco had gone to Oswego, and he arrived just after he had left. He followed him to the lake and wanted to call him back, having learned that a messenger from the Nanticokes had arrived. But Ganassateco had gone on, promising to return in 5 days. Garistagona told us that the council would probably meet tomorrow and deliberate on our offers. He also related that 5 chiefs and 3 other Indians of the Zisagechrohne had been here, and had made a present of many beaver skins to the Grand Council. He said that they had also made peace with them and renewed their covenant, and that the hatchet which they had raised against the 5 Nations was now buried, (i. e., a war would not be carried on). The Indian who was an envoy from the Nanticokes and Tuscaroras, also lodged in our house. All that we could therefore do was to await Ganassateco's return, and ask the Lord to direct all our affairs in accordance with His divine will.

Saturday, 30 June-11 July. To-day we slept late, as we were very tired from our journey. Our friends set a bountiful breakfast before us, to which we did ample justice, though it consisted only of Indian corn boiled in water. We were almost famished, and though we ate frequently through the day, we could scarcely satisfy our appetites. So that our hosts should not be astonished at our dreadful hunger, we told them how we had nothing to eat by the way, and had not been able to procure food in Gajuka. They showed much pity for us, and exerted themselves to entertain us as well as possible. The old Oneida chief then visited us, and was very conversational. The messenger from the Nanticokes delivered the message to him, which he was to lay before the Council, and present the fathom of wampum belonging to it. The messenger had become acquainted with us in Wajomik. We asked him whether the Nanticokes had not commissioned him to bring the matter of a blacksmith before the Council, but he knew nothing of it.

Several chiefs visited us. They were all very friendly, and glad to see us again. In the afternoon the old Oneida chief came to see us, and said that they would assemble and would be pleased to have us present. We went with him to the house where the sachems were convened: They assigned us seats in their midst, and questioned us concerning our journey to the land of the Sennekas, wanting to know how we had found matters there, and whether they had been at home. We told them that they (the Sennekas) had all been drunk during the whole of our stay there, at which they laughed. The Sennekas appear to have the reputation of being hard drinkers.

The old Oneida then presented the cause of the Nanticokes. It treated of the war with the French Indians. They returned the fathom of wampum to the messenger, and said it was of no consequence, because they had made peace with the Zisagechrohne. Afterward they spoke to each other about our affairs, and expressed much regret to us that we should be long delayed, but Ganassateco, who had our affairs in hand, was absent, and they could take no steps in the matter until his return. They would, however, do so much as to send a messenger to Oswego, to recall Ganassateco, and tell him that we were here, awaiting his return. This pleased us very much. They seemed very kindly disposed and told us their names, which we put down, as an act of great importance to them. We made them a present of a piece of tobacco, which they greatly appreciated.

A feast, to which we were also invited, was then held in the house. The occasion was the going to war to-morrow of 20 warriors. The repast was held in the house of the chief, and all was conducted in a very ceremonious manner. Every one brought his kettle. The chiefs sat together, and our seats were in the midst. After the usual ceremonies the meal was served by two servants. They had boiled a whole pig with Indian corn, and the servants continued helping the guests until the supply was exhausted. As we had no kettle or dish, they furnished us with a kettle and filled it very full. We were still hungry from our long fast, and ate the food with great relish. When we had emptied our kettle they filled it again, and we took it home with us. Our hunger had been fully appeased for the first time in many days. The chiefs and ourselves then returned to our huts. Afterward the warriors had a dance at which the chiefs were not present, as they said it was only for the young people. David and I retired, having talked over our matters together, asking the Lord for His gracious direction.

Sunday, 1-12. We spent a quiet morning together. In the afternoon we called on the old chief Gaschwehtio, and found him very polite and sensible, a man of great decision of character. He conversed freely with us. He remembered that Brother Joseph had been in his house, and asked whether he had gone over the great waters, and when he would return. The chief also began to speak of our errand, viz.: to have permission given to several of our Brethren to live among them and learn their language. He did not think this plan possible, for he said that the Indians here sometimes drank very hard, and in their carousings they might harm the Brethren; yea, even kill them. David, however, told him that he had spent a long time in Shomoko, and that the Indians there were more addicted to drink than those here, but up to this time they had never harmed us in the least, for they loved us. Thereupon he wanted to know if we could not learn the language in Shomoko. We told him that the Maquai spoken in Shomoko was very poor, and that the language could not be properly learned, as they were not masters of it themselves. He agreed with us fully and said they spoke miserably, but that here and in Anajot they spoke more beautifully, and had a much greater choice of words than Gajukas and Sennekas. We afterward visited another chief, Sequallisere, also a very sensible man. He would like us to have lodged with him, for he said that his house was always quiet, and there was never any drinking going on there, and consequently no noise like that sometimes heard in the town. He lives far away, close to the trail leading directly to Tiaoga, along the forest. Gaxhayen lived there before this man. We then returned to our hut. Several Indians from Oswego had arrived, and brought tidings that Ganassateco would be here in 4 days.

Monday, 2-13 July. I rose very early and considered our matters prayerfully. It seemed best for us to wait patiently. Many Indians visited us; they were all very friendly and had much to say to us. David went down to the creek, while I remained and wrote. Several Indians from Oswego, relatives of Ganassateco, called. They were very pleasant people, and seemed at once to feel quite at home with us. In the evening the old Oneida invited us to visit Anacharisso, a fine looking young man, one who feels friendly to us and is a member of the Council. He regaled us with bread and bear's fat, and was very kindly disposed. Whenever he saw us pass his house he called us in and offered us food. After we had had some conversation with him we returned to our hut. In the evening the Indains danced around our house till after midnight.

Tuesday, 3-14 July. We walked down to the lake, which is about 10 miles from here, hoping possibly to meet Ganassateco. On the way we saw many beautiful springs at which we met Indians. The creek that passes Onondago here flows into the Zinochsae. The lake flows E.S.E. and W.N.W., and discharges at the latter end. Ganassateco did not arrive, and we went back to our hut. Our hosts entertained us with a bountiful repast on our return. Several old squaws got drunk, and made a great noise in our quarters during the evening. The Indians again had a dance.

Wednesday, 4-15 July. The old Oneida chief came early in the morning and had much to say to us. He said, as we had now been in the land of the Sennekas, in Gajuka and Onondago, he would propose that we should go to Anajot with him, and thence to the Susquehanna, taking an Indian along who would help us to construct a bark canoe, and we could then travel by water to Tiaoga. Thus we could also visit his land and town. We would have had no objection to his plan, had it not been for our long detention here. We retired, asking the Lord to direct us in our perplexities.

Thursday, 5-16 July. I did not feel quite well, and we remained quietly in our hut, waiting further developments in the course of our affairs. In the evening we visited Anacharisso, and talked over many things with him. He described the most direct trail leading to Tiaoga, said it was a very difficult one to find, but much nearer than the one going through Gajuka. Anacharisso regaled us with chestnut milk. He was very kind in his attentions. In the evening several drunken squaws again made a great noise in our hut.

Friday, 6-17 July. I wrote very industriously to-day. We ordered some provisions for our journey, flour and Cittamun, so that when Ganassateco should return and our matters have been dispatched, we need not be delayed for lack of provisions. Our plan was to proceed, not by Gajuka, but by the more direct way to Tiaogo. The Indians, and Anacharisso in particular, were opposed to this, and said it was not prudent for us to take this trail. We might lose ourselves in the forest, because it was a difficult one to find, and so overgrown with grass that it could not easily be distinguished. The Asseroni (Europeans) would say that the Indians had murdered us, and evil might thus be the result. Therefore they persuaded us to take the sure path, with which we were already familiar, and on which we could not go astray. We then returned to our hut, and were regaled with corn and chestnut oil, a new dish to us, but one which we found very palatable. Afterward we spent a quiet evening together.

Saturday, 7-18 July.   We felt a little worried about our long delay.   David went out and met the old Oneida chief, who had much to say.   He concluded by inviting us to dine with him, because he believed that it had been a long time since we had eaten meat.   Now he wished us to eat some good fat bear meat at his house.

A white man arrived in the town, and as no one could talk to him David was sent for, in order to ask him whence he came and whither he was going.   He came now from Fort Williams, and was on his way to Oswego to visit his brother there.   His account was very confused, and it was difficult to understand him.   We came to the conclusion that he had run off from his master.   The old Oneida then came and called us.   We went with him to his hut, and he set before us a meal of bear meat and corn bread.   The white man was there also.   He talked much and very confusedly, on subjects which had no connection whatever.   He railed at Conrad Weisser.   We had nothing to do with him and let him talk.   It was well for him that he cannot talk to the Indians.

We then left and crossed the creek, in order to visit the chief Sequallisere.   He welcomed us very kindly and conversed freely.   He told us that he had never been in Philadelphia.   It was a subject of great regret to him that so many of their chiefs died, especially on journeys like the last one to Philadelphia, when they lost several and some of the most important of their number.   On that account, he said, he preferred to stay at home.   There he need dread no sickness.   We discussed many things with him concerning our Brethren, telling him where we lived and what is our errand to the Indians, assuring him that we came because we love them, and not in order to gain any profit for ourselves.   We mentioned the names of all our Brethren who had Indian names, and then returned to our hut.

In the evening the Englishman came to us, and said that he could speak the Cherokee language quite fluently.   We inquired whether any Indians could speak it, and found one, who at once began to speak to the Englishman, but he soon discovered that the latter could speak only a few words. After he had gone the Indians asked us whether he was drunk.   David said, No; but they insisted on his having taken rum, for he talked nothing but nonsense.   David told them that he thought he was not in his right mind. We then heard that Ganassateco had arrived at the lake, and would be here to-morrow.

Sunday, 8-19 July. Ganassateco's daughter came home early, and he and his wife soon followed. He brought me a letter from Aaron Stevens, the interpreter from Albany, in which he writes to inquire as to our business in Onondago with the Nations. We asked Ganassateco whether the man had given him no other message. He said, No. We wished to know whether Ganassateco had not told of our errand in Onondago. He said that Stevens had asked what it was, but he had answered that we had best report for ourselves. We told him that we had waited here a long time and our matters had not yet been decided. We therefore urged him to use all influence to have the chiefs assemble, and consider what answer they could give to our propositions. As we had learned that they had brought rum with them, we begged him to urge their assembling, the sooner the better, before they should begin drinking again; otherwise nothing would be done. Ganassateco promised to do this. He had brought an English flag with him, and told us that there were a great many traders in Oswego, who had 100 huts there. We felt very thankful not to have gone.

David went to the Oneida, Garistagona, and had a conversation with him, in which he urged him to make preparations for the Council to convene, for rum had again been brought to the town, and they would, no doubt, soon begin their carousings, and our affair ought certainly to be decided before they begin drinking. He said that this was true, and it was just that our affair should be presented. Ganassatecò, however, was the man to expedite matters. He could do nothing but use what little influence he possessed. Ganassateco again visited us and related much of Oswego, and we told him of our journey to Zonesschio, and in what condition we had found it. He expressed his sympathy for us.

Soon after we saw that the chiefs assembled and remained in session a long time. Afterward they came to us and seated themselves around our fire. Ganassateco spoke as follows, saying: Our matters, or the proposals we had made to them were of great importance, and were so many in number that they could not be dispatched speedily; and they would therefore, prefer to send us a messenger to Wajomik or Shomoko, who would bring us their decision, for we were, no doubt, very anxious to start on our journey home. Therefore he returned us our belt and fathom of wampum.

We then replied: Brethren, it is true that the affairs which brought us here are matters of great importance. On that account we have given you ample time to consider, and for the same reason we undertook our journey to the land of the Sennekas, with your consent, in order that you might have sufficient time to discuss everything. As we have seen and heard, you have however done nothing, and we have come a long distance because we wished to receive your decision from you here in Onondago. Our Brethren would feel very much grieved if we returned without an answer. We do not mind waiting a day or two longer, if you will give us a decisive reply. The propositions we have made to you are not evil or dangerous ones, or matters which require much deliberation. You can soon tell what your feelings are in regard to them. Make another attempt, and consider our matters to-day, to-morrow or next day, for we wish to bring an answer ourselves from the Council in Onondago. Our Brethren will be best satisfied with this. Hereupon we again handed them the belt and fathom of wampum.

They talked over the matter and agreed to come together to-morrow, to consider what answer they should give us. Toward evening we saw that all preparations were being made for a grand drinking bout. The house was cleared, which is no good sign. We asked permission of the wife of Ganechwatikhe to spend the night in her house. She consented willingly and fastened the house very securely, so that no one could molest us. They soon began to drink and to make a great noise, but yet it was nothing compared to Zonesschio. The old chief Gaswechtio, however, came into our hut. He was very affectionate and called David his son. We spent the evening by ourselves.

Monday, 9-20 July. We rose early. To-day we both felt as if something must be decided, though we could not see how, for the drinking had continued throughout the whole night until morning. Then all had grown quiet. Ganassateco soon came to see us ,and was quite himself.

He had evidently exercised great self-control and had not become drunk, and thereby gave us proof of his interest in our affairs. He at once told us that the Council would soon convene, after which they would come and report their decision. He then told us much about Anajot, the adjacent country, and the lake there. He said that Onondago Lake empties into the river which flows from Gajuka, with which Oneida Lake unites, and they flow on, emptying into Lake Ontario. Ganassateco was very intelligent, and glad to be with us. He said that he had heard we had gone to the lake to meet him, and wondered whether we had seen the salt springs. We told him we had gone too far to the right, and had thus missed seeing them.

In a few hours Ganassateco came and called us, and said that the Council was now in session. We accompanied him to his house, and found them all assembled around his fire. They seated David in the midst of their circle. As I was to occupy a very high seat I was placed behind David. They all looked very friendly, sensible and intelligent. Thereupon Ganassateco spoke as follows:

Brethren Gallichwio and Ganousseracheri! You have been sent by your Brethren here in this country, and by the Brethren Tgarihontie, Johanan and Tgirhitontie across the great waters, to bring us a message. You have also brought letters from your Brethren across the seas. We herewith present this fathom of wampum to you and your Brethren over the great waters. Accept this as an Indian letter to take with you. We are very grateful to your Brethren for having sent you.

David received the fathom of wampum from them, translated what had been said, and handed it to me, after which Ganassateco continued:

2. Brethren, you have been sent by your Brethren, Johanan, Tgarihontie and Tgirhitontie, across the great water, and by your Brethren, Ganachragejat, Anuntschi, Tschigochgoharong and Tganiatarechoo, on this side of the great water, in order to renew, confirm and make their covenant with us much greater than it has ever yet been. You have made a proposition that several of your Brethren should live among us, for two years or more, to learn the language thoroughly, and thus be enabled in future to make known your views more clearly. (At this point he held a

lengthy discourse on the reason of our coming to the Indians, explaining that we had not come from any motives of self-interest.) He then continued thus: Well, Brethren, we herewith covenant with you that we, the Aquanoschioni, will be and remain your Brethren, and our covenant shall not be separated or torn asunder. Two of your Brethren are to dwell among us and learn our language. They may come next spring or summer, and remain a year or two, or even longer, until they have fully mastered our language.

We said that the two Brethren ought to spend some time, not only here in Onondago, but also in Anajot, in Gajuka and in the land of the Sennekas, in order to become familiar with all the different dialects. The chiefs all approved of this plan, and said: Yes, it would be very well to do so. The old Oneida chief, in particular, sanctioned it in an emphatic manner; he was specially pleased to have us visit him. Ganassateco then handed the belt of wampum to David, and said: This is the belt, and this is what it signifies. David then translated all, and handed me the belt. Ganassateco continued:

3. Brethren, you told us that on your journey through Wajomik, the Indians there, the Shawanese and Nanticokes, applied to you for a smith to mend their guns and hatchets, and whatever was needed in that line, desiring that this smith should live among them in Sochantowa. To this we do not consent for the present, but think that the Indians there may go to Shomoko. The distance is not very great; we are much farther off from the smith than they are, and we desire the smith to remain in Shomoko. He has fitted up his house nicely there, and we therefore hand you this fathom of wampum, to say that the smith is to remain living in Shomoko, and if the Indians need his services they can go there.

David took the fathom of wampum, handed it to me, and interpreted their words. Afterward we made some remarks and said: The Indians are leaving Shomoko in great numbers, and if they all left the smith might also move away, and then the Indians would find it difficult to find one. The chiefs, however, remained firm, and we let the matter drop.

4. He continued: Brethren, you also proposed to make a journey to the land of the Sennekas, to visit the three chiefs, Achsochqua, Garontianechqui and Hagastaes, and

asked our consent for this purpose. Now you have been in the land of the Sennekas and have returned. We give you this fathom of wampum as a token that this journey was undertaken with our consent and entire sanction. David accepted the fathom of wampum, and gave it to me, translating what had been said. We then told them that we had thoroughly understood all they had said, and as soon as we arrived at home we would send a report of it to our Brethren, and in particular to Johanan, across the great water. Thereupon they ended the meeting by the usual cries, common to the close of the Council, and we were both obliged to repeat them also. They then separated, and we could see that they themselves were glad to have our affairs at last settled.

We returned to our lodgings, and after some deliberation concluded to start to-day. We called Ganassateco, and told him that we intended to leave, and he at once told his wife to prepare some provisions for our journey. We said, however, that this was needless, as we had already made the necessary preparations. He told us that he had distributed the presents, which we had given him for his chiefs, before he went to Oswego. We recognized many articles which they were wearing. He gave us many greetings for our Brethren, and named all their Indian names, counting them on his fingers so that he might not forget them.

We then packed up our things. Many young people looked on in astonishment. When they saw that David's pack was very large and mine was small, several of them said that Ganousseracheri had so much to carry, and Gallichwio had only a small bundle. Then Ganassateco said that I was a great man, not accustomed to carry heavy burdens. We then said farewell to Ganassateco and his household. They really seemed to feel sad at our leaving; they had enjoyed our society and liked to have us around them. They stood and gazed after us as far as they could see us. Ganassateco accompanied us out of the town; we took a very affectionate leave of him and went on our way rejoicing. Our feelings in leaving Onondago we can scarcely describe. We actually felt some regret. This morning we could not fully understand the Daily Word, but now we found its peculiar application to our journey. We felt ashamed of

our want of faith and thought.   It is the Lord's doing.   To
Him belongs the glory.

We ascended the first Prince's Peak.   It was very warm
but we felt thankful and happy.   We were overtaken by a
very heavy shower and thunder storm.   Several Indians on
the way asked if Ganassateco was at home.   They informed
us that our Gajuka had left Gajuka 4 days ago for Ganatocheracht.   In the evening we arrived at the French Camp
and lodged there.   Water was very scarce there, as almost
all the streams were dry.   We spent a happy evening together.   Our hearts were filled with gratitude to the Lord
for all the wonderful love and care which he has shown
toward us in our great perplexities.

Tuesday, 10-21 July.   We rose at daybreak, and after
we had eaten some Cittamun we started on our journey.   It
was very warm and we found but little drinking water, as
almost all the creeks were dry.   The gnats were so annoying that we scarcely knew how to keep them off.   We came
to John's Beach on Lake Sganiatarees.   There we found the
kettle which we had concealed when we passed here the last
time.   We went on across the creek which flows from the
lake, and at noon reached Lake Achsgo, where we rested and
refreshed ourselves with Cittamun and water.   Here we
waded through the lake and reached the other shore, much
fatigued by the exertion.   We went on, however, and met
an Indian on his way to Onondago.   He asked us if we had
no bread.   He said he had nothing to eat, as there was a
famine in Gajuka.   We gave him a loaf of corn bread, and
went on through the wilderness, where the gnats were
exceedingly troublesome.

In the evening we arrived at Ganatarage, and found the
house closed where we had lodged before, because the
Gajuka's mothr, who had occupied it, had moved to the
plantation.   However, several children ran and told her
that we had arrived, and she sent her son, a polite young
lad who felt kindly toward us, to bring us to her home.   He
took my pack and carried it to her house.   She at once
prepared a couch for us and appeared very glad to see us.
She thought we already were in Ganatocheracht and informed us that our Gajuka, her son, had started from Gajuka 4 days ago.   She went out into her plantation and
brought in an armful of green cornstalks, as she had noth-

ing else to give us. We gave her some of our corn meal, and asked her to cook it so that we might have something to eat.

Wednesday, 11-22 July. After we had rested we started, and at noon we reached Gajuka. The chief Onechsagerat, was not at home, having gone to the chase because of the great famine in the town. We put up with our old hostess, who, when she saw us exclaimed, O, we must soon die! She gave us a very cordial welcome and was very glad to see us. Said they had no food, unless her son went out with his bow and arrow, and was successful enough to shoot some little birds. They had lived on these for some time. This is a neighborhood in which spring is very cold and wet, and the Indian corn is apt to freeze.

We told our hostess that if she could get us some Indian corn in the town we would gladly buy some. She went around the whole town and could get but a hatful, and the price of that was so exorbitant that, for the same money, we might have bought several bushels in Pennsylvania. However, we were glad to get even this small amount. The son of our hostess had a cock which he gave us, and we made a meal of it. We made him a present in return. We inquired whether we could not engage an Indian there to take us higher up the lake, in a canoe. The lake extends for at least 50 miles, and we might pass it in a day. This would be a great help to us, for our packs were very heavy. The squaw took great pains to find an Indian who owned a canoe, but without success. As the canoes are all made of birch, the few which were to be had were cracked and dried up by the heat of the sun. We were obliged to start on foot, and could not therefore make the trip in one day, but will require two days to make it. We passed a happy evening together.

Thursday, 12-23 July. We made an early start. A heavy dew had fallen during the night, and the grass was very wet. The heat was intense, and we felt it greatly all day. At noon we came to Tschochniees. We found the Indian and his wife in pitiful circumstances. Their son was lame, in consequence of his having fallen on a stone and injured his leg, and the man was old and could not hunt, so they had nothing to eat. We went on farther and in the evening we encamped near the lake, where we slept comfortably.

Friday, 13-24 July. After an early breakfast we started. We named our quarters the 1000 Mile Station, because we had traveled exactly 1,000 miles. David carried the corn meal which was left over from our breakfast, in a kettle. After we had gone some distance we met several Indians who had known David in Shomoko. They called him by name. We gave them what food we had remaining from our breakfast. When they had eaten it they gave us a piece of dried bear, which they had brought from the chase. At noon we reached the lake. We ate some Cittamun, and drank some lake water, which was very warm. We were caught in a very heavy thunder storm and shower, and as we had no hut we were thoroughly drenched. In going through the tall grass of the plain we became very wet. It was a difficult matter to find our way through the plain, because it was so overgrown that often we could scarcely distinguish our trail, and were obliged to proceed at a venture. A heavy thunder storm came up. As night was approaching we resolved to take shelter in a hut of straw and grass which we found. It gave us good protection from the rain, and we spent the night there.

Saturday, 14-25 July. We started early and were obliged to climb a very high mountain. I was very fatigued as our packs were heavy. We hastened on, however, though the way was difficult, and lay over many hills and through swamps. When we reached the Pentecostal Spring we halted and enjoyed some Cittamun and cold water. From there the way grew very bad. We went on till in the evening we reached the War Camp. By the paintings on the trees we at once discovered that our Gajuka had been there. He had shot 3 bears and 3 deer, and had slept here for 3 nights. All this we could tell from the horses and figures painted on the trees. We spent a comfortable night here.

Sunday, 15-26 July. After our usual breakfast we made an early start, as we wished to reach Ganatocheracht to-day. We ascended and descended the high mountain and came to the creek Ganhotak, and at noon reached a place called the Rapid Messenger. Here we halted and refreshed ourselves with water and Cittamun. At last we emerged from the wilderness, and felt very thankful to the Lord for having helped us thus far. On our way we forded the creek several times, and at evening arrived at Ganatocheracht, where we went to our old quarters and received a kind welcome. The man, however, was absent on the chase. Our outlook for provisions was very poor. When we were here before we had left some Indian corn, which we now shared with the squaw. This evening we felt very tired, having walked more than 40 miles. We retired for the night with thankful hearts.

Monday, 16-27 July. To-day we rested. David repaired the canoe, which was leaky, and made all preparations for our journey by water. The squaw made bread for us. We made her a present of a stroud, which we had brought from Bethlehem, and gave it to her as a token of our appreciation of her faithful care of our goods; nothing had been spoiled. After a pleasant evening together we soon fell asleep.

Tuesday, 17-28 July. At an early hour we made all preparations for the journey. It was my birthday, and I poured out my heart in prayer unto the Lord. David got the canoe ready. The river was very low, and we felt fearful about descending the falls going into the Susquehanna, as it is very dangerous going down stream because of the swift current. For this reason we would have liked an experienced Indian to take us, but could not find any. David and I had to venture alone, and proceeded without serious difficulty into the Susquehanna. Sometimes, however, we ran against rocks, and David was obliged to carry the canoe over them, yet without any serious harm to it.

On our way down the Susquehanna we had a view of Joseph's Heights on our right, and the Meadow of Roses on our left. Here David landed on the plain in order to shoot some turkeys. When he got in the grass, which was very high, a rattlesnake darted toward him and would have bit his leg, had it not been for the thick buckskin leggins, which were heavily ornamented with fringes. It was the longest and thickest rattlesnake he had ever seen. David was much frightened and at once returned, allowing the turkeys to fly off unharmed.

We passed many rapids, where the current was very swift. To-day we have advanced about 50 miles. Toward evening we passed over falls so steep that our canoe nearly filled with water. We landed and looked for a place on a high bank of the shore, where we might be safe from snakes.

Wednesday, 18-29 July. Having breakfasted we went on our way. On account of the very shoal water David was often obliged to wade in the Susquehanna, and draw the canoe after him. At noon we came to a spring, where we rested and partook of some food. The spring we named Michael's Spring. Farther on David shot some ducks. Night was coming on, and we could find no sleeping place because of the snakes. Finally we were obliged to camp on the shore, near the Susquehanna. We built a large fire, rested well, and named our quarters Camp Distress.

Thursday, 19-30 July, In the morning we found ourselves enveloped in a very unhealthy and dense fog. David went to an island to get some bark to mend our canoe, which had leaked very badly yesterday. He brought back many cherries of a kind we had not yet seen. They tasted like ordinary cherries. When the canoe was mended we sailed on, and came to the Indian town of Onochsae. No one was at home, so we went on till we reached a hunter's lodge, where we spent the night.

Friday, 20-31 July. It rained all day and we were obliged to remain stationary. I was not very well. David mended our shoes and we spent the day resting by our fire.

Saturday, 21 July-1 Aug. This morning there was another dense fog. At times it thundered and rained. We started, however, and passed over some steep rapids. The Otcongo sorcerer, who was going down the Susquehanna, came towards us, and we paddled along for some distance, side by side. He inquired for news from the Nations, and handed over his kettle into our canoe, bidding us eat and drink. After he had talked with us for some time we left, and went to Tenkhanneck, but found no one at home. Soon after we came to the town where Anton had lived. We landed and inquired for Anton and Nathaniel. The Indians told us that they had left, long ago, for Gnadenhutten. We continued, passing Joyful Welcome, and encamped in the evening, after sunset, quite near to the gates of Wajomik. Today we had traveled over 50 miles. After singing hymns of prayer and thanksgiving we laid down to rest.

Sunday, 22 July-2 Aug. We started quite early. The

fog was heavy and unhealthy, as it is almost every morning
along the Susquehanna. After going through David's Strait
we passed by Hazirok, the boundary of Wajomik. We
greeted it by firing several salutes. It was with peculiar
feelings that we again entered Wajomik, and our hearts
were filled with gratitude. We paddled on rapidly and
with difficulty, the water being low, passed over the upper
falls of Wajomik. At noon I was taken down with a very
severe attack of fever, and lay down in the bottom of the
boat and covered myself, while David paddled on. We came
to the Shawanese town, but saw no one, and about 5 o'clock
we reached the town of Nanticokes. The old chief and
several Indians soon came down to the shore to meet us.
They were much surprised to see us, as they had taken it
for granted that we had returned by a different route, or
had been taken sick. They were very kind and cordial.
The old chief invited us to his house, and at once had a
couch prepared for me, so that I could lie down. David
made some tea for me. I perspired, and toward evening
felt a little better. We had hoped to meet some one from
Bethlehem or Gnadenhutten here, but were disappointed.

Monday, 23 July-3 Aug. Many Nanticokes visited us
in the morning. They were all very friendly and kind.
They inquired whether a smith could be sent them, and
wanted to know what answer the Council in Onondaga had
given. We told them that the 5 Nations, at the present
time, thought it proper for them to frequent the smithy at
Shomoko, and wished the smith to remain living there.
They also asked whether the 5 Nations intended soon to
come down. We had some bread baked for our journey.
Afterward David and I visited the Hill of Peace, and considered whether it would be best for us to proceed to Shomoko, or push on directly to Gnadenhutten, and decided on
the former plan. We were glad to be among this people,
and prayed that soon they may be counted among the Lord's
people.

Tuesday, 24 July-4 Aug. In the morning there was
again a heavy fog. We waited till it cleared. We then
made preparations to start, took leave of the Nanticokes,
and got into our canoe. At the falls we got out and looked
around, to see where we could most easily pass. We came
down the middle without much difficulty, and without

striking the rocks. Then we went on. Once we got into a hole, and were carried so far down the river that we ran aground, and were obliged to draw the canoe to land.

We passed Onoussera Tavern. Soon after I had a severe attack of fever. A heavy thunder and rain storm came up, and as we had no hut and nothing with which to build one, I had to lie down on the rocks near the shore, and David put coverings over me. When the rain had ceased we went on and passed Wombhallobank, where we halted and David made some tea, for the fever left me very thirsty. Toward evening we encamped 2 miles above Neskokepo, and built a hut as well as we could. We named our quarters the Merciful Samaritan, and spent a happy evening together.

Wednesday, 26 July-6 Aug. (Some error here if following dates are correct.) We left our quarters. On the way I again had an attack of fever, but we kept on and at noon arrived in Shomoko with our Brethren. They were exceedingly glad to see us, and particularly as our coming here was a perfect surprise to them. None of the Indians were at home except Thachnechtoris, Shikellimi's son. The others were all out hunting. I had to go to bed very soon. We felt very thankful to be re-united. Toward evening, after I had perspired freely, I felt better.

7th and 8th August. We rested. I had no fever and I felt much better. I talked some with our Brethren, and told of our journey, which was of great interest to them.

Sunday, 9th. We spent a happy day together. In the evening we spoke to the Brethren, and especially on the subject of our mission to the heathen. We then enjoyed a blessed Communion together.

10 and 11 August. I was pretty well, only weary, having no fever. Many Indians visited us, among the rest James Logan, Shikellimi's son. He rejoiced greatly to see us. David told them much about the Aquanoschioni, and said they were fine, worthy and sensible people. He told them how kindly they had received and entertained us, and brought a greeting to the whole of Shikellimi's family from the old chief in Gajuka, Onechsagerat, who knows them well. They all listened with great attention.

Wednesday, 1-12 August. We traveled from Shomoko to Neskopeko by water. Brother Anton Schmidt went with us to take back the canoe.

Thursday, 2-13 August. We arrived there at noon. We went into the town, but found few of the Indians at home. We visited the old chief Nuteemer, who rejoiced to see us. Our stay there was very short, and we hastened on. Brother Anton went with us a short distance into the forest, and then we took leave of each other and he returned to Shomoko, whilst we went as far as Frederick's Tent, and spent the night there.

Friday, 3-14 August. We started very early on our way to the Deer Mountain. A refreshing breeze from Gnadenhutten revived and strengthened us. As we passed John's Rest we greeted it, and came to the Schrautenbach just as a heavy shower and thunder storm came on. We were obliged in haste to seek a shelter from the rain, and as there was no hut there, we lay down in the fork of a large tree, and spread a covering over us, in order not to get thoroughly wet. After the rain was over we decided to remain there, because it would be very wet going through the bushes, and I did not feel very well. We built a fire, dried and warmed ourselves, and named our quarters the Onondago Post House.

Saturday, 4-15 August. We rose early and hoped to reach Gnadenhutten in time for the Love Feast, but were unable to do so. We went on as far as we could, over the Wolf Mountain, then over Pilgrim's Courage to the spring at the foot of the mountain. Here David and I rested, and then proceeded on our way to Gnadenhutten. There all the white and brown Brethren and Sisters rejoiced greatly to see us, and especially as they had heard from Brother Martin, who had been in Wajomik, that I was sick. In the evening I spoke to the brown Brethren and Sisters, and told them of our journey, which gave them much pleasure.

Sunday, 5-16 August. After we had had a good night's rest, and had seen all the Brethren and Sisters well and happy, in the afternoon we left Gnadenhutten for Bethlehem. On the way we were delayed by a heavy rain, and did not reach Bethlehem until an hour after midnight.

GEN. JOHN S. CLARK'S NOTES ON CAMMERHOFF'S JOURNAL.

Gen. Clark, of Auburn, had this journal translated, and afterward sold the manuscript to the N. Y. State Library. With others it was destroyed by fire, but I had copies of all. I give a portion of his notes, and the dates used are those of the New Style. Cammerhoff used both. Gen. Clark had the first award of the Cornplanter medal for Iroquois research (1904), as was his due, and his valuable work is well known. He wrote little of an extended nature, but was an authority on local matters. We owe to him our knowledge of the Oneida fort which Champlain assailed in 1615. The diary of 1750 was translated by Miss Clara Frueauff of Bethlehem, Pa.

May 20. He said "Reichel translates this, "Went a short distance lower down opposite the great plain, and pitched our tent on a knoll." It appears to have been above the falls and below the Nanticoke town, named "Hill of Peace."

Wamphallobank. "Several falls were Nanticoke Falls."

29. Gachanai is Lackawanna Creek.

June 1. Sto-ke Creek: "Is this Bowman's Creek?"

4. Onochsae at Meshoppen.

5. "Horned Tree" at Black Walnut or Skinner's Eddy.

6. "Dangerous Cataract;" Wyalusing Falls.

Spain might refer to Mexico or Florida.

7. Rose Meadow was Wysaukin.

8. Oskoehka is Towanda Creek, below Towanda. Joseph's Heights, between Sugar Creek and Ulster. "Narrow path," narrows at Breakneck Hill. There is now a good road cut along the base of the mountain.

9. Long Island, at the West Branch, now Lock Haven.

10. Is Nochwaio a name for the Tuteloes? Shomoko is Shamokin, and Anajot is Oneida.

June 12. Skehantowa (great plains) is the Iroquois name for Wyoming. Ganhotak Creek seems Newtown Creek, and the country as described in Sullivan's Campaign.

14. The lake is probably Cayuta. A second Sto-ke Creek appears, and Clark gives a map and notes of vicinity of Ithaca. Thus we have Kayeghtalagealat, (valley between mountains), from map in Secretary of State's office; Oneida

dialect. Gariiataregechiat, which A. Cusick defined " From
here we see the lake," a first good view, etc. Nochwaio,
(place of flags) he thought was Cayuga inlet; Notantakto
(to go around the bend), Six Mile Creek; Nogaene, Fall
Creek; Gaheskao, Great Gully Brook; Neodakheat, (head
of the lake) Ithaca; Sto-ke, Butternut Creek; Tianontiaou,
eastern base of Saxon Hill; Tschochnioke, Taughanick
Creek.

16.   Tschochniees, probably Payne's Creek; Gientachne,
Salmon. Creek.

17.   Ganiatarage, on Backus place, 1½ m. north of
Union Springs. Tiuchheo or Tichero. Among unidentified
sites in Cayuga Co. was one on lot 95, Fleming, east side of
Wheeler's Creek, 2 m. southwest of Fleming Hill. One a
mile southwest of Fleming Hill, and still another a mile
west.

27.   Ondachoe he thought was on Sheldrake Point. The
stream was on Fatzinger's farm in Fayette, 8 m. from
Cayuga Lake. Ganazioha was Kendig's Creek, 2 m. from
foot of the lake.

28.   Old Ganechstage was at White Springs farm,
south-west of Geneva; Onnachee, 4½ m. west of Flint
Creek; Otochschiaco, now Fall Brook, Hopewell.

29.   Lake Onachee, or Canandaigua.

July 1.   Lake Noehnta, Hemlock Lake, creek the same.
Another creek at Livonia. Ohegechrage was Conesus Lake.

2.   Here Tgarihontie is said to have been adopted by the
Senecas.

26.   " We have evidence here, very conclusive, that
Ganatocherat was on the north side of the river, opposite
Wellsburg." An evident error.

REV. WM. M. BEAUCHAMP'S NOTES ON
CAMMERHOFF'S JOURNAL.

May 28.   Gajuku sometimes appears for Cayuga village.
Most of the Moravians had Indian names, and Martin
Mack's was Ganachragejat (one who heads a troop). Ske-
nantoa (great plain) was Wyoming, equivalent to Shenan-
doah. The early form of Wyoming was Wajomik. The
Tuteloes once lived in North Carolina and Virginia, but are
now extinct. They were allied to the Saponi tribe, and both

came north before 1750, and first came to Shamokin, then
to Waverly, N. Y., and then to Cayuga Lake,

29. The Delawares were tributary to the Five Nations,
and were moved about at pleasure. Aquanoschioni is a
variant of the Onondaga term for the Long House or confed-
eracy, which is Konosioni, the real or original house. To
this the Tuscaroras were added, as we build a woodhouse,
but their chiefs are not mentioned in the great condoling
song. Tohekechnati was the Black Prince, who died in
1749.

30. Peach and apple trees were soon planted by the
Indians. Gnadenhutten (tents of grace) was a favorite
Moravian name, and five successive villages were so called.

June 1. Stoke Creek, perhaps from Atoge (north) or
Atoka (cranberry), Tenkhanneck is now Tunkhannock.

June 4. Otcongoe or Ote-kon (magic charm or power),
from otcon (spirit) and goa, (great) from his reputation.

6. The nation differing in speech from the Iroquois
and Delawares, was probably a tribe of the Andastes, as the
Oneidas could hardly understand them. As these occupied
the Susquehanna at an early day, the Iroquois could hardly
have met another nation there. The comment on the Tuscaroras is judicious. The Shawanese (southern people)
were a wandering people, thought to have once lived in New
York, the Iroquois expelling them, and later south of the
Cherokees and Catawbas. They are the Satanas of Colden.

8 Tioga was a frequent name, meaning the forks of
two large streams. About this time Weiser thought the
Zisagechrohne, or Missisauguas (big mouth) had about
2400 warriors, but this is a large estimate. Their name
refers to the mouth of their river. Onohaghquage (place
of hulled corn) is now Oquaga.

9. They took the Chemung branch and came to Gana-
tocherat (village at the end), the last of the Cayuga towns.
This was on the flats southeast of Waverly. Zonesschio is
Geneseo. It means a beautiful valley.

10. Maquais for Mohawks. Anajot or Oneida, here has
the French sound of Oneiout. There is yet a place on the
Chemung, not far from Waverly, known as Tutelo or Tute-
lar, which seems the place mentioned across the Chemung.
It is a moderate walk from the Chemung to the Susquehanna
near Waverly.

12. Gallichwio (a good message) was the name given Cammerhoff, April 15, 1748. In the Seneca form this is one title of Handsome Lake, the prophet. Horses were much used at this time by the Indians. Gen. Clark thought Ganhotak was Newtown Creek, but this is too far west and Wynkoop Creek seems better. It may be derived from Gahato (log in the water), Morgan's Seneca name for the Chemung.

13. David did all the fishing and hunting. Kassickahe (to make a high forest) from the tall trees. Painted posts had many uses.

14. Ganiatarenge (at the lake) is now Cayuta Lake. Cataraqui (fort in the water) is sometimes applied to Lake Ontario and St. Lawrence River. The Seneca name for Ontario was Lake Niagara. Tiochtiage is the name of Montreal, and Tekiatantarikon (double mountain) that of Quebec. Another Sto-ke Creek appears, with the same meaning. The Ohio could be reached with canoes by a short portage to Chautauqua Lake.

Etachioni is the wild mandrake or May apple. Tianontinaou is the eastern base of Saxòn Hill.

15. Untagechiat has been defined as the hill from which a fine view is had, equivalent to prospect hill, but I would render it, end of the mountain, as being more literal. Nochwaio (place of rushes or flags) is Cayuga inlet. Notantakto (to go around the bend) is Six Mile Creek. Nogaene is Fall Creek. Ganiataragechiat (end of the lake) at Ithaca. Morgan has a variant, Neodakheat, with the same meaning. Like all distances in this journal, Cayuga Lake is made too long. Tschochnioke is Taghkanic Creek, where the main fall is 216 feet high and a mile from the lake. The rare duck hawk breeds there. Onochsoe is a cave.

16. The French Indians may have been captive Hurons or merely Indians from Canada. Zeisberger gives Tiochtiagega as the Onondaga word for French, derived from the name of Montreal. Gientachne is Salmon Creek. Gatabes for Catawbas. The Iroquois had long wars with them and the Cherokees. Tshochniees on Payne's Creek. Gaheskao or Great Gully Brook. In Onondaga this would be great arrow. This village was Cayuga by name.

17. Tiucheo or Tioherio is river of rushes, an old name. Sannio, by a change of persons would be Gannio, to pass the

river in a canoe, and a ferry there was needed by foot pas-
sengers. Ganiatarage varies in form and one letter changes
the meaning.

18.   Garontanechqui (horse) may be Crane's Creek or
another large stream. Lake Ahsgo or Owasco (bridge over
water) is 12 miles long and has a broad sandy beach. The
largest clay pot ever found in New York was recently ex-
humed there, but is pre-Iroquoian. Sganiatarees (long
lake) or Skaneateles lake, is 15 miles long, and they followed the trail east to Nine Mile Creek, near the present
trolley line. A Cayuga chief, whom they met in the morning, had the frequent local name of Sagogechiatha, (he
keeps them awake) borne by Red Jacket, who probably had
a Cayuga father.

19.   The "French Camp" was near the spot where the
electric road from Auburn reaches Nine Mile Creek. The
first Prince's Peak is between this creek and Cedarvale, and
the second between there and Onondaga Valley, which they
reached near Dorwin's Spring. Canassatego's house was
very large and the English flag showed his partisanship.
Indian women made a frolic of hoeing corn. Messages were
intoned. Both names for the Nanticokes mean Tide Water
People, but referring to a bay. Swatane was Shikellimy's
Oneida name. Thachnechtoris and Sojechtowa (John Shikellimy and James Logan) were his elder sons.

20.   Zinschoe or Swenochsoa (house on a bank) is Onondaga Creek. When Weiser came, a few weeks later, but
one house remained east of the creek.

24.   A bronze tablet on St. James' Church, Skaneateles,
now amrks the site of "The Pilgrims' Hut at St. John's
Beach." Their journey was about 16 miles.

25.   At Owasco Lake the spring was east of the sandy
beach. Cittamun is a Delaware word, properly Psindamun
(roasted meal).

26.   The elm bark straps, braided by Indian women,
were very strong and may still be had. They are passed
over the forehead or shoulders to the burden behind.

27.   Iroquois mortars are sections of large logs, about
30 inches high and deeply hollowed at one end. They would
serve as tables by reversing ends. Deidrich Willers thought
Ondachoe was on Sheldrake Point, which seems too far
south. The town is said to have been "in the west," and

may have been in Varick. He thought they landed on lot 51 in Fayette. Canoga, Red Jacket's birthplace, is not mentioned. He made Golden Brook the present Silver Brook, lot 27, and thought Ganazioha (where there is sand) was Kendig's Creek. Nuquiage was on Rose Hill farm, and gave a Cayuga name to Seneca Lake. Tionctora is Cross Lake, properly given as Tionctong afterwards. Charlevoix called it Tiocton, and J. V. H. Clark, Teungtoo. The Onondagas now know it as Teu-nen-to, (at the cedars).

28. Ganechsatage is the same as Kanadesaga (new settlement village), variously spelled and often removed. The old town had been at the White Springs, 1½ miles southwest of Geneva, and later was at that place. Hon. George S. Conover made many valuable notes on these sites. It was not a town destroyed by DeNonville, but replaced one. Onontio (great mountain) was the name given Gov. Montmagny of Quebec, and continued as a title. Axoquenta is now Flint Creek. Onnachee or Onaghe was on lot 20, Hopewell, and in this journal only was Canandaigua Lake called after the town, which was on the south side of Fall Brook, then called Otochschiaco, (bilbery or red bearberry.

29. The bridge differed from the one at Onondaga. Canandaigua is the last of the "finger lakes," tributary to Seneca River, and this is the first mention of the village as Ganataqueh (chosen town). Earlier travelers have mentioned the clan totems on houses.

30. Hachniage or Honeoye (finger lying) was also the name of the lake and falls. Asseroni (makers of knives) was a name for the Dutch, applied to others.

July 1. Oil Spring had an early fame, and was a later Seneca reservation. Hemlock Lake and creek were called Noehnta, a corruption of Ohneta, *hemlock,* and Conesus Lake Ohegechrage.

2. The Twightwees were Miamis. Indian ladders were notched posts

4. Fish were often shot with arrows.

9. The pheasant of some States is the partridge of New York.

14. From the creek Onondaga Lake has here the name of Zinochsae.

17. "Corn and chestnut oil." The Indians were fond of nut oils.

20. Canassatego died soon after, and Cammerhoff the following year.

22. Iroquois canoes were usually made of elm bark.

27. Stroud, a cloth made in England for Indian trade.

DIARY OF J. MARTIN MACK'S, DAVID ZEISBERGER'S AND GOTTFRIED RUNDT'S JOURNEY TO ONONDAGA IN 1752.

As Mr. John W. Jordan, Librarian of the Pennsylvania Historical Association, has already published Mack's diary, with notes, this will be partly summarized. After Cammerhoff's trip in 1750, nothing was done till 1752, when Mack, Rundt and Ziesberger went to Onondaga by way of Albany. The latter two were to remain and study the language, while Mack's stay was to be brief. He was born in Wurtemberg, April 13, 1715, went to Georgia in 1735 and to Pennsylvania in 1740, was largely employed in missionary work, and died in Santa Cruz, W. I., Jan. 9, 1784. Charles Gottfried Rundt was born at Konisberg, May 30, 1713, came to New York in 1751, and died in Bethlehem, Pa., Aug. 17, 1764. David Zeisberger was chosen to compile a lexicon, which, in English, German, Delaware and Onondaga, as prepared by him, was published in Cambridge, Mass., in 1887. Though imperfect it contains much of value. The words seem quite as often Mohawk as Onondaga.

"After leaving the singing service," July 26, the party left Bethlehem, arriving at New York July 30, and leaving there on a sloop, Aug. 3d. They were in Schenectady on the 11th, and next day came "to Williams' fort, a Maqua town, where many Indians live, who were baptized by a minister of the church of England, by name Ogilby. We found but few at home. Conrad Weisser's son resided here last summer, to learn their language." At another time also the Moravians called Fort Hunter, William's fort.

On Sunday, "we were obliged to rest all day."

On their way on Monday, "we left the Low Dutch and entered the High Dutch settlements," stopping 8 miles east of Canajoharie, the Indian town.

"Tuesday, August 15. . . . At 8 o'clock reached Canajoharie, a Maqua Indian town, where Bro. David and

Post were arrested seven years ago, and carried to prison in New York. Bro. David showed us the house in which they then lodged. . . . The castle, which was built during the last war, is half a mile from the town. . . .We continued for eight miles through the woods until noon, when we came to the Great Falls. . . . In the afternoon we crossed over the river. . . . Here we met about one hundred Indians, mostly from Anajot and Cayuga, who live in these parts and dig roots, which are very good in all kinds of sickness. The Indians sell them to the people hereabouts, or exchange them for goods with the traders."

"Wednesday, August 16. . . . About 10 o'clock reached the last house between here and Onondaga, where we found many Indians. . . . After being here half an hour the Indians that we met yesterday arrived, and with them the chiefs of the Oneidas. . . . We heard that a large party of Indians lay drinking near the river side, about half a mile from here, and near where we must cross. . . . In the afternoon the chief came to us and inquired as to our business in Onondaga. Bro. Hill told him the whole object, but he did not seem satisfied and left us. During the evening the chief of the Oneidas, and a Seneca" came on the same errand. Explanations were useless. "They were very bitter, and told us several times, 'Don't you take it upon you to go any further, for if you do you will see what will come of it; for we have heard no good of you, and have been charged not to let you go any further; therefore you shall go back to-morrow.' The Oneida chief, who was at the Council two years ago, was not with them." A conference was agreed on for next day.

The Germans in the house told them it would be impossible for them to go on saying "Nine years ago there were also two persons who had a mind to go to Onondaga to learn the language, but the Indians sent them back, and if they had gone there they would have been killed," referring to Anton and Pyrlaeus.

"Thursday, August 17.—The four Oneida chiefs met this morning, with twenty of their nation and a chief of the Tuscaroras. We then went to them, when they immediately bade us sit down." Explanations were heard "with great attention. A chief then asked whether we had a belt of wampum to the Council at Onondaga. Bro. David replied, 'No, but we have some strings of wampum.' These were handed to them, and explained according to the instructions given us at Bethlehem."

The result was good. The chief said: "You may go on to Onondaga, and lay your proposal before the Council. This, we chiefs say to you; ye may go in peace, and we are glad that we have heard of your affair."

"The chiefs . . . at parting called us 'their brethren,' and also told us their names, being Huyenjot, Hachtachguosde, Tgawio, Onontio, Guntaantie, Kontartie, Satiunganichnarontie, Ognico, Iagotisgenogechtie, and Iagothonto, the speaker. They also informed us that on our way up we must pass through several towns, among the first two Tuscarora towns, where we should tell the chiefs that the Oneidas knew of our going to Onondaga. At the last town a chief would go with us and hear our proposals. Upon proposing to them that two of their chiefs should go with us, they replied that it was not necessary, for they had listened to and know our message already, and you may appeal thereto if you are asked about us. We observed, however, that they sent out messengers, and soon after learned that they were sent to the Cayuga and Seneca country, to tell the chiefs to appear at Onondaga, to hear the message of the Brethren."

They took leave of their German host, who was amazed at the change in affairs. "By night we reached a fine creek, by the side of which we refreshed ourselves, and after a happy singing hour went to rest under the trees."

"Friday, August 18.— . . . . We set forward early this morning. . . . At noon we met an old Seneca, who informed us that he had been appointed, by a messenger to accompany us to Onondaga. In the afternoon it rained in torrents. Two hours before night we reached Anajot, where, finding only a few women at home, we continued on to Ganatisgoa, a Tuscarora town. Here we found almost thirty houses, large and regularly built, with a wide street through the middle of the town. We soon obtained lodgings in a hut, and were joined by two old Senecas, who had been hunting not far from hence, and were also on their way to Onondaga.

"Saturday, August 19.—The watchword. . . . In

the morning the Tuscarora chief who lives here, came to see us, and told us that yesterday he had received an account of the matters we had to lay before the Council at Onondaga, from the Oneidas. Being lame and unable to attend the Council, he requested us to tell him of our matters, which we did, to his great satisfaction. The Senecas started with us. Before noon we came to a few huts occupied by some Tuscaroras, and in the afternoon to a town of the same tribe. The Senecas stayed here all night, and told us that they would overtake us in the morning. We went on a little farther and lodged in a cold and dark wood." A huge tree fell close beside their fire, but they closed the day with a singing hour.

Sunday, August 20.—The Senecas joined them at 8 in the morning. Lodgings were bad and Indians drunk. "At noon some Indians belonging to Onondaga met us. We then came to a place where many posts were standing, from which we concluded that a town must have stood there formerly. The old Seneca told Bro. David, that when he was a child of eight years of age, Onondaga stood on this spot, but was burnt by the French. In the afternoon, between 4 and 5 o'clock, with the Watch words. . . . we arrived at Onondaga. We were taken to the hut of a chief, who was absent and did not return until evening. Several chiefs, hearing of our arrival, came to visit us. We also learned that some of the chiefs had gone to Canada, and would not return until autumn.

Monday, August 21.—Many visitors called on us this morning; among the rest a very old chief, who told us that the Council would meet during the day, and would listen to what we had to tell them. In the afternoon we met the Council, but found only Onondagas present. To them we related the object of our visit, and gave them one string of wampum after another. When we finished, the wampum was returned to us by a chief, who said: 'We only had a mind to hear what you had to offer. We will let all, both Cayugas and Senecas that are called hither, come, and then you shall declare your matter publicly, that they may also hear it,' which was according to our desires.

Then a servant laid an affair relating to the Catawbas before the Council. First of all, the servant laid an instrument, which they use in time of war, at the feet of the chiefs, declaring at the same time that the Catawbas would now fain have peace with the Six Nations. Next he laid down a pass, which the Catawbas had brought from the Governor of Charleston, sealed with the King's seal. This they handed to Bro. David to read to them. The contents of it were to this purport: The Governor desired the Six Nations to be willing to make peace with the Catawbas, assuring them that the Catawbas would faithfully keep to it. He also set before them the harm that arises from their being at war—that both were only weakened thereby—and yet they are children of the same land. The Governor in every article called the Six Nations "Brethren." In conclusion, he assured them that the Catawbas were true friends of the English. The chiefs then asked us what we thought of the matter. We replied: "It is good; we find nothing bad." They appeared satisfied with our opinion, and from their conversation it is likely a peace will soon be concluded. All night long it was very noisy, as many of the Indians were drunk.

Tuesday, August 22.—We were awakened early this morning by many drunken men and women coming into our hut, but when they commenced to fight among themselves we thought it prudent to withdraw, and passed part of the day in the woods. In the afternoon one of the Seneca chiefs visited us, from whom we learned that they thought of leaving for their town to-morrow. Upon hearing this Bro. David went to the Onondaga chief. He began of himself to make excuses, that he had been unable to call the Council together to-day, because so many Indians were drunk, but he hoped it should be done. to-morrow. Then Bro. David said: "I have heard that the Senecas that are here will leave to-morrow, which we shall not like. We would rather that they should hear our matters." The chief then promised to speak to the Senecas. After dark the chief came to us, and told us that the chief of the Cayugas had arrived, upon whom the whole affair had waited, and that the Senecas would also stay to attend the Council.

Wednesday, August 23.—In the forenoon a chief came and told us that the Council would assemble in the hut where we lodged, which it did. There were about thirty present, among whom there were four Senecas and the Cayuga chief; the rest belonging to Onondaga. We were placed next to the Cayuga chief, as Bro. David understood their language best. He was quietly told of the object of our visit, and what every string of wampum meant. Then he desired the Council to attend, and taking the first string of wampum, he sang in the Indian manner the names of all our Brethren, mentioning at the same time Bro. Johanan as a great and mighty man. "These men," he continued, "are sent by Bro. Johanan, T'girhitontie, T'garihontie, Anuntschie, and the rest of the Brethren on this side and on the other side of the great water, to bring good words to the Six Nations. They know that the chiefs of the Aquano-schioni will take all in good part." Then the string of wampum was hung on a pole, with the usual *Juheh!* of all present.

"The second string was then taken up: "Gallichwio," he continued, "had gone home, and that the Brethren would let the Six Nations know how dear he was to us, that we loved him much and them also—that he loved the Indians very much." . . . . Then was the string hung upon the pole, and the Council sung *Juheh!* The third string was then held up, and he sang as follows: "That T'girhitontie, Anuntschi, and Anousacheri—who was present—had returned from over the great water, and brought salutations from T'garihontie and Johanan his father."

Our message being ended we delivered our presents to the Cayuga chief, when he said: "T'girhitontie, Anuntschi and his Brethren had sent presents." These were two pieces of linen, each 22 yards, some thread and tobacco. They were laid, being a present, upon a blanket. They then conferred together, when two servants took the presents and divided them into three parts. Then the chief arose, gave one part to the Cayugas, another to the Senecas, and the third to the Onondagas. The latter was again divided into two—one part for Upper, and one for Lower Onondaga. Our strings of wampum were divided in the same manner; whereupon the whole was confirmed with a loud *Juheh!* We were then told that the chiefs would meet and consider our message, and they would give us an answer to-day. They then took leave, shaking hands with us all.

About four o'clock the Council again assembled. We were desired again to sit by the Cayuga chief, whereupon he took a string of wampum in his hand and lifted it aloft,

saying, "We have heard and understood that our Bro. T'girhitontie, Anuntschi and Gallichwio, with those over the
great water, among whom there is a great man who has the
affairs of the Brethren in hand, send good words to the
Aquanoschioni.   Brethren we have heard and understood
all. We are glad and thankful that theyhave sent Ganachgagregat, Anousseracheri, and the white Brother (Rundt).
It rejoices us to hear that thou and thy Brethren are well,
and sit in peace by your fires."   Then he handed us the
string of wampum.

Taking up the second string he said: "T'girhitontie, thou
and thy Brethren, and those over the great water, inform us
that our and your Bro. Gallichwio went home a year ago.
Now, Bro. T'girhitontie, the Aquanoschioni say to thee,
use thy best endeavors to find us such another person among
thy Brethren, for we know that Gallichwio truly loved the
Aquanoschioni—in whose heart was no guile."   This was
confirmed by the whole Council with a *"Juheh."* The string
of wampum was then handed to us.

With the third string in his hand, he continued: "Bro.
T'girhitontie, thou hast let us know that, together with
other Brethren, thou hast been over the great water and art
now come back, and hast brought salutations from our Bro.
T'garihontie and his father Johanan.   Thou must salute
them from us, the united Six Nations.   Bro. T'girhitontie,
thou hast also assurred us that the brotherhood between us
and you stands fast, and you hold it fast.   We also hold it
fast."   Here the speaker locked his hands together and
lifted them up; showing how firmly they kept the covenant.
"Thus minded," said he, "were all the chiefs of the Six
Nations," which was assented to by all present.   Then they
delivered to us the string of wampum.

Next he related that Bro. Gallichwio, two years ago,
made a proposal of two Brethren living among them and
learning their language: "And as thou, Bro. T'girhitontie,
and thy Brethren, have again taken this matter in hand,
we think wisely, and have sent Bro. Anousseracheri and his
white Brother, whose name we do not know (Rundt) ; we
are pleased, and think that a good work is set on foot thereby. It shall be as you desire, as all the chiefs are of the same
mind.   The two Brethren shall live a couple of years among
us and learn the language, that we may tell one another the

thoughts of our hearts. Then they may go to the Cayugas and reside there some months, and also to the Senecas." When he finished a string of wampum was handed to us, and the whole was confirmed by three *"Juhehs,"* in which we joined.

It was suggested that the two Brethren should visit the houses in the town, and whenever they have an opportunity, to converse with the Indians. When the Council meets they may attend, so as to learn the ways and manners of the Indians in propounding any matter; that when the Brethren have a message for them, they may know how to deliver it. The chiefs asked us where we wished the two Brethren to live, while they remain in Onondaga? We replied, "we have not thought much about it, but would leave it to the Aquano-schioni, and take their advice." "It is well," said they, "for we have not considered about it, but will do so soon, and give you an answer before Ganachgagregat goes away."

They also spoke about the maintenance of the Brethren, and said, "If the Brethren will frequently visit in the houses they will be supplied with victuals, but especial care shall be taken of them where they lodge." When all was concluded, the servants brought in two kettles of boiled Indian corn, when we ate socially together.

We have been thus far well and happy, and have not seen in any one a dark look, nor heard a contrary word. They have acted toward us in a brotherly manner. Even the children were quite free with us. We wished that our Brethren, who were engaged in our work among the heathen, could have been present at the Council. . . .

Thursday, August 24.—This morning we were visited by several Indians from the next town, five miles distant from here. Some of them were present at the Council. The women were friendly, invited us to come to their town, and gave us apples. Our friends, the Seneca chiefs, returned home to-day. Their names are Thagachtatie, Julchcotanne, Ataneckenni, Thojanorie; the Cayuga's, Giottononannie. The names of the Onondaga chiefs are Otschinochiatha, *the thick*, Ganatschiagajio, and where we lodge, Garachguntie. In lower Onondaga are these chiefs, Zargonna, Ganochronia, and the Tuscarora, Thequalischki.

Friday, August 25.—Our matters being so far advanced, we considered together about the return of Bro. Mack to

Bethlehem. The head chief sent for us, as he had something further to speak about. When we entered his hut he bade us sit down, and asked if Ganachgagregat would leave to-day. We told him that he would, and that we would go with him to Anajot and then return. He then said, "Very well. We have spoken together about the residence for the two Brethren, and as soon as they return they may select a house to their own mind, for the doors of all stand open. They have full liberty to go where they will, and live where they please." We thanked him and then retired.

In the afternoon we visited the chiefs and many of the Indians in their huts, and the chief with whom we lived ordered some victuals prepared for us. Two hours before night Bro. Mack set out for Bethlehem, with Bro. David and Rundt, who go part of the way. When we had walked six miles we came to a fine creek, where we staid all night. Bro. David caught eight fine trout, which we ate for supper. Before lying down to rest we kept a happy singing hour. . .

Saturday, August 26.—After praying and singing we at once started on our way, hoping to reach Anajot to-day, which is 45 miles from Onondaga. At 10 a. m. we reached the first Tuscarora town, Ganochserage. The chief there called us into his lodge and treated us to Quashes and Pumpkins. After partaking we traveled on, passed several Indian houses and also met several Indians.

Two hours before dark we reached the second Tuscarora town, Ganatisgoa. The Indians are nearly all away, hunting roots. At evening we came near to Anajot, but as we wished to be alone together, we selected an agreeable spot and remained there all night. We kept a blessed Lord's Supper together, and then retired to rest.

Sunday, August 27.—Having rested well, we arose early and sang some verses. After passing through Anajot we came to a hill, about a quarter of a mile beyond where we rested. Here we must part. We sang some verses, wept like children, and blessed one another—so we parted. Bro. David and Rundt, on their return, will visit in Anajot and the Tuscarora towns. My eyes are not very dry, all day long, and I cannot express what I felt at parting with my two brethren. At night I reached Kash's.

Monday, August 28.—To-day I remained here and visited the Oneidas who live hereabouts. Some of the chiefs were very friendly. They gave me something to eat, and asked where I had left my companions. When I told them, they gave me to understand their satisfaction by friendly looks.

Tuesday, August 29.—In the morning I left Kash's, and went down into the Maqua country. Toward night I passed through Canajoharie town, and came *Wednesday, August 30*—to William's fort. Here I learned that Conrad Weisser's son had returned to learn the Indian language.

(Thence Mack went on, reaching Bethlehem Sept. 23d. The separate Journal of Zeisberger and Rundt follows.)

Sunday, Aug. 27th.—The hour of parting from our good Martin had come, an event we had been anticipating with sad hearts for some days. Early in the morning we accompanied him to the hill near Anajot, and took an affectionate leave, commending him to the Lord's protection. We returned to our quarters, oppressed by a great sense of our loneliness here in the wilderness, and determined with the Lord's help, to lessen our mutual burdens, and to stand by each other in good and evil days. After making our packs we pressed forward to the first town of the Tuscaroras, Ganatisgoa, and halted at the house of the chief Sequarissere, where we had lodged before. He was not at home, but his wife shared her scanty provisions with us. Several Indians immediately visited us and inquired as to the object of our visit in this region. We told them quite frankly, that we expected to sojourn in this part of the country for some years, in order to learn their language. Our intention was to spend some months in Onondaga, for the present, and next year to proceed to their neighborhood, where we would also remain for some months. They seemed much pleased and approved of our plans.

We then proceeded to another place, where we found two huts of Tuscaroras. An old man bade us enter and conversed with us, wanting to know why we had come, and where we were going. After we had answered all his questions he expressed himself greatly rejoiced, and thought our undertaking praiseworthy. Thence, after passing a few Tuscarora huts, we went on to Ganochsorage, a town of the Tuscaroras. We stopped but a short time, as there were some drunken Indians who soon called on us, and might have become troublesome. It being early we went on as far as a creek, and took up our quarters for the night.

After we had refreshed ourselves with some pigeons, which we had shot during the day, and fishes we had caught in the creek, we lay down to rest, but could not sleep because of the gnats which tormented us.

Monday, 28th.—We made an early start and went on through the woods, arriving in good time at Onondago. There we returned to our former host, and remained at his house until we had found a suitable dwelling. The inmates of his house welcomed us warmly, and rejoiced to see us again.

Tuesday, 29th. We went to the upper end of the town to visit, but found no one at home, except an old man, who was quite alone in his hut. He had never heard of us, because, as he said, he never went into the town and few persons came to him. He concerned himself little about what happened there, for, according to his own account, he was not very bright, and could not understand their affairs. Thereupon we went to several other huts, and also visited our neighbors. We found but few at home, as most of them were out gathering roots. Some drunken Indians chased us on our return, so that we were obliged to retire to the woods till they were gone.

Wednesday, Aug. 30th. During the forenoon the chief, Otschinachiatha, came to our host, and charged him to make an effort in our behalf to find lodgings for us in the town, as we were strangers there, and did not know what situation would be most desirable. David told him that we had already been looking around, but had been unable to find any suitable place. We felt that the chief was really solicitous for our comfort, and cared for us like a father. We are truly grateful to have found a man like him. Afterward some women held a strange gathering in our house; they threw dice in order to divide the clothes of one who had died. In the meantime we went out and shot some pigeons.

Thursday, August 31st.—We again visited in the town, and called on a young chief, Anaharissa, with whom David was well acquainted. He was very friendly, inquired particularly about Gallichwio, whose death he deeply regretted. Later we visited Ganechwatikhe. He had seen and visited our Brethren in Philadelphia. He did his utmost to show us how kindly he felt toward us. He told his people much about the Brethren, and of what he had seen and heard in Philadelphia. Afterward we came to the house of the late Ganassateco; it was almost deserted. We found but one young man there. He well remembered that Ganousser-acheri and Gallichwio had lodged there.

Several chiefs assembled in our house toward evening. A string of wampum had arrived from Mr. Johnson, who sent word to the Indians to gather as many roots as they could, as he expected to be there in 10 days and purchase them. After this message had been delivered, the chief Otschinachiatha again brought the subject of our lodging-place before them, and bade them consider where we should stay. The matter was then discussed, Hatachsoka, a chief, said that he would gladly receive us in his house, if it were a better one, but he had nothing but a miserable hut on his plantation. Hereupon our host, Ganatschiagaje, announced that he would like to keep us in his house, if the rest were satisfied. They decided that we were to remain, and commended us with due solemnity to the Council, saying that if they had any matters to confer upon they would meet in our house, in order that we might listen, see and learn how negotiations were carried on, when conducted according to their method. We expressed our sincere thanks for their kind efforts in our behalf, and felt truly grateful that they, by their exertions, had now provided us with a home. They advised us to do much visiting; all houses were open to us, and we could have ample opportunity to learn and converse with the people. We said we would certainly not fail to do so, and would make it a point to visit faithfully. Our efforts to obtain suitable lodgings had been quite unsuccessful, and we felt truly grateful to the Lord for having thus removed all difficulties.

Friday, Sept. 1st. Ganechwatikhe called to see us in the morning and asked us to be his guests. We accepted his invitation, and he regaled us with roasted pigeons and very good bread. He seemed very kindly disposed, inquired whether Tgirhitontie was well, and asked if Johanan and Tgarihontie were still across the great waters, and whether they will soon return. David related to them of our Brethren, and told them how Tgarihontie had gone to Greenland, and that perhaps he was now on his homeward journey. He expressed great surprise to hear and to learn that Tganiatarechoo had crossed the great waters last winter.   After having conversed with him on many subjects, we went to the house of the chief Anaharissa.   He was not at home, but the old squaw whom we found was very kind, and at once entertained us with nut oil and salt.   From there we returned to our quarters.

Toward evening the chief Otschinachiatha came to see us.   He despatched our host, Ganatschiagaje, with a string of wampum to Mr. Johnson, to bring him the message that he might come whenever convenient.   He mentioned what he should bring, and what things were most needed by the Indians.   He, however, forbade his bringing any strong drink, except what was needed for his own use, as they did not wish to have the Indians get drunk.   The chief also told him to tell Mr. Johnson that two of the Brethren from Tgirhitontie were here, and that they had brought only good tidings from our people, and that he hoped to hear the same from him.   In the evening we spoke to our host about our sleeping-places.   We proposed making them more comfortable with boards, which we would procure in the woods, an arrangement of which he fully approved.

Saturday, 2d.—We spent the day quietly, though there was much going on out of doors.   In the evening some French traders came to our house, but when they saw it was fully occupied they left, without saying a word to us.

Sunday, 3d.—The French traders came to our house early in the morning.   They could not understand English, but one of them could speak the Maquai language quite well.   They asked the Indians what kind of people we were, and where we came from.   They gave them as much information as was necessary, and the traders left us perfectly undisturbed.   Because of the disturbances in our house, on account of the great number of strangers, in the afternoon we went out into the woods to gather roots, in order to be able to buy several blankets, as the nights were growing cold.   David was in great danger of being bitten by a rattlesnake in the woods.   It occurred to him that it would be well for him to be careful of snakes, and as he looked down a rattlesnake thrust its fangs toward him, and looked very angry but could not reach him.   On our arrival at home we found that the French traders had taken lodgings in our house, and had begun to carry on their trading. We kept to ourselves and no one annoyed us.

Monday, 4th.—There was much disturbance going on in our house to-day, for all were engaged with the traders and the house was continually filled with Indians. No one troubled us and we preferred remaining quietly at home, as there were drunken Indians in the town. With the roots which we had gathered we bought a blanket from the traders. In the evening a few Indians who had come with the traders from Canada, conversed with David, and told him of their mode of worship and their priests. They spoke highly of them and their kind treatment of the Indians. They were both Onondagas; one of them lived in Canada; the other spent most of his time there. They said that they had lately heard that the English laid claim to a town in Onontio's country, and this fact would most likely occasion a war in the spring. David assured them that he had heard no such report and did not credit this one, as many falsehoods and evil reports were circulated about the English among the Indians, and it was unwise to believe them.

Tuesday, 5th.—We went out visiting and called on Ganechwatikhe, with whom we conversed about the Brethren, a subject which he himself introduced. He told us that he thought of visiting them next summer and inquired about the nearest way. David advised him to go by water as far as Wajomik, where the Nanticokes could certainly give him exact directions, as they were well acquainted with the Brethren. On this occasion we told him that many of the Nanticokes had recently visited Bethlehem, and had been much pleased with it. We afterward went to our lodgings.

Wednesday, 6th.—There was much coming and going of Indians in our house, but we remained quiet and undisturbed.

Thursday, 7th.—As soon as we arose we heard great weeping and lamentations by the members of our household. Shortly afterward a number of old women assembled, and began to weep and moan most pitifully. The reason for all this was because one of their relations had died during the night, and now, for a certain time they were to lament every day at sundown, and every morning at sunrise. We went into the woods to dig roots, and returned in the evening.

Friday, 8th.—The trader departed with his wares, and the house returned to its usual quiet. We spent the day writing.

Saturday, 9th.—We enjoyed a quiet morning together. In the afternoon we visited the chief Hatachsoka. We met an Indian whose acquaintance David had made in Shamokin. He was much surprised and pleased to see us. From there we returned to our lodgings and passed a quiet evening together.

Sunday, 10th.—We intended to visit in the town, but learned there was much drinking going on there, so we concluded to remain at home. In the afternoon some warriors set out, after having gone through various ceremonies, sung their war song and fired a great many shots. They marched through the town in order to make a display of their whole procession. David went to the creek and succeeded in catching some fish. The Indians were surprised, as they were not in the habit of catching any here. He shared them with our hostess.

Monday, 11th.—We went to the woods to gather roots, and bought shoes and a few necessary articles from some French traders who had arrived.

Tuesday, 12th.—We visited the chief Hatachsoka, who takes great pains to teach us the language. David conversed much with him, and put down a number of words.

Thursday, 14th.—We visited several huts, but found few of the inmates at home, as they had gone to gather roots. We therefore soon returned to our lodgings.

Friday, 15th.—Several chiefs assembled in our quarters. They had received a string and belt of wampum from Canada, with the news that one of their number had died there. The belt signified the announcement of the death, and the string expressed the desire that the Council might not think ill of the chiefs in Canada because of the occurrence. After they had duly considered the subject with each other, the chief Otschinachiata asked David whether he had perfectly understood the matter, and he then explained it to him in particular, whereupon they partook of a meal together and then separated. We then went into the woods, where David split some boards for us, and Bro. Rundt gathered roots.

Saturday, 16th.—We went into the woods in order to enjoy a time of quiet meditation, to-day being a special day for prayer and thanksgiving among our Brethren. As we were caught in a shower we hastily built a hut which served as a shelter. We prayed fervently that the Lord might make Himself known to this Nation, among whom we dwell, and claim many among them as His children. Toward evening we returned home and spent a quiet evening together. (No journal for several days.)

Tuesday, 19th.—We spent another quiet day, making ourselves acquainted with the people and their language.

Wednesday, 20th.—There was much drinking going on in the town. We went into the woods to gather roots. Many half drunken Indians called. They were all good humored and did not molest us.

Thursday, 21st.—David went out to shoot game for the household. A great many drunken Indians gathered around the house in the evening, and kept up such a noise that we slept little during the night. However, we felt sure of the Lord's protection.

Friday, 22d.—A wild scene presented itself to our eyes in the morning; many intoxicated Indians went in and out of our house. Our host advised us to remove our guns and axes, as there were a great many drunken Indians in the town, who were greatly excited by strong drink, and it was very probable that they would come hereabouts. We at once resolved to spend the day in the woods and thus avoid them, a plan which met with the approval of our hosts. We started with our gun, axe and kettle, and first of all went hunting, in order to get some provisions, as we had fared scantily during the last few days. After having been successful in securing some game, we entered a very wild cedar swamp and camped near a creek, to which we gave the name of Cedar Creek. Here we enjoyed a meal and rested until toward evening, when we returned and found that the noise and confusion had greatly abated.

Saturday, 23d.—As most of the inmates of our dwelling went to Tiojataiksa, the nearest town, and there was much drinking and carousing still going on, we remained at home and spent much of the day writing. We were truly thankful to have found lodgings in the quietest dwelling in the town, where there was but little or no drinking going on, a great exception to the generality of the houses, in most of which many were drunk. Our house was at some distance from all the others, so that we experienced but little annoyance of any kind.

Sunday, 24th.—We spent a quiet Lord's day until toward evening, when suddenly the house was filled with drunken Indians, who kept up their savage yells through the whole night. We commended ourselves to the Saviour's keeping, and rested in the assurance of His watchful care.

Monday, 25th.—Drunken Indians overran the house during the whole day. They, however, seemed kindly disposed toward us, especially the men, who did not molest us in any way. A few of the women found fault with our presence, and wanted to know what business we had here. David asked them if they did not know that we had been staying here for some time? They said they had been in perfect ignorance of our sojourn. David then told them that their ignorance was of no consequence, as the chiefs of the town had been fully informed, and that was sufficient; they might make all their inquiries about us of them, whereupon they left us.

The chief Otschinachiata then visited us; he was half drunk, but showed himself very friendly. He spoke in high terms of Gallichwio, saying that he had been a truly good man, without deceit. He lamented his death greatly, and said that the great God, who has His dwelling place up in the heavens, had allowed two of our best men to die, viz: Gallachwio and Ganassateco; he wanted to know whether we thought that was right. The chief said that God might have permitted them to remain longer among us. Afterward he spoke of Tgirhitontie, and wanted to know why he did not visit them. David told him that he was much engaged at home. The chief urged his coming in the spring, as they had not yet made his acquaintance.

Tuesday, 26th.—We went visiting across the creek, where we saw that there were no drunken Indians. We conversed much with the chief Hatachsoka concerning our Brethren. He would like to visit them in the spring. On our arrival at home the chief Otschinachiata again visited us in a half drunken state. He talked much of Tgirhitontie and our Brethren, and showed himself very friendly toward us. Finally he inquired for Bro. Rundt's name; as he could not pronounce it, he said he should be named Thaneraquechta, of the tribe of the Great Turtle. He then took leave of us, after having talked for several hours. We retired to rest with grateful hearts.

Wednesday, 27th.—David performed the surgical operation of bleeding a sick Indian. Twenty warriors started out, and at the moment of their departure they fired off their guns, and created a great sensation. In the afternoon David went off deer hunting with one of our Indians. In the last house of the town he found a Low German, who lay there sick. He was greatly rejoiced to see a white man. David could not remain, but promised the man to visit him again.

Friday, 29th.—We visited the Indians living at the lower end of the town, and came to the house of the chief Sorichona, who was very friendly and conversed freely with David. We then called on the sick German, whom the Indians declared to be weak-minded; his disconnected conversation led us to thing that their opinion was correct. He had come here from Oswego with his goods, and had been unable to proceed on account of sickness. He took little notice of our presence. Next we called on the chief Gachsanagechti, who is the principal chief of the town, and after whom it has been named Tagachsanagechti. He is quite aged, and takes little interest in what goes on in the town. As we did not find him at home we soon left. In the evening David had a discussion with an Indian from Canada, who lives in our house; he had been baptized by the French. (Discussion omitted.)

Saturday, 30th.—We visited our neighbor, Otschinachiatha, who was very friendly and talkative. He asked us where we expected to spend the winter. We told him perhaps in Cayuga, and in the spring we intended making a short visit here, and then purposed visiting our friends in Bethlehem again. He thought our stay here very limited, and said we would scarcely be able to learn their language in so short a space of time, as it is the most difficult of all nations. David told him that we would not forsake them, even if we left them for a time, but that we would visit them frequently, and after our return from Bethlehem, next summer, we would make them a visit. He seemed pleased with our plans. He spoke of Thaneraquechta as being almost too old to learn the language. After having talked with him for some time we returned to our lodgings, and found some bread, brought us by unknown friends.

Sunday, Oct. 1st.—David went with one of our Indians to visit the town of Tiojatachso, siutated on a hill 4 or 5 miles from here. Bro. Joseph had visited there 7 years ago. David returned in the evening.

Monday, 2d.—We made many visits in the town, among the rest to Anaharisso. He was very friendly, and we conversed much with him. He asked whether Bro. Rundt already understood the language. He thought it would be better if each of us lived alone with the Indians; we would learn their language more quickly when separated, as when we were together we spoke much Asseronish (German), Afterward we went to the creek to fish. Later the chief Otschinachiatha sent an invitation for us to come to his house, which we accepted. He regaled us with bear's meat, shot by his son. The meal was most opportune, for we felt the need of strengthening food. The chief made many inquiries, and wanted David to tell him about his journey across the great waters. Finally he spoke of the Nanticokes, who live in Wajomik, and said that many of them had been in Anajot last spring. One of them had been here and had put down 20 belts. From his remarks we were led to suppose that there was a good understanding between them. After some more conversation we returned to our lodgings.

Wednesday, 4th.—All the inmates of our house having left, we remained at home to guard it. In the afternoon we had a visit from the sick German trader. He complained bitterly of his miserable quarters, and the hard treatment he had received from the Indians with whom he lodged. He said he had scarcely enough to eat during his illness; they gave him nothing but pumpkins—severe diet for a sick man. From all that the man told us we came to the conclusion that we had been exceedingly favored in finding such good lodgings, and that our hosts had, thus far, treated us with marked kindness. At times provisions had been scanty, but in our greatest need food had always been sent us from elsewhere.

In the evening, as we sat around the fire, one of our Indians told much of his town, Gachnawage, in French Canada. He told us that the priests there preached to the Indians, and forbade their drinking, dancing, going to war,.

etc.; the Indians, however, did not heed them, notwithstanding their having been baptized. Whenever they feared meeting the priests, they ran into the woods and drank as hard as ever, and then came home. The priests would then reprove them from the pulpit, because of their disobedience. (David gave his views, which I omit.)

Friday, 6th.—To-day we made our visits at the upper end of the town. The Indians told us that drunkenness was one of the greatest curses here. They said that a drunken warrior, who had gone off with others, had torn out the nose of a warrior. One old Indian asked David why the whites would persist in making strong drinks? They were the cause, he said, of the Indians becoming drunk and ruined thereby. David told him that rum was a medicine, and used as such could do no harm, but because they made ill use of this medicine, they were the cause of their own misfortunes. They listened to us and said we spoke the truth, for they knew by experience that an overdose of medicine often resulted in death.

The Indian continued, saying: How was it that Asseroni also got drunk? David answered and said that it was only too true; that they committed the same faults as the Indians, but we and our Brethren did not do so, as we thought it very wicked to rob ourselves of the understanding which God himself had given us. After having conversed on these things for a long time, we went back to our lodgings and sat by the fire until late, talking and thinking of the friends at home.

Saturday, 7th.—It rained hard all day and we remained in our quarters. Toward evening we visited our neighbor, Otschinachiatha, who again treated us to some of his excellent bread. We talked over various matters with him and then returned to our lodgings.

Sunday, 8th.—There was much drinking going on. We visited the chief Hatachsoka, and were pleased to find that his son, whom David had bled, had quite recovered. One of the baptized Indians in our house was quite drunk. When he became sober in the evening he began to cry nad lament bitterly.

Monday, 9th.—Some of the chiefs and warriors as sembled at our lodgings. They had received several strings and a belt of wampum from the Twightwees, who live above the Ohio. These brought tidings that the tomahawk had already been raised and that the Twightwees aimed it firmly against Onontio in Canada. We also learned that Mr. Johnson would not make the visit here we had so long anticipated, as we had hoped to buy a few blankets from him with the roots we had gathered. In the evening they began drinking and carousing, and carried it on during the whole night. Though they entered our sleeping apartments they did not molest us in any way.

Tuesday, 10th.—We started out to make some visits, but as most of the Indians were not in a condition to be talked to, being still under the influence of rum, we soon came home. David went out to shoot. During his absence the Low German, the sick trader, visited Bro. Rundt. He had much to say to the Indians in the house. They made great fun of him, as they looked on him as not quite right. In the evening our young people went to the dance. We spent a quiet evening together.

Wednesday, 11th.—We went to the German trader's as he intends to go to Oswego to lay in a stock of goods. We asked him to bring different things for us, among the rest blankets and a small kettle, which he consented to do. A great many drunken Indians were around the neighborhood, so we went home. In the afternoon we went to the creek to fish, and brough home a good mess of trout.

Thursday, 12th.—Early in the morning David bled one of the Indians in our house. Afterward we went to the lake, as we were in want of salt, and wished to provide ourselves with some for the winter. We found three huts at the lake inhabited by Indians. We inquired where the best salt spring was to be found, as there are a great number there. One of the Indians, named Ganneshora, invited us into his hut, to boil salt at his fires, saying that the spring there was the best one. At first we did not accept of his offer, as we wished to be alone, and, beside, there was but little wood to be found in the neighborhood. However, as we were going farther away from the lake, in order to find a place where there was more wood, he came running after us, and begged us to accept of his hospitality. He though we might be short of provisions, and he was bountifully provided, and we should certainly not hunger with him. We yielded to his persuasions and returned with him, at which he was much pleased, for he had at once recognized David, and bade us welcome as Brethren. It would have been a great pity if we had not remained with the Indian.

We at once made our preparations for boiling, during which the Indian talked much, and showed himself most kindly disposed. Toward evening David went to the creek which flows into the lake, in order to fish. He caught but little. The Indian had gone out to shoot, and presented us with a duck which he had shot. He greatly regretted not having any fresh meat to give us. In the evening his wife returned from the town with bread and provisions which he shared very freely with us. . . . . . In the evening David and the Indian conversed at length by the fire. . . We told him much about the Brethren, to which he listened most attentively till late at night.

Friday, 13th.—This morning we had much conversation with the Indian. He asked us whether we would return to the town to-day. He would have liked us to remain longer with him, and said that he had provisions in abundance, and that we should not suffer want. Later, Gannechwatikhe, who was also there, invited us to his hut, and treated us to meat. He and the Indian with whom we lodged, advised us not to spend the winter in Cayuga, but rather to remain in Onondaga. For, as they said, we now felt a little at home with them, and had learned to understand their language tolerably well, but if we went to Cayuga we would be obliged to learn a different language, and that might mix the two. Hence it would be better to learn one language thoroughly and then proceed. Besides, they said, provisions were scarce in Cayuga, and that we would have to suffer want. Here there was no lack of food. We told him we would go there and if we were not satisfied we would return and remain here.

Soon after a boat with French traders arrived, who, when they saw us, were very anxious to talk to us. As they spake neither English nor Indian, they could not be made to understand what we were doing, when they saw us boiling salt. We again returned to the town. In parting our Indian said: "When shall I see you again?" "Perhaps never." He was a very polite and modest Indian, who tried to show his friendly feeling toward us in every possible way. We took leave of him and returned to our lodgings.

Saturday, 14th.—We heard this morning that a number of warriors were to leave, and would pass over the "Great Island," accompanied by several inmates of our house. We therefore wrote a letter to our Brethren in Shomoko, and enclosed one to our friends in Bethlehem, venturing to run the risk of its arriving or not. If it did reach our Brethren they would be glad to hear how we were. We directed the letter to be delivered to Sneek in "Great Island." He knows the Indian that will take it, and the latter will ask him to send it to Shomoko. Toward evening we visited the chief Otschinachiata. From him we learned that two vessels with Germans had arrived in New York, and one in Philadelphia. He also told us that traders had been in Anajot, and had many inquiries, but the Indians could give them but little information.

Sunday, 15th.—We remained at home to-day and wrote. The warriors set out to-day. The Indian who was to take our letter remained, in order to wait for our host, Ganatschiagaje, who had been sent as a messenger to Mr. Johnson, and who had not yet returned.

Monday, 16th.—We heard, early in the morning, that Johnson's boat had arrived down at the lake, and that there were two Englishmen in it. The Indians having invited us to go with them, we did so, in order to show them who we were, as they had no doubt heard of our being here. By the time we reached the shore we found nearly the whole town encamped on the ground. Mr. Johnson's agent had pitched a tent, in which he and the chiefs from Onondaga were seated.... They bade us enter and sit down, which we did after having spoken a few words of welcome.

After they were all assembled, the Indians made him a present of half a bushel of roots, whereupon the agent read the speech which Johnson had given him in writing. An interpreter, whom he had brought with him, translated it but not very fluently. The sum and substance of the whole speech was to tell them why he had delayed coming, and that, because the season was so far advanced, he had sent but one boat. This one came only as a pioneer; next spring he intended to send several. Thereupon he presented them with two kegs of rum, and the trading began. The people rushed with such great eagerness that they nearly tore down the tent. We soon saw that this was no place for us, and as the people pressed so closely we could not say a word to him, and soon returned to our lodgings.

Tuesday, 17th.—We remained at home and attended to various matters there, as we knew that few inhabitants of the town could be found in their homes. Ganatschiagaje returned to-day and seemed very glad to find us still here. David went down to the creek and caught a good mess of trout. We spent a pleasant evening, talking much of the friends at home.

Wednesday, 18th.—Almost all the inmates of our house went to the nearest town, and we therefore stayed at home. There was much drinking going on here. We were especially annoyed by it during the night, as the drunken Indians kept up a continual yelling, and constant running in and out of our house. We committed ourselves to the Lord's keeping.

Friday, 20th.—Early in the morning David went out hunting with the Indians from our house. He pursued and wounded a deer, until night overtook him, and he was obliged to stay in the forest all night, without capturing the deer. He had strayed into a cedar swamp and could not get out.

Saturday, 21st.—He came home early in the morning, at which the Indians rejoiced greatly. It had already been reported over the whole town that he had gone out hunting, and as he had not returned at night it was most likely he had lost himself in the woods. We were very thankful to be together again. One of the Englishmen lodged at our neighbor's, but as he did not inquire about us, we thought it best not to go to him.

Sunday, 22d.—We visited our neighbor, the chief Otschinachiatha, and talked much with him, making use of the chance to find out if Johnson or the Englishman had asked about our mission here. As far as we could find out they were perfectly indifferent regarding us and our work. The chief treated us to a very bountiful repast. Both he and his wife told us that whenever we were hungry, we should either come ourselves or send one of the children in our house, and let them know, and they would always send us food. We thanked him most heartily for his kind offer, and accepted it as coming from the Lord, who cares for us and will not have us suffer want. The chief continues to show himself as kind to us as he did in the beginning of our stay, and never ceases to provide for all our wants.

On our return to our lodgings our host, Ganatschiagaje, told us that in two days he expected to start off to war, and would not return till late in the spring. As the Indian who was to take our letter to Bethlehem was still here, we asked our host to take charge of it and deliver it himself, to which he agreed. We made known to him our plan of going to Cayuga shortly, and of spending the winter there if possible. We expressed our gratitude for having been permitted to remain so quietly and undisturbed in his house, for here we have been least annoyed by the drunken Indians. He spoke very kindly, and showed himself greatly pleased at our having lodged with him. Later, David went out fishing and brought home a large quantity. We spent a quiet, happy evening together.

Wednesday, 25th.—Our host set off this morning, and promised faithfully to deliver our letter. We wished him a pleasant journey, and rejoiced greatly at having this opportunity of sending news to our Brethren before winter sets in. In the afternoon we went out fishing and were very successful. Our hostess was quite alone with us in the evening. We sang hymns as we sat by the fire.

Thursday, 26th.—A terrible storm from the south has been raging for three days. At times we feared houses would be carried off. There was a continual crashing of trees falling in the forest. We were very glad not to have started on our journey to Cayuga, as had been our intention. The autumn seems to be a very stormy, rainy season in this vicinity. Indeed it has been so ever since we came. If the weather is fine one day, it rains and storms the next; hence traveling in the woods is very unsafe. A dog was beaten to death in our house this afternoon. When we asked for the reason of such an act, we were told that the dog was to be dressed and eaten. Fortunately the preparation was to take place elsewhere. These and similar occurrences convinced us that in future, if at all feasible, we must try to conduct our own housekeeping, for such things often happen among the Indians, and in spite of times of very great hunger, we could not overcome our aversion to eating animals of that kind. The subject of our evening's talk by the fire, was mainly the welfare of these poor heathen, who are still so far from the Saviour and His love.

Friday, 27th.—All the inmates of our house went away, and we passed almost the whole day alone. Toward evening we visited our neighbor, Otschinachiatha, and talked with him on many subjects. There was a drunken revel going on in the neighborhood, causing great carousings. We remained quietly in our lodgings.

Saturday, 28th.—We longed to hear from our Brethren, but of course we can expect no tidings. In the afternoon we went visiting, from one end of the town to the other. We found only a few women at home, the young people had mostly gone to war, and the rest to the chase. There were few inmates in any of the huts. On one of our visits we found the old chief, Gachsanagechti, who has been lying ill for a long time, and can neither speak nor hear. However, he looked at us very kindly, and by the look on his face showed his pleasure at our visit, also extending his hand in token of his joy. We spent a quiet evening.

Sunday, 29th.—Several warriors from Canada came here from Ganachserage, and lodged in our house. One of their number recognized us, as he had seen and spoken to us on our journey hither. He talked much with David and asked about our plans. When he heard that we meant shortly to leave here, he said that we were not doing wisely; we ought to stay a year at least at each place, for we could not possibly learn the language in two or three months. We told him that it was our intention to return and spend some time here again.

Monday, 30th.—One of the warriors conversed freely with David. He told the latter that he had been baptized, showed his calendar, by which he can see, from day to day, whether it was the Sabbath or any other holiday. These baptized Indians are commonly in a miserable condition. Not the least change seems to show itself even in their outward state, and instead of being more honorable, they seem to live a more dreadful life than the others, and at the same time are very conceited because they bear the name of Christians.

Later we visited the chief Otschinachiatha, who asked us if we had no wish to spend the winter here, as many had advised us to do. We answered that we had not yet fully decided. We intended to visit Cayuga, but whether we would deem it best to stay there we could not say. We could easily see that the chief would be pleased to see us remain. We therefore took the matter into serious consideration. After prayerful meditation we resolved to undertake the journey as soon as possible, before winter sets in, as our road is a very difficult one. We would be obliged to go over many creeks, pass over mountains and cross two lakes. We were badly provided for the severities of winter, and so David decided to go down to the Falls, on the way to Oswego, having heard that a trader was there, in order to buy several blankets and other necessaries with the roots we had gathered. They proved to be a great treasure to us, as we were out of money. We saw how the Lord provided again for us in this respect, and made money to grow for us in the forest, so that we might procure our greatest needs.

Tuesday, 31st.—Early in the morning David went down to the lake, to speak to the chief Hatachsoka, who owned a canoe, in order to ask him whether he would be willing to take us to the Falls (Gasquochsage). He consented to do so and David returned.

Wednesday, November 1st.—In the evening David started on the lake with the Indian in his bark canoe. A dance was carried on in our house in the evening. The Indians seemed to enjoy it in their way.

Thursday, 2d.—A feast was spread for the evening, at which many Indians were present. It had been prepared by the warriors from Canada. The dancing was kept up till morning.

Saturday, 4th.—At the close of their revelings the warriors became very drunk. They left in the afternoon. Toward evening David returned. He and the Indian had reached the Falls (Gasquochsage) on the day they left here, and had stayed there over night. As he could not get what he needed from the trader, he went to Oswego the next day, the trader sending the Indian along to get new supplies. Below the Falls they crossed this river, and then went on foot. On the way they met the chiefs Gaschwechtioni and Sequalissere from Onondaga. They came from Canada, where they had spent the whole summer. They welcomed David very kindly, and showed their pleasure at meeting him, as they knew him very well. They gave him food, and offered him a canoe, which was to go down to Oswego. As they could thus travel by water they arrived there about noon. He soon went to the Captain in the fort there, who received him very graciously and refreshed him with food. The Captain asked David about the object of our mission, and he showed him why we had come, and told him that we expected to remain among the Indians for some time, in order to learn their language. To all this the Captain made no objections. His wife, who has been here only a few months, said she thought she had seen David in Albany two months ago. She invited us to visit her this winter, for she said it was a rare thing to see a white man in this region.

When David had made his purchases—everything was terribly dear—he returned the same day, in order to reach his home as quickly as possible. The Indian went with him a short distance, but being already drunk, he did not go very far before he returned, in order to get more rum. David therefore went on his way alone to the Falls. Here the Indian, who was sober by this time, caught up with him. At the Falls he found six boats, with Germans busy unloading them, and then taking the loads by land to Oswego, to which place they brought stores for the winter. Their time was so fully employed by their boats and their merchandise, that they had little to say to David and his comrade. David and the Indian proceeded, spending another night in the woods, and reached the lake on the next day about noon. The journey, which is usually made in 5 days, they made in 3½. We felt very thankful to be reunited.

Sunday, 5th.—We made all our preparations to go to Cayuga to-morrow. We visited the chief Otschinachiatha, who was building a house, and told him of our intention to leave next day. In the town there was much drunken carousing, and we had many visits from those who were drunk. An old chief visited us in the evening. When he heard of our intention to go to Cayuga he was not at all pleased, and said we did wrong not to remain here and learn their language perfectly. He asked why we wished to mix our language and not learn any thoroughly. We told him that we would visit the place, and if we did not find it advisable to stay, we would return and spend the winter here. This arrangement seemed to satisfy him. The chief

Otschinachiatha sent for us later, and regaled us with pork and bread in abundance. He said it would be well for us to satisfy the cravings of our appetite before starting out on our journey. He showed us much kindness and talked very freely.

He said, Brethren, I see you depart with great regret. However, I dare not bid you stay, for I cannot annul or destroy what Tgirhitontie proposed and the Council decreed. It is my duty to see that the wishes of the chiefs are carried out. However, if I were permitted to advise you, I would say, stay here; you shall suffer neither want nor hunger, and in Cayuga I fear that you may be exposed to hardships. We told him that we would not decide where to stay till our return. It was clear to be seen that the man felt kindly, and that he and his household had become attached to us. Indeed all the chiefs urged us to stay. Some drunken women made a great noise till late and disturbed us very much.

Monday, 6th.—We set out early on our trip to Cayuga. In the beginning of our journey we ascended the first Prince's Peak. It was a most wearisome ascent, as we were burdened with heavy packs. This was Bro. Rundt's first experience of this kind, and he felt the fatigue very much. We soon ascended the second Prince's Peak, which is even steeper than the first; then entered the French camp, Tistis Creek, and passed over another very steep hill. The continued ascending of hills to-day made us very tired, and we felt completely worn out, as we had been lately suffering from general debility. It began to rain in the evening, and we built ourselves a hut as shelter for the night.

Tuesday, 7th.—We made an early start so as to reach Cayuga to-day. Soon we arrived at John's Beach, Lake Sganiatarees, where David had lodged several times with Bro. Cammerhoff. About noon we reached Lake Achsko, through which we had to wade. It is quite long and the water at this season of the year being already cold, we were completely chilled by it. Passing on farther we went through the "Salt Desert" and came to Ganatarage, the first of the Cayuga villages. Here we entered but found only the female part of the community at home, as the males had all either gone to war or were engaged in the chase. At first the women looked at us in great wonder, and did not know what to make of us. Their first question was to ask where we came from? We told them from Onondaga. They then asked if we were traders? We said, No. Were we blacksmiths? No. David then asked them if they knew Ganousseracheri? This at once gave them a clue as to who we were, and they replied, laughing, that he had visited them two years ago, with Gallichwio. They received us most kindly and had much conversation with David, who told them that we expected to spend some time among them, and had come to speak with the chiefs of this place. This information pleased them. News was brought that traders had come to the lake with rum for sale. Most unwelcome news for us, which led us to fear a sad time at Cayuga. Being very weary we soon retired.

Wednesday, 8th.—We started early in the morning for the next town, where the chiefs of this vicinity live. On our way we met many Indians who were going to the traders, and who thought we belonged to them. As we approached the town we met two chiefs from there, Onochsagerat and T'gaaju. The former at once knew David, and was very friendly and glad to see him. They told us that they were on their way to the traders, but would return toward evening. They directed us to a house a short distance from the town, and bade us remain there till they came back, as they wished to talk with us, which we agreed to do. The inmates of the house at once surmised that we had come from Onondaga, and when we told them that their surmises were correct, they understood who we were. We remained there till evening, when the chiefs returned, bringing with them a keg of rum, a present from the traders. The chiefs bade us welcome by drinking a glass of it.

We then spoke to them and told them that our errand was well known to them, as one of the chiefs had himself presented our cause to the Council at Onondaga. After spending almost three months there, we had come in order to see if it would be advisable to spend the winter here, and for this reason we wished to speak with them and hear their opinion. They replied, saying that they remembered all that had been said and decided on in the Council about our affairs. They held a short consultation and then told us to take up our abode in the dwelling of the chief Tgaaju, who is the sachem of this neighborhood. We explained our gratitude for their kindness in not only giving us permission to remain, but also in at once providing a dwelling for us. They at once went to the town and took us to our quarters, assigning a place to us where we might sleep and live. Our presence, in a short time, was known over the whole town, and many Indians visited us. They remembered Ganousseracheri, whom they had learned to know two years ago, and all seemed glad to see him.

(I omit details of the assault on David by a Dutch trader. The former nearly lost his life, but was saved by the chiefs.)

Thursday, 9th.—We rose early and considered what we had best do. Finally we decided to return to Onondaga earlier than we had intended. The trader would probably spend the winter here, and in this event, we could not remain. We told the chief that we meant to leave to-day, and he tried to have us stay till to-morrow. We made all our preparations, and when we saw that the drunken revelers **were growing more terrible,** and that all in our house were frightfully drunk, we thought it time to take our departure. We picked up our packs, left the house, and passed through the town without anyone's saying a word to us. We hastened on as fast as possible, as we feared that the drunken Indians might start in pursuit of us, and hinder our going. We reached Ganatarage safely, and found but one woman at home. All the others had gone to the revels. She had just prepared a meal, which she invited us to share. She also gave us bread for our journey, for which we felt very thankful, as we had been forced to leave the town without provisions. From there we hastened on, fearing that we might meet drunken Indians returning from the town. Our hearts were heavy, but the Lord watched over us most mercifully. After a very hurried march we crossed Lake Achsko, the waters of which are very cold. In the evening we built ourselves a hut and laid down to rest, thankful for the Lord's great protection amid all dangers.

Friday, 10th.—We made an early start. As we were scant of provisions we did not take a meal until noon, when we felt very much exhausted and weary because of our heavy packs. The noise of howling wolves had greatly disturbed us during the night, and they kept it up in the morning. We then crossed Lake Sganiatarees and rested at noon at John's Beach. Here, on our former journey, we had buried in a hollow tree our kettle, some provisions and a few trifles. Two Seneca Indians joined us at this place; one was from Zonesschio, and the other from Ganechsatage, places very familiar to David, as he had traveled there with Br. Cammerhoff. The one from Zonesschio said that he had heard much of Ganousseracheri from Iesharenies, the Seneca who had spent last winter in Bethlehem, and had related much on his return. He invited David to visit them on his return home. They traveled with us as far as our night lodging, and David conversed much with them. In the evening we found a few huts in the woods; the Indians occupied one and we another. Notwithstanding our being greatly fatigued we retired in a very happy frame of mind.

Saturday, 11th.—After a very good night's rest we started early in the morning. Our way led us over a very steep hill, whih we ascended ,and then continued on in good spirits, reaching Onondaga at noon. There we took the shortest path to our lodgings, recalling with pleasure what a quiet and peaeful time we had spent here, with none to molest us or make us afraid. For the present it would seem as if Onondaga were the only place for us to stay, for though the Indians in Cayuga seem to feel very kindly toward us, and have great faith in the good intentions of the Brethren, yet we could see no way of living there under present conditions. To-day we stayed at home, glad to rest.

Our hostess inquired how we had been pleased with Cayuga. We told her that the Indians there were much given to drink, and that on that account we felt very uncomfortable, and therefore thought of spending the winter here. At this time we spoke to our hostess about her lodging us during the winter. We told her that heretofore we had been her guests, but we thought it would be an imposition for us to remain with her as such, for we knew that she had harvested but little corn. For this reason we did not wish to stay on the same terms, but would make her a proper compensation when we went home in the spring. We meant to buy our own corn now, from those Indians who had some to spare, for we saw that the squaw needed what she had for her own use. Our hostess seemed much pleased with this plan, for, as she said, she had many children and much people to feed; if possible she would like to buy some corn herself. She was very friendly, and fully satisfied with our plans.

Sunday, 12th.—In the morning we visited the chief Otschinachiatha. He at once treated us to a meal, and was much rejoiced to see us back again. We told him about our journey to Cayuga and of our experiences there. We told him how the chiefs and all the Indians had received us very kindly, and had even appointed a dwelling for us. Afterward, however, we saw that it would not be well for us to remain, for, in the first place, they were frightfully addicted to drinking and were seldom sober; and in the next place a trader had come there, who was a dealer in rum. He would not suffer us to stay, said he was our master, tried to excite the Indians to kill us, and in his anger tried to stab David with a knife. The Indians kept him off, and told him we were not the kind of people he claimed we were. He would not hear anything that they said, but insisted that we should not remain. . . . . . The chief asked for the trader's name; he did not know him. Then he said: I am glad that you have been there, and have seen for yourselves that you could not remain, and that it is now your own desire to stay here. I had no authority to command you to remain, and yet I was very anxious that you should do so, and live near me. I am sure that no one will have any objections to this. He said that we were safe from Asseroni and traders. They dared not put on any airs while here.   They came and attended to their own business, and went away immediately afterward, without venturing to engage in any quarrels.

We saw plainly that the whites have more respect for Onondaga than for any other town, for when they come here they are obliged to conduct themselves properly and quietly. They are not allowed to bring any rum here, at least not publicly, for they are afraid of the chiefs, who will not permit it. The chief then said: You are my nearest neighbors; when the building of my house is ended my sons will go to the chase, and you shall receive meat and never suffer hunger. When our Indian Brethren visit Tgirhitontie he entertains them, and gives them as much to eat as they want, therefore you shall not starve, for you are our Brethren and we are one. Furthermore, he continued, you can see and know for yourselves, that the chiefs here

think well of you and your Brethren, and things like those
you have just experienced in Cayuga you need never fear
among us. We try to do what is right, and wish to have
nothing to do with ought that is evil.

His sons came home and he told them of the treatment
we had received in Cayuga, and asked them if they knew
the trader who had wanted to kill us. No one knew him,
and he determined to make inquiries, till he should succeed in discovering who the fellow was who dared to take
such liberties in their country. We then spoke to him about
our means of support, told him we would like to buy some
corn, as we feared becoming a burden to our hostess if we
remained till spring, for we knew that her supply of food
was scanty. We mentioned the fact of our having spoken to
her on the subject, and said that she seemed perfectly satisfied with this plan. The chief said he would hold a meeting
with his people to-morrow or next day, and would then give
us an answer. We conversed with him on various subjects,
and then returned to our lodgings.

Monday, 13th.—Our hostess having gone away with her
whole family, we spent most of the day at home. Toward
evening we enjoyed a pleasant walk in the woods. To-day
we remembered especially the Lord's gracious dealings,
and felt sure that He would never forsake us in the future.

Tuesday, 14th.—We visited our neighbor, the chief, during the morning, and found him busily engaged with the
building of his house. Not wishing to disturb him we
remained but a short time. In the afternoon David went
out shooting.

Wednesday, 15th.—One of our neighbors invited us to a
meal, at which he entertained us most bountifully with the
meat of a bear which he had just shot. The meal was most
opportune, for our hostess had not yet returned, and our
larder was well nigh empty. It often happens that when
we are very hungry, and don't know where to look for
food, some one comes and invites us to a most bountiful
meal, or food and bread are brought in a basket to the
house, and often by some unknown donor. Thus we see how
the Lord cares for us, and will not let us suffer hunger.

Thursday, 16th.—We were still alone in our lodgings.
We wrote and attended to various matters. In the evening
we sat by the fire and sang hymns, having a strong sense

of the Lord's watchful presence amid all our perplexities.

Friday, 17th.—In the morning David went to Otschina-chiatha's who at once spoke of our wish to purchase some corn. He told us to bring him that with which we wished to buy it, and he would call a meeting of those Indians who still had corn left, and propose the subject to them. We still had 1600 black and white wampum beads left; these we gave to the chief, and he at once convened the people in his house. The proposals were conducted in a very solemn manner, and treated with due importance. The chief began by producing the wampum, which was placed in the middle of the circle, so that all could see it. We remained silent spectators during the whole affair, and were in no way obliged to take part. This we were very glad for, as we greatly preferred that all should be done according to the good pleasure of the Council, and not after the manner of the traders.

While they were conferring about the price, we went home, and when they had decided, the squaws brought a quantity of corn to our lodgings. We saw that they had acted very generously toward us, as they had given us corn of both kinds. The one kind is especially good for bread. The Indians had also brought us some beans. In the evening, in course of conversation, we had a good opportunity of telling our hostess that in the spring we would certainly remunerate her for all she had done for us during the summer. We learned that a trader in Oswego had busied himself in the matter, and wanted to know from the Indians what we paid them, saying that in all probability we would pay them nothing at all. We assured the woman that we expected nothing from her gratuitously, but meant certainly to pay her for all she did. We would like to have cancelled our debts now, but were unable, as we could carry but little with us, owing to our fatiguing journey. Our hostess seemed satisfied with our explanations.

Saturday, 15th.—We partook of the first meal of bread, baked from our own corn. Toward evening a woman arrived at our house from Oswego. She had brought three kegs of rum, and we at once foresaw that for several days that there would be little rest or comfort in store for us. The Indians at once began their drinking carousals and continued them the whole night, making a terrible noise, the like of which we had never heard here. We could not sleep a minute and tried to be patient, committing ourselves to the care of the Lord.

Sunday, 19th. At the first faint dawn of day, for which we had longed during the whole night, (for that seemed to us as long as three nights), we took our kettle and axe and took refuge in the woods, where we cooked some of our own corn. It was a very good thing for us to have it, for otherwise we would have been forced to fast to-day. David got wood for our fire near by. In the afternoon we returned to our lodgings to see how matters looked by that time, and found no prospects for a better night. However, as it was raining, we could not lie down in the woods, and at this season it is not easy to build a hut there. An old woman came to our house and offered us a basket of pumpkins, which she would give us if we would go for them. Br. Rundt went with her to the upper end of the town, and saw that all was quiet and undisturbed there. In the evening we visited a chief, an old friend of David's, who lived there, and we spent the night there. The people received us very kindly, and seemed much pleased that we should have taken refuge with them. However, we had not been there a long time before some drunken Indians came, and we saw that they had brought rum to the house for sale. Notwithstanding their arrival we slept soundly, and no one molested us.

Monday, 20th.—Early in the morning our host and hostess were invited to the town to the drinking festival. They urged us to stay in their house, as it would not be advisable for us to occupy our lodgings in the town. We felt very grateful to them for this arrangement, and were glad to do so. In the afternoon, however, they returned in a drunken state, bringing a number of drunken Indians with them, so that we soon saw that we could no longer rest here in peace and quiet. We, however, spent the night here, as we did not know whether the carousing was not even greater in the town.

Toward evening we walked out to the plantation, and talked over the possibility of staying through the winter under these circumstances. We had learned that more than 20 kegs of rum had been brought to the town, and as there

were but few people there this amount of liquor would last
a long time.   During the summer we could manage more
easily than in winter, when the snow was 4 or 5 feet deep,
and there would be no place to find a refuge in case of need.
Besides, as most of the men had gone to the chase or to
war, the people staying at home consisted chiefly of women,
and there seemed but little for us to do.   No snow has fallen
as yet, and the weather has been very favorable, so that we
feel as if we might venture to begin a journey home.   We
asked the Lord for His aid and counsel in all perplexities.

Tuesday, 21st.—The drinking and carousing began
early in the morning, and a great number of drunken Indians came to our house.   The rum was sold here, and we
plainly saw that we could not think of staying any longer.
We therefore started off for the town and went to our
lodgings, where all had grown quiet and we could rest undisturbed.   We spent much of the evening talking, and at
last concluded that it would be wiser to go home now, and
come back in the spring, when the Indians had returned,
than to spend the winter here.

Wednesday, 22d.—In the morning David went to Otschinachiatha, and told him of our resolve to leave, as we
thought it better to make the journey now than in the
spring.   At first he seemed a little startled and had nothing to say.   David asked him what he thought of our plans.
He replied that he could say naught against them, for we
were our own masters, but we could easily see that he felt
hurt, because the announcement of our purpose had come
to him so suddenly.   When he heard, however, that we
would return in the spring, he was reconciled, and asked
when we would leave and what route we would take.   David
told him we would start as soon as possible, as snow storms
might be expected, which would prove a great hindrance
to our journey.   If the weather continued so pleasant we
would go via Diaoga, through the forest. (We had no money
to travel by Schenectady, and would on that account journey
through the woods.)   The chief asked us to let him know a
day before we started, so that he might have a talk with us.
He then described our route, and advised us to buy a canoe
in Diaoga and go by water, for in case of snow storms we
could go on more easily in that way.   He had much to say to
David, was very lively, and seemed well satisfied.   We

learned from him that a blacksmith, whom Mr. Johnson had sent to work for the Indians, was expected shortly.

Thursday, 23d.—We made all preparations for our journey, and told our hosts of our intent to leave. They were much amazed at our sudden change of plans, but seemed satisfied when we gave them our reasons for so doing. We told our hostess that we would leave our things, and the corn which we had bought in her care, so that when we returned in the spring we would find some food, for then corn would in all probability, be scarce. She promised to take good care of everything. A chief came home from the chase and visited us. In the woods he had been told of our adventures in Cayuga, and we gave him a full account of everything. He was very friendly.

Friday, 24th.—David went to Otschinachiatha in the morning and told him of our purpose to leave to-morrow. He said that he felt great concern about our journey, as snow had fallen during the night. This was the first snow. He feared we might perish by the way, and no one would know what had become of us. David told him that we intended to travel by Schenectady, and would then have but 3 or 4 days journey through the woods, before coming to the dwellings of white men. This plan seemed to please him, and he said now he could rest satisfied, and think of us without worry.

Toward evening we ascended the hill near our house, and prayed God to pardon whatever faults we may have committed. Afterward we visited several neighbors, who expressed much surprise at our determination to leave. They were all very friendly, and we saw that they regretted our going. We assured them that we would return early in the spring. They provided us bountifully with fish for the journey. Late in the evening we visited the chief Otschinachiatha. He told us to greet Tgirhitontie and his Brethren, and bade us tell him how we had fared in Onondaga and Cayuga, and assure him, at the same time, that his Brethren would have been differently treated here in Onondaga than they were in Cayuga. He said he would often think of us, and rely on our promise to return in the spring. We spoke to him about the intention of several chiefs of Onondaga, who had wished to go with us to Bethlehem, to visit the Brethren there. We urged them to carry out this plan, and told him that our journey now need not interfere. Afterward we took an affectionate leave of his whole family, and told them of our intention to start on the morrow at break of day. On our return to our lodgings we were much annoyed by the noise of drunken Indians.

Saturday, 25th.—We rose early and made our packs. Our hostess took much pains to do all she could to add to our comfort. We settled our accounts with her. She had supplied us with food, and we felt glad that she was pleased with our payment. Latterly we had entertained many fears on that score, not knowing whether we would be able to satisfy her expectations. The Lord has helped us in this matter, and removed all difficulties.

As soon as it was day we took leave of the inmates of our house, and started on our way rejoicing. The members of the household watched us as long as they could see us. We felt that that they had not grown tired of us, but were sorry to see us depart. On the top of a hill near Onondaga we kneeled down and thanked God for His gracious help thus far, and invoked blessing on Onondaga and its inhabitants and that He would reward them richly for all their kindness toward us, and not remember any of their evil deeds.

Our way led us through the forest, where there was much snow, and it was often difficult to distinguish the trail. We reached Ganochserage, a town of the Tuscaroras, in the evening, and went to the chief's house, where they all remembered us. The Indians received us very kindly, made a special fire for us, and David related much of Onondaga. They wanted to know whether we would not in future come and stay with them.

Sunday, 26th.—We made an early start, and were very glad of the company of a Tuscarora Indian, who was going on business to Diaogu, as he proved himself to be a very efficient guide. We passed through two Tuscarora towns, Tiachsochratota and Titiachrungwe, and rested in the latter. The people showed us great respect, because we came from Onondaga. We then went on to the last town of the Tuscaroras, S'ganatees, and called on the chief where we had lodged before, and had found only women at home, as all the men had gone to war or to the chase. Our Indian guide wanted to spend the night here, but when he learned that

we wished to proceed, he went with us and we reached
Anajot in the evening. As soon as we reached the town
most of the inhabitants who were outside, recognized us,
and called to us, "Welcome, Brethren!" We were led to the
chief's house, who greeted us saying, "Welcome, Brethren!
I rejoice to see you in good health."

Another came and greeted us in the same way, and these
were the two Indians who had at first been very unfriendly
toward us. They had changed so completely in their manner to us, that it was hard to believe them the same people.
They at once sat down beside us and conversed, asking if
we had spent the whole time in Onondaga, and how we
had been pleased. We told them that we had visited in
Cayuga and had spent a quiet time in Onondaga. They
invited us to remain with them, and were amazed at the progress which David had made in the Onondaga language.
We told them the cause of our journey home, and that in
the spring we would return. After much conversation
they brought forward the subject of the history of the
land on the Juniata, and told us, when we come home, to
say that they were deeply grieved to see white people living
on their lands. They wished to have them removed, so that
their people need not kill their cattle, and thus cause dis-
sension in their land, a thing they wished to avoid. David
answered them, saying that they had nothing to do with
affairs of that kind, but as they wished it he would make it
known. They were very modest and friendly and showed
us great respeect. The chief told us that he had met Bro.
Martin in Diaogu on his journey home. The Indians said
that in the spring the affairs of the Nanticokes, Shawanese
and Mohicanders had been transacted in this house, in the
presence of a great concourse of people.

Monday, 27th.—Quite a deep snow had fallen during the
night. We took leave of our hosts and made an early start.
Because all the swamps were full of water, we were obliged
to pass over a very bad road. We did our utmost to pass
through the forest to-day, but did not succeed. On the way
we met Indians from Anajot who were traveling in the
same direction, and who accosted us in a very friendly
way. In the evening we camped in the woods under an old
Indian hut, and built a good fire. The two Senecas who had
journeyed with us from Cayuga arrived, and were much

surprised to find us here. There was a heavy frost during the night.

Tuesday, 28th.—We were obliged to pass over a dreadful road in the morning, through a swamp. At noon we reached the river, it was very high and dangerous to ford. We called for a long time, then fired several shots, till at length a negro came and told us there was no canoe there, and we would be forced to wade. We, however, saw no possibility of doing this, for the current was very rapid, and the water so deep that it came up to our shoulders. We therefore begged the negro to come and convey us across on horses, to which he consented after much delay. Having reached the shore in safety we went to the house of Kash, a German settler, who received and entertained us most kindly. He was surprised to hear that we had spent so long a time among the Indians, and thought we must have fared very well. He asked whether we had made much progress in learning the language, and gave us tidings of Bro. Martin.

Th rest will be summarized.

They had but five shillings left, and offered to pledge or sell their gun and blankets, if Kash would advance them money. This he would not do, and they went on to another German house, where they stayed all night, leaving their gun and blankets with the settler, for safe keeping. They reached Indian Canajoharie in the evening, meeting drunken Indians there. Thursday they came to more German houses. At noon on Saturday they crossed the river at Schenectady, and were at Albany after dark. On Friday, Dec. 15, they were in Bethlehem, "with hearts overflowing with gratitude."

GEN. J. S. CLARK'S NOTES ON JOURNAL OF 1752.

I use but two of these. Ganatisgoa, a Tuscarora town, 6 m. south of Oneida Castle, on Cowaselon Creek, Stockbridge. Anajot, or Oneida, on the head waters of Sucker Brook, a tributary of Oriskany Creek, southwest corner of Vernon.

JOHN W. JORDAN'S NOTES ON JOURNAL OF 1752.

A few only are given. He made many personal notes. John Martin Mack, a member of the party, was born in Wurtemberg, April 13, 1715, and came to Georgia, 1735. He was awhile at Shecomeko, N. Y., and went to the West Indies in 1762, becoming a bishop and dying at Santa Cruz, Jan. 9, 1784.

Aug. 11. Schenectady was settled by Curler in 1661, and was destroyed Feb. 9, 1690. In 1752 it had about 250 houses.

12. Mr. Jordan naturally mistook William's Fort (Fort Hunter) for the one at Rome. Rev. John Ogilvie was born in New York and was a graduate of Yale. He took the Mohawk mission in 1748, being rector of Trinity Church, New York, later, and dying Nov. 26, 1774. Samuel, son of Conrad Weiser, was born April 25, 1735.

14. The Low Dutch were Hollanders, and the High Dutch were Palatines.

15. Beside the others, Post and Zeisberger were arrested at Canajoharie in March, 1745, brought back, and then released April 10th. The Oneidas called ginseng, Kalondaggouh.

16. Heckewelder called the Oneidas W'Tassoni, or stone pipe makers, and the Senecas, Maechachtinni, or mountaineers. These were Delaware names. Gallichwio (a good message) a name given to Cammerhoff by Shikellimy in 1748, was the name of an Oneida chief living at Anajot. T'gerhitontie (row of trees standing), was a chief's name in the Bear clan, but given to Spangenberg in 1745, at camp in Lewis township, Lycoming County.

23. It is not known when Zinzendorf received the name of Johanan. Watteville was Tgarihontie and Zinzendorf's son-in-law. Nathaniel Seidel was given the name of Anuntschie (the head) by Shikellimy in 1748. At the same time Mack received the Cayuga name of Ganachgagregat, (he heads a troop).

REV. W. M. BEAUCHAMP'S NOTES ON THE
SAME JOURNAL.

Aug. 12.   William's fort, at a Mohawk town, was mentioned earlier, and can only be Fort Hunter. This name was occasionally used.   Thus Col. Woodhull, 1760, left Schenectady, going west.   "We camped two miles below Fort William," and then went on to Little Falls.

14.   High and Low Dutch settlements refer to people from Holland and Germany. The latter were Palatines.

15.   The Indian village of Canajoharie may once have been at Fort Plain and even near the present place, but was then at Indian Castle in Danube. He says it was 8 miles below the Great Falls, now Little Falls. This was the historic Canajoharie, where Brant and Hendrick lived. The roots dug were for the most part ginseng, which the Moravians also dug at Onondaga, where it was called Da-kyen-too-keh (the forked plant).

16.   Beyond Kash's their way led through the woods and away from the river. Pyrlaeus and Anton were those turned back nine years before. Gen. Clark said that the original Kass farm was in the present town of Schuyler, given to Johan Jurg Kast and his children in 1724, a tract of 1,100 acres on the north side of the river.

17.   Wampum was necessary as credentials. They explained the messages contained in it, and thus showed their true character. The first town was Anajot or Oneida; the second a Tuscarora town, called Ganatisgoa.

18.   Ganatisgoa means large village, and is the Canadesseoah of some maps. It becomes Sganatees by contraction.

20.   They passed the old fort, south of Jamesville, burned in 1696. That the original pickets could be seen 58 years later would be indeed remarkable, but the place was again occupied; perhaps till 1720.

21.   Servants were also mentioned by others, and were usually captives. The English called the Iroquois brothers; the French termed them children.

23.   Rundt was termed a white brother because not yet adopted.

24.   Otschinochiatha, here called *the thick*, has his name defined as the *sinew* elsewhere, which is correct. He is usually termed the Bunt, a Dutch word for bundle or

bunch, but his Indian name is variously spelled. He lived to great age and retired from office on this account. Upper and Lower Onondaga may refer to the situation on the creek, but the former may be Tueyahdasso. Anajot, here reckoned as 45 miles from Onondga, was probably about thirty.

25. They rested by Butternut Creek.

28. Ganochserage, or Canaseraga, the western Tuscarora town, was about midway between Onondaga and Anajot or Old Oneida. It was east of Chittenango Creek, and then some distance from it. The hills south were once named from it, and even Cazenovia Lake was known as Canaseraga.

30. Throwing dice was either the deer button game or that of the bowl.

Sept. 1. DeWatteville was adopted into the Onondaga Turtle clan in 1749, as Tgarihontie (messenger). Ganatschiagaje means an *old* or *black kettle*. Tganiatarechoo (between the lakes) was Prylaeus.

10. Onondaga Creek was an early salmon stream.

White cedar is yet abundant near Onondaga Creek, and Bartram spoke of it in 1743.

23. Tiojataiksa was Tueyahdasso, now Indian Orchard in LaFayette.

26. Sagosanagchti (very weak, but bearing the names on their shoulders) is the fuller form of the Onondaga Council name, Seuh-ro-keh-te, (bearing the names). It was sometimes the title of the head chief and applied to the town.

Oct. 1. Tiojatachso closely approaches the present.

9. The Twightwees were the Miamis.

12. The salt spring found by Le Moyne was of considerable size, and at some distance from the lake. The Indians did not then use salt. Afterward they dug pits along the shore to secure it.

17. Onondaga Creek again proved a good fishing place.

31. They wished to go to Oswego Falls, which the Onondagas still call by its early name.

Nov. 6. Tistis was Nine Mile Creek, (nine miles from Onondaga Creek), which Morgan called Usteka, (bitter nut hickory). Tistis, however, suggests Otisco. The Prince's Peaks were east and west of Cedarvale.

8.   Tgaaju was then a noted Cayuga chief, whose name has been mistaken for that of Logan, who was called Soyeghtowa.

26.   The Diaogu to which they went was at the mouth of West Canada Creek, Herkimer, N. Y.   Tiachsochratota was not far from Canastota, and the name is suggestive. Titiachrungwe or Tiochrungwe (in the valley) was farther east.   Sganatees at first suggests Skainadoris, (long lake), the early name of Madison Lake, but it is contracted from Ganatisgoa.

29.   At Kash's they were on the north side of the river, crossing it 8 miles east.

DIARY OF BROTHER DAVID ZEISBERGER'S AND
HENRY FREY'S JOURNEY AND STAY IN
ONONDAGA FROM APRIL 23D TO
NOVEMBER 12TH, 1753.

The first part will be summarized.

On Monday, April 23d, they left Bethlehem, arriving at Maguntsche in the evening.   Leaving there next morning they reached Heidelberg and lodged with Jacob Miller. Wednesday night they were at John Loesch's.   On Thursday they went toward Shomoko, lodging at Benigna Creek, on Christian's Ruh (Rest).   Their camp fire spread in the night, but was soon quenched.   Friday night they reached Shomoko.   The Indians there visited them.   Some Oneidas called next day and discussed their plans.   They chose a tree for a canoe, and on Sunday rested.   The canoe was begun on Monday and finished on Wednesday, May 2d. " We launched it and nearly made ready for the journey," starting the next afternoon, going 6 or 7 miles, and making a hut for the night.   Friday they went on, but the Susquehanna was rising and they proceeded slowly, camping above Fish Creek.   Saturday the river was much higher, and they remained "and spent a happy Sabbath in the woods."

They had made a sail and on Sunday went on their way. " We could sail as fast against the stream as if we were flying away.   In two hours we passed Nescapeke and the

falls." They camped at Wamphallobank. The water fell
a little on Monday, and from an Indian chief they learned
that the Nanticokes had not yet started. They passed the
Wajomick fall and reached the Nanticoke village in the
afternoon, having a warm reception. Some Tuscaroras
were still with them, who had been in Bethlehem. Here
they lodged. On Tuesday the chiefs and people came to
see them off.

On the way they saw a few huts of friendly Indians.
Rain came and they stopped early and built a hut.
Wednesday the river was still rising, but they reached Hazirok in the evening, where there was a Menissing (Mini-
sink) town. All the Indians knew of Bethlehem, and had
confidence in its people. At noon they soon left Wajomik
and Hazirok behind. On the right was Snake Mountain,
and on the left the Dragon's Head; these continued to Tioga.
"We passed a few more huts and an abandoned Indian
settlement, where Anton and Nathaniel had once lived.
Here the Susquehanna makes a great curve toward the west
and northwest." They supped on some pigeons and a duck.

Thursday, May 10, they started early, the river again
rising, and saw a few huts. "Toward evening we passed
an abandoned Indian settlement," making slow progress.
Friday morning they reached Tenkhanik. The Delawares
had gone some miles above and had two huts. At night
they found three good deserted huts and had good quarters.

Saturday was cold, "and about noon reached Onochsae.
There is a hollow mountain here, whence the place derives
its name. We found two huts here, but only Delaware
women were at home. They were very coarse and rude.
We soon left, and saw three new huts at which they were
still working." These were on the other side of the river,
and they rowed past. Three Indians followed them in a
canoe and brought them back. "One of them knew Br.
David very well. It was Otcongaa, a Delaware. He was
said to be a famous sorcerer. . . . One was an Oneida
from Anohochgrage. His father is a chief among the
Oneidas, whom Br. David knew well. . . . When they
heard that we were going to Onondaga they were astonished
beyond measure at the great distance of our journey."
They wanted rum. The Indians of this neighborhood

were of quite a peculiar type.   Br. Henry to-day celebrated
his thirtieth birthday.   It was the first he had spent in the
Indian country."

Sunday, May 13, was very cold, and "we could hardly
stand the sailing."   The main course from Wajomik to
Tioga was northwest.   They killed a deer in the river with
a hatchet, took what meat they wanted, and hung up the
rest for the Nanticokes, who were following.   They slept in
an empty hunter's lodge, remaining there Monday, baking
bread and roasting meat.   Deer often came to their hut.
Tuesday was cold, but they got on well, passing "Mon
Plaisir in the Desert."   Two canoes from Tioga passed
them "on their way down to the next town, to the Bear
Feast."   One Indian said "that of the Tuteloes, who once
lived near Shomoko, some had moved up from Tioga to
Cayuga, others to Anochochgrage."

Wednesday, May 16, there was ice, with a strong northwest wind.   "We passed two huts inhabited by Indians.
At night we encamped on the Shomoko road, which comes
from the great desert and here touches the Susquehanna.
Br. Joseph and party had taken this route when he went
to Onondago. . . .   The wolves made a terrific noise
around us during the night."   Thursday they reached
Tioga.   The huts were Delaware.   Some Cayugas were
some way up the west branch.   The north branch was
taken by the voyagers.   "It is the largest; the other is
about as large as the Schuylkill.   Now we were obliged to
grope our way as well as we could, being quite unacquainted
with this district.   So much we learned from the Indians,
that no branch turns off until Zeniinge, when we must turn
to the left."

Friday night they "encamped on the road that goes
overland to Onondago, and here touches the Susquehanna."
Early on Saturday several Delawares passed them going
from Tioga to Anohochgrage.   "We asked them how far it
was to Zeniinge, but the place was unknown to them.   They
told us, however, that it was two days' journey to Anohochgrage. . . .   We, also, now went on our way, passing
Owego, an old deserted Indian town, where the overland
road turns off to Onondago from the Susquehanna.   Bro.
Joseph, with his company, had followed this road. . . .
Along the Susquehanna, from Tioga to Zeniinge, the country

is quite pleasant. We also had a strong and favoring wind, so that we could sail quickly a long distance."

"*Sunday, 20th.*—We rose early and went on our way, pssing many deserted Indian camps. We soon drew near a hut which stood quite alone, in which was a Cayuga woman who talked a little with us. . . . We went on and saw more huts, built near each other. The name of this town is Tschachnot, (Chugnutt). Delawares and a few Cayugas live here. We landed and inquired how far we were from Zeniinge. They told us there was no road of any kind. The Indians, who were familiar with the neighborhood, go through the woods, and lose themselves almost every time. We certainly could not find our way out again. The best way was up from Owego; it was easy to find as it was more trodden. . . . We therefore concluded to take the road from Owego to Onondago. Bro. David had once before taken this road, and though many years before, he could at least recall the general directions. Thereupon we returned to Owego. . . . On that day we went as far as Owego, encamped on the creek, and found, later, that the Indians had stolen our bread."

On Monday they went up the creek, " searched for the Onondago road and found it. We carried our canoe to a safe place, where the creek was quite deep, and sank it. We packed our bundles and prepared to foot it." Some things they hid in a hollow tree. On Tuesday they started early over a poor trail. This they lost and regained, and at night this happened again. Wednesday they followed the trail along the creek, losing it often. " The Indians had no proper trail, but where they cannot distinguish it each one runs through the woods according to his own judgment. Thus it often occurs that from two to three miles, and often farther, there is no visible road." Toward night it was lost for a long time but regained.

"*Thursday, 24th.* We continued our journey but soon lost the trail. After long search we found a trail that led us across the creek. We thought it an Indian trail, but on careful examination found it was a bear track." They again reached the road. " Without a compass we would have been in a bad case in the forest. . . . After going several miles farther the road turned off from the creek, now very small, and the trail ascended a mountain." They deliberated. " Providence directed us to turn back and go to the Nanticokes, whom we imagined by this time in Zeni-inge. We did so." At night they shot a duck and lodged in an old hut. " In the forest there is no game of any kind. It is very different from ascending the Susquehanna by water. There is no dearth of food there, game being always abundant." Friday was a trying day, but they got one duck. Saturday they started after eating their last biscuit, and reached Owego at noon. They got out their flour, raised their canoe and shot some game.

Sunday, 27th. They went down the creek to the river, where they met two Cayuga Indians from Tschachnot, who told them if they had gone a day longer they would " have had a good road, because two roads meet there, and a road branches off, turning toward Cayuga lake. It is much frequented."

" We inquired whether the Nanticokes had passed. They told us that they had spent the night about a mile farther up, and were about starting. We then went on, soon catching a glimpse of the Nanticokes, who were busily engaged in preparations for departure. As far as the eye could reach you could see one canoe behind the other along the Susquehanna. We soon overtook them and met a few canoes. They were glad, and greatly puzzled to know how we had crossed the country, and pleased to have us travel with them. We told them how we had wandered around in the woods, and had suffered much from hunger because our supply of food was exhausted, and we could no longer say we would take dinner or supper, but had to wait till we could find something, and the Lord helped our needs. They told us they had heard of our going this way, and had feared we might have much trouble, knowing what the Indian trails were. They at once brought us bread and sapan, so that we might refresh ourselves again, for they could well see that we were very weary. They showed us much pity, and said we should not go hungry as long as we were with them. They, indeed, had but little left, but as long as they had any food we should share it with them. For, they added, We are brothers; we are one. We learned that the two Indians who had met us, had meant to hunt up our canoe and take it away, as it would be of service to them, but they had missed the chance.

We then followed them. There were 25 canoes and we were the 26th. Three canoes were still behind and would follow. At noon they stopped to dine; they gave us food to eat. Now that the whole company, with all their utensils and cattle were together, they presented quite a lively appearance, not at all like a scene in the wilderness, but like one in a large city. We journeyed with them and then encamped. Shot several pigeons on the road, and tore off bark for our hut, because it looked threatening. We took it along in our canoe, building a hut in the evening in Nanticoke Town. In the evening Chief Patrick brought us food into our tent. The Tuscarora also visited us with his wife, and brought us bread. We had many visitors in our tent in the evening, and they were all exceedingly glad to have us with them.

Monday, 28th.—As the sky looked very dark the Nanticokes took a day of rest, and we did the same with them. One of them had shot a deer during the morning, and they shared it with us. We had many visitors during the morning, among the rest interpreter White told us that a few days ago they had met a messenger with two strings of wampum, one of which was from the French for the Six Nations, and the other from the Six Nations to all the cities and settlements of Indians, in order to let them know what Onontio and the Six Nations intended to do. Onontio, or the Frenchman, said to the Six Nations: They should allow them to pass through their country, as they had their hatchet in their hand, and would clear out of the way whatever impeded them. He promised to do them no harm, but would pass peaceably through their land to Ohio. The second string, from the Six Nations said about this: All nations of Indians had not heard what Onontio meant to do. On this account they had sent 900 braves after him, only to see what his intentions were, and if they saw that he wished to do them harm then they would at once punish their father Onontio. (By this name they have called the Frenchman, and he and the others have called them his children). We rested well to-day and the Nanticokes fed us bountifully, so that we again gained strength. The Tuscarora and his wife also visited us, and invited us to travel with them to Anajot, from whence it is about 50 miles to Onondago. We

did not refuse, neither did we accept, but waited to see how
the Lord would direct.

Tuesday, 29th. We again broke camp with the Nanticokes and sailed up the Susquehanna, passing Tschachnot,
an Indian town where Delawares and a few Cayugas live.
A little farther on we saw several huts. Toward evening
we came to the Fork, where the Susquehanna divides. The
one stream comes from the east, and is the branch coming
down from Schohari, on which Anohochgrage, a large town
of the Tuscaroras is situated, about 30 miles from here, and
where they have a minister. The other flows from the
north, and is a branch on which one can go by water both
to Anajot and Onondago, a day's journey to both places.
We now remained for the night in the Fork, and put up our
tent among the Nanticokes. The branch which turns here
toward the north is about as wide as the Lehigh at Bethlehem. The other that flows up in an easterly direction is
a little broader. Both become very shallow at some places,
so that during the summer, when the weather is very dry,
it is scarcely navigable with a canoe.

Wednesday, 30th.—Again we stayed quietly with the
Nanticokes, because it rained and thundered very much,
and we had built a good hut in a dry place. In the morning
eight Oneidas and Tuscaroras came down from the town.
Nanticokes went to meet and welcome them; they also took
two Nanticoke chiefs along in their canoes, up into the
town. During the day we had many calls from the Indians.
We saw and heard that they hold the Brethren in Bethlehem
in great esteem. They said they never had seen a people
of that kind, who lived so intimately and so peacefully
together as the Brethren, and that they must soon visit
them again.

Thursday, 31st.—We started pretty early with the Nanticokes, sailing northerly up the branch, and when we had
gone about 6 or 7 miles we reached Zeniinge. A Nanticoke,
with his wife, sailed with us in our canoe. As we saw that
the only three houses were crowded, we built a hut on the
right bank of the river, right among the Nanticokes. In an
hour's time a whole city had arisen. We halted there and
waited to see how the Lord would direct us to proceed, for
we were not to go to Anajot, though it had been proposed
to us. We went to the old chief Cossey, and told him our

distress, as we had nothing to eat, and did not know where we could get anything, asking them to sell us a little corn. He said he would see and talk with the chiefs, and ask them to gather something for us. They did not wish to sell us anything, because we were Brethren, but they would all contribute, and we should not suffer or want. They thought it a disgrace to sell us food, as we are their Brothers, because, as they said, we had helped them in distress when they had nearly died of hunger. They held a council, and gathered nearly half a bushel of corn and sent it to us by White, their interpreter. We thanked them very much, and promised to serve them again when we had an opportunity.

Soon after the council was convened; we were also invited to be present, so that we could hear what message the Six Nations had sent them. We joined them, and when all were assembled the Tuscaroras from Anohochgrage, and the Oneidas who had come down from Anajot arose, walked around in a circle, shook hands with every one, and solemnly welcomed them, saying: Brothers, we are glad to see you here in Zeniinge. After these words they welcomed us in the same way. Some of them knew Bro. David, as they had seen him in Anajot. Thereupon a Maqua from Anohochgrage made a long speech, consisting entirely of compliments. Then he brought out two strings of wampum from the Tuscaroras in Anohochgrage. The one was intended to welcome them, and to express their pleasure at the arrival of the Nanticokes in Zeniinge. The second was to say that the land lay open to them from their Fork up as far as the old Indian town. There they could live and plant where it suited them best. Then a present of several sacks of corn was given to the Nanticokes, in the name of the Tuscaroras. They were given them for planting. Various matters were then discussed with them. They also talked over many things with us. They asked us where we were going, and what our intentions were, which we told them. They bade adieu to each other and again separated, and we returned to our tent.

Many Nanticokes visited us, and also some of the inhabitants of the place, who are partly Onondagos and a few Shawanese. A negro, a fugitive, also visited us. He had lived several years among the Indians. He offered to travel with us to Onondago, as he said he was perfectly familiar with the road. However, we did not pay much attention to him, as we did not trust him, and we afterward learned he had never gone that way before. In the evening four Indians of the town came down the river on a hunting trip. They visited us at once. One of them knew Bro. David well at Shomoko, and was glad to see him. They had heard of us, but did not know what kind of people we were. They were very friendly, and the Indian who knew Bro. David at once offered to go with us to Onondago. It is four days' journey by water from here. We told them we would give them an answer in the morning. We saw that the Lord Himself had made this opportunity, without any effort on our part, and we were thankful and happy.

Friday, June 1st.—In the morning we spoke to White about our canoe, which we wished to leave with them till our return; he at once agreed to this plan. Bro. David then went to the Tuscarora to ask the time of his departure for Anajot. He said he could not tell yet, as his child had been taken sick. Bro. David told him we would take the shortest way by water, with an Indian for our guide. We were glad the matter of our journey was decided in this way, as, because of their kind efforts to travel with them, we feared to give offense if we refused to accept, and in this way we can use our own pleasure in journeying when and how we choose. David went to the island to engage the Indian to go with us. He, however, did not meet us, as he had gone down the river to Tschachnot.

Many Nanticokes visited us in our hut, Chief Cossey among the rest. He pressingly invited us to visit him in Onondago, which we promised to do. He said that when we came again, they hoped to entertain us more comfortably, as now their stores of food were almost exhausted. We asked them for a little food and flour for our trip, which they gave us. They have not only treated us as friends, but as Brethren, for they have but little themselves, and have shared with us in their poverty. . . . In the evening we witnessed the sorceries of the Indians with a sick child.

Saturday, 2d.—As the Indian who was to go with us had not returned, we could not leave. The Nanticokes broke up their camp and went to the place they had selected, three

miles farther down the river. They bade us farewell in a
very kindly way, believing that we would, perhaps, start
to-day. They all invited us, most pressingly, to visit them
in Onondago. We stayed in our tent, and spent a happy,
quiet day together. . . . Many of the Indians visited
us. One woman, who knew Br. David well, said to him:
You, Ganousseracheri, you are quite at home in our country
and among the Aquanoschioni, but here you are such a
stranger and cannot find your way. Br. David told her
that if we were to come again, we could certainly find our
way more easily. This was our first visit here.

Sunday, 3d.—We had to stay here to-day, as the Indian
had not yet returned. Our ability to proceed caused us
some anxiety. Our supplies were scanty, consisting of but
a little corn, which the Nanticokes had given us. If we
used this we would have nothing for our trip, and it was
perfectly impossible to procure food of any kind here.
Famine prevails all around and the Indians subsist on the
various roots and herbs they find in the woods. We wished
to buy a half bushel of corn from a Shawanese woman, and
offered her 100 black wampun for it. She, however,
refused to sell, saying very truly: What good would the
wampun do her, if she must starve in consequence? We
pitied her, though we were in the same trouble.

About noon the Indian who was to go with us came
home, and visited us at once. He forthwith agreed to start
to-morrow morning, saying to Br. David that when he was
in great trouble in Shomoko, Br. David had shown him kindness; hence he could not refuse to go with us. . . . Br.
Henry went down to the Nanticokes to see if he could get a
little corn for our journey. The old chief Cossey made us
a present of some, and would take no pay for it, because, he
said: We are Brethren, and must help each other in
distress whenever it is possible.

They were about planting corn, and all working together, old as well as young, the men hoeing and the women
planting after them. They work in this way, so that none
may remain idle and neglect to do their planting. When all
has been planted each one receives his piece of ground,
allotted to him to be tilled. This suffices for all their wants.
Br. Henry helped them work till they returned to their
homes. They ate together and asked Br. Henry to be their

guest. In the evening the Indian who is to go with us, came with his brother, who is also going along, to spend the night with us, as we were to make a very early start.

Monday, 4th.—We set off early with the Indians, rowing up the branch. The water was very swift. At noon we arrived at the third fork of the Susquehanna from Shomoko, not counting Hazirok, which divides Wajomik. The branch on the right hand, which turns to the north, is called Anajota, and leads to Anajot, about a day's journey from a lake. The branch on the left, turning to the northwest, is the largest, and is called Tiohujodha. After having eaten some sapan, and fish which the Indians had caught on our way, we continued up the branch Tiohujodha, which is not quite as large as the Schuylkill, and made good progress to-day. While sailing, the Indians again caught a great amount of fish, enough to appease our hunger and have some remaining. The Indians shot a wolf that was walking along the shore. During the afternoon we had a heavy thunder storm, with much rain, so that we were thoroughly drenched. For quarters at night we had a miserable dark hole. The evening meal was of turtle eggs, which we had gathered on our way.

Tuesday, 5th.—A few Oneidas, on the chase, visited us in the morning. They had thought we were the same who were in Onondago last year. They came from Anohochgrage and were very friendly. We invited them to breakfast with us. They were baptized Indians, and said grace before and after meals. Before leaving they made us presents of venison and bear meat. We went on our way and soon passed the fourth fork. The branch on the right, turning toward the north, is called Schio. We continued our course in the Creek Tiohujodha, which is the largest, and flows for the most part, northwest and west. It is generally as wide as Antony Lane in Pennsylvania. The Indians again caught a great quantity of fish, and while we were resting at noon two deer came into the creek, of which they shot one. Now we were abundantly provided with food. In the afternoon we met a canoe, sailing down the stream, bearing an Indian and his wife from Onondago; they both knew Br. David very well. As we had no more salt we bought some from them. We made a halt early in the evening, because the Indians wished to roast and enjoy the venison, which they did.

Wednesday, 6th.—This morning we made a very early start, so as to end our journey by water. The Indian was sick to-day, having no doubt eaten too much venison. He was lying down in the canoe all day long. Our journey was specially pleasant during the afternoon. The water was deep and the current not rapid. The creek seemed to grow wider as we ascended. This seems to be the case with most streams here; they seem to be very much the same from beginning to end, as no creeks empty into them, and they usually rise in some lake. The Susquehanna consists principally of lakes, hence it comes that it varies but little in width from Shomoko to Tioga, and from Tioga to Zeniinge, as no creeks of any importance flow into it. Thus it is not surprising that the Susquehanna continues to rise for such a length of time, and then grows so very high, because, reckoning in scant measure, its source is 400 miles from Shomoko, and by exact measurement it would doubtless be 60 miles more.

In the morning we reached the fifth fork. The branch on our left, called Onogariske, about twice as large as the Monocasy, turns to the west and flows from a lake. We would have ascended it, but, as the creek was too shallow, we continued our course in the Tiohujodha and went on a little farther. Here we concluded our journey by water for the present, being 50 miles from Onondago by land. We gave our canoe to the Indians, who on their return were to deliver it to the Nanticokes for safe keeping.

We had ascended the Susquehanna as far as it was navigable in a canoe; had the water been higher we might have gone half a day's journey farther, on to the lake, and would then have but 30 miles by land. The ascent of the Susquehanna by water, if any one knows how to row, is by far the most pleasant and convenient mode of traveling. Having tried both ways of journeying I speak from experience. By land the trip is fatiguing, even on horseback, and on foot it is still more so, because for more than 100 miles the traveler must carry his food on his back, and this burden is almost unbearable. By water Onondago can be reached in three weeks from Shomoko, and all supplies carried along. There is nothing to be dreaded, as above

Wajomik there are no dangerous places, except now and
then where the current is rather rapid.   Our journey this
time, was greatly lengthened by our ignorance of the way.

Thursday, 7th.—In the morning we started early, with
the Indians, into the forest.   They thought they would find
a trail, but we could see no traces of it, and they fared no
better than we had formerly done.   They ran here and
there in the forest, till at length they found a path.   They
went on very rapidly, as they had determined to reach
Onondago to-day.   We kept up with them for some time,
but our packs were so heavy that we found it impossible to
go on in this way.   Not knowing our way we concluded to
lighten our loads, and hide some of our things in the woods,
and thus better keep up with the Indians.   We crossed a
mountain, and then the Creek Onogariske, which, had the
water been higher, we might have ascended in a canoe.

Our course lay westerly till we reached the trail that
comes up from Owego, and is quite clearly defined here.
We then proceeded toward the north.   As we now saw that
our path was good and plain, and that the Indians hurried
on very fast, we let them go on.   We followed as quickly as
possible, however, and at noon reached Lake Ganiatareske,
in which the creek rises, and soon after empties into the
Creek Tiohujodha, the largest branch of the Susquehanna.
At noon we camped near the lake and boiled some sapan,
and then went on through the woods, finding a path in the
afternoon which turns to the right.   We took the trail to
the left, because the other turns so far northeast.   We came
to a large lake which Bro. David remembered to have seen
nine years ago, and by this he knew that we were on the
right road.   He knew the place where Bro. Joseph had spent
the night with his company, and was much pleased to find
the names they had cut into the trees.   We went farther
down, and toward night found a hunting lodge where we
spent the night, very thankful to have been helped thus far.

Friday, 8th.—We started again and went on as rapidly
as possible, not knowing how great the distance was.   We
descended quite a steep mountain, and saw that a change
and separation took place in the waters, and that the Susquehanna lies much higher than the waters which flow into
the St. Lawrence, as it suddenly descends a mountain, and
yet we had not ascended any.   At the foot we came to a

creek which flows north through Swenochschoa. The lakes
on the mountain, of which there are three close together,
flow in a southeastern direction. The trail leads down along
the creek, and is as crooked as snake fences, because of
the trees which often lie across the road, and the number of
sloughs. In the afternoon we emerged from the wilderness, and hoped soon to reach Onondaga. The path changed
and became more passable, and before we knew it we
reached the town. We passed through the plantations,
where the Indians were hoeing the corn. They hailed us,
saying: Welcome, Brethren! and appeared glad to see
us.

Soon after we met the chief Otschinachiatha, who was
very friendly. He said we would probably find our house
closed, and the greater part of the people in the plantation.
He told us to open the house, as it was ours. We went to
our former lodgings. Our housekeeper soon came home
and was glad we had returned. She told us her troubles;
she and her children had nothing more to eat. She had taken
good care of all that we had left with her for safe-keeping.
In the evening the Chief Otschinachiatha came with several
other chiefs, and welcomed us very kindly, inquiring
whether we had brought any message from Brother Tgirhitontie, so that they might be guided by it and take counsel together, and that we might give utterance to our
thoughts and say what were our wishes. We said that we
should be very glad to have them do so, and thanked them
for their offer. This time we had but little to say; if convenient, however, we would be glad to hold a meeting with
them and express our wishes. The chief then said they
would meet to-morrow in our house, and he would have us
make the needful explanations to him, so that he might
make all known to the Council in the proper order. We
told him that this pleased us, and asked him to come to us
whenever convenient to him.

Then they showed a belt of wampum from Onontio. A
small letter attached to it showed that it had been sent by
Asseroni, and not by the Indians. The Governor of Canada
made known to them, in this way, that he was on the way to
Ohio with all his men, and held the tomahawk firmly in his
hand, and would destroy all who opposed him. He assured
them, however, that he would do no harm to the 6 Nations,

but only meant to attack the English.   They also told us
that they had sent away all their young men to Ohio, to see
what were Onontio's intentions, and to find out if he wished
to do them any harm.

They talked on various subjects with us, and we told
them of our journey, described the course we had taken and
how we had fared.   Among the rest they told us that the
trader, who had treated Bro. David so badly in Cayuga,
had passed through here soon after we left.   He had spent
several days here, had been drunk and had done much evil,
squandering all he had.   After much talk they took leave of
us and went home.   We soon retired and felt comfortable.
The Daily Word to-day was a great comfort to us: "The
windows from on high are open."   Isaiah 24:18.

Saturday, 9th.—Chief Otschinachiatha came to us early
in the morning; we explained to him all that we wished to
tell them.   Soon after the chiefs who were at home
assembled and welcomed us most kindly.   The Chief seated
himself beside Bro. David, who again repeated to them, so
that they all might hear, the following words: Brethren
of the Six Nations!   Our Brothers Ganousseracheri and
Thaneraquechta returned last autumn, and brought us the
good tidings that they sat in peace and quiet around our
fire, and smoked their pipe, and no harm came to them.
Now we have also learned from them that you would prefer
to have them remain longer with you, and learn your language thoroughly before proceeding elsewhere.

Then Br. David took the string of wampum in his hand
and said: Thus says Br. Tgirhitontie: Brethren, you
Aquanoschioni!   You have had a wise thought.   I and my
Brethren are of the same opinion as you, and we are
pleased.   Permit our Brethren to dwell in peace and quiet
around your fire in Onondago, as they have done in the
past.   As Br. Thaneraquechta finds difficulty in learning the
language, we have sent another in his stead, who already
understands it, and perhaps may be able to learn it more
easily.   The Chief sang this to the Council with the usual
ceremonies.

Then Br. David took the second string, and said in the
name of Br. Tgirhitontie: Brethren, you Aquanoschioni!
The last time our Brethren came and brought you the news
of Br. Gallichwio's death you made known to us, by a

string of wampum, that we should look around and seek for another man like Gallichwio, for he had a great affection for the Indians. Now we have seen and found a man, who, like the late Br. Gallichwio, loves the Indians. He has crossed the great water, and perhaps you will some day have a chance of seeing him.

The Chief, as usual, told them all this by intoning. We gave them a roll of tobacco and they seemed much pleased. Afterward we talked with them on many different themes. We told them that Br. Tgirhitontie had crossed the great water and would return again. Two messengers were immediately afterward sent with one string to the land of the Senecas, and the other to Anajot, by way of Ganochserage, so that all the nations might get the news.

Sunday, 10th.—In the morning Chief Hatachsocu came and begged Br. David to come and bleed his son, who was sick, which he did. We then visited Otschinachiatha, who asked if we would stay longer with them than at our last visit. We replied that we meant to spend some time with them, unless something occurred to compel us to leave, as for instance, having no more food. For this reason we would like to have planted something, though it was doubtful whether anything would grow so late in the year. We saw that he was not against our doing so, and so went to choose a place for planting. Without special reason, however, we changed our plans and decided not to plant.

During the afternoon warriors came from the war and brought a prisoner with them. We were invited to listen to them. When they had all assembled, the captain gave an account of their whole journey, and went into the most minute details of all that had happened to them, telling where they had been treated kindly or badly by Indians or Europeans. We drew a lesson from this, viz, that everything is made known to the Six Nations, and we learned how to treat the Indians as they passed through Shomoko.

Monday, 11th.—We returned to get all the luggage we had left behind, but found that the Indians who had been with us, had gone back without our knowledge, and had stolen all our things.

Tuesday, 12th.—During the day, which we spent in the woods, we prayed the Lord earnestly, to direct and guide us

in these days of great perplexities, for we heard of nought
but war and rumors of war.

Wednesday, 13th.—We returned to our lodgings.

Thursday, 14th.—Br. David visited Otochinachiatha,
who told him that some of the chiefs had returned from
Oswego, and brought the news that the French had crossed
Lake Ontario in great numbers. They had never seen so
many people together, and they feared evil results from all
this. Then Otschinachiatha said to Br. David that he would
like to make a communication to him, but feared we might
misunderstand him. He then said he had heard several
chiefs speak of our being here as unsafe during the war
time, as they did not know how matters would turn out with
the French. Therefore as soon as the war cry came from
Cayuga, and matters looked dangerous, they would say to
us: Brethren, depart now; it is time; go and tell our Brethren the state of things here.

David told them we were glad to know this, and would
surely follow their directions, begging them always to deal
plainly with us and make known their wishes. Otschinachiatha said there was no present cause for our departure,
for, as soon as they had news that we must leave, we could
at once go into the woods, whither they would follow us.
We felt disposed to stay and wait till the danger seemed
more imminent, having perfect trust in the Lord's guidance.
To-day's text seemed suited to our circumstances.

Friday, 15th.—We went into the town. Br. David bled
a woman, who had formerly entertained Gallichwio at her
home. Warriors returned in the afternoon, and brought
three children as prisoners. We also had visits from
drunken Indians.

Saturday, 16th.—The Indians had a feast in honor of
the returned warriors, which consisted in a rum drinking
carousal. Our hostess was asked to attend it, hence we went
into the woods. When we returned in the evening, and
found that the situation looked threatening, we decided to
go into the woods again. Our host advised us to leave
quickly (we, however, were not greatly alarmed), because
they feared that the drunken Indians might harm us.
Scarcely had we left the house when they bound one of
their number. We spent the night in the woods, sure of the
Lord's protection.

Sunday, 17th.—In the morning we again returned to our lodgings, and found the noise somewhat less. Our hosts were not at home and we were quite alone. We wrote and enjoyed a quiet season together. All were drunken in the town.

Monday 18th.—Their drinking bout continued. We returned home to see to various matters. As the supplies of our hostess were exhausted, we shared what little we had with her. Famine prevails everywhere, and the Indians live mainly on the rooots and herbs they find in the woods. In the afternoon we visited the chief Sequalissere, who was very friendly. He inquired where we lived. We tried to explain it to him as clearly as possible; he has never been in Philadelphia or that vicinity. Oh, how ardently we wished they might visit the Brethren. They would have different impressions of us, which would carry more weight than if we spent a year among them.

Tuesday, 19th.—The drinking continued. We remained quietly at home.

Wednesday, 20th.—The Indians were all half drunk. We spent the day at home writing. In the afternoon we went out hunting.

Thursday, 21st.—We were quite alone all day, and thought much of our friends at home.

Friday, 22d.—We enjoyed our morning devotions of song and prayer. As there was nothing to be done at home, we went into the woods for several miles, and built ourselves a hut, where we spent the night.

Saturday, 23d.—A quiet, happy day, in which we thought specially of our friends in Bethlehem.

Sunday, 24th.—We went home, having shot only a few pheasants and ducks. There was a great uproar in our lodgings; a woman had come there with rum, and was offering it for sale. We regretted having left the woods, and wished we had stayed in our hunting lodge. For some time we were quiet spectators, but at last we took refuge on the hill, where we built a fire and spent the night.

Monday, 25th.—Scarcely had we left Otschinachiatha's house (he was not at home), when an old woman, who was there, came and urged us to stay with her. She said that all were drunk in our lodgings. We accepted her invitation, and she at once prepared some food for us, entertaining us as well as she could.

Tuesday, 26th.—We wished to see how matters were in our lodgings, but the old woman would not consent to our leaving. She said that the rum was still being sold; hence we remained with her, and found that she was glad of our company. Our hostess supplied us bountifully with food, and said we should not suffer want, as she had plenty to eat.

Wednesday, 27th.—We remained with the woman, chopped her wood and helped her in various ways.

Thursday, 28th.—The wife of our host Ganatschiagaje, asked us to cut down some trees for her in the plantation. We did so, for her and for some other women, who had made the same request.

Friday, 29th.—We returned to our lodgings and spent a quiet, peaceful day.

Saturday, 30th.—Toward evening Andres Hattelios, arrived with some news from Virginia. (Andrew Montour.)

Sunday, July 1st.—We made an attempt to visit Andres, but found him absent, and went on to the house of Anaharisso, where we were received with much kindness. Andres visited us during the afternoon, and conversed much, asking about different Brethren from Bethlehem whom he knew. He showed much affection and attachment for the Brethren, and said that he had long wished to visit Bethlehem, but had never been able to do so. He well remembered the journey he had made with Zinzendorf to Wajomik, and later with some other Brethren to Bethlehem, and afterward with Br. Joseph to Onondaga, where he had received pleasant impressions of the Brethren. We had felt much pleasure at the thought of getting a letter from the Brethren in Shomoko, but were disappointed, and only learned that they no longer lived in the old house. Andres was not aware of the fact that they had built a new house, and had thus passed without seeing them. He was much surprised that we had been able to exist during the famine among the Indians. He said he could endure it no longer. We spent a pleasant, happy evening together.

Monday, 2d.—In the morning we visited Andres, who had invited us. He offered to forward a letter for us if we wished to write. We accepted the offer very willingly.

Tuesday, 3d.—It rained hard, and we spent the whole day indoors. Toward evening we visited Otschinachiatha's house, where we found a woman who talked much of a visit she had paid Philadelphia. She had lodged in Zinzendorf's house, and said that meetings were held there twice a day, and the Brethren showed much kindness. She was the wife of the late Gaxhayen. Another old woman told us that in her youth two French priests had lived in Onondaga, and had taught the Indians. At that time Onondaga was situated several miles farther east. It had, however, been destroyed by the French, and was afterward rebuilt where it now stands.

Wednesday, 4th.—We went out visiting, but found hardly any men at home, as all who were able had gone fishing, in order to procure food.

Thursday, 5th.—We wrote and spent a pleasant day. We visited in several houses, but found few Indians at home.

Friday, 6th.—The chiefs, who had returned from the chase, convened to-day to consider the message from Virginia. We were summoned to appear, and after Andres had made a speech, they handed Br. David the Governor's letter to the Six Nations, asking him to translate it, no doubt in order to find out whether it agreed with what Andres had said. Br. David excused himself on the plea of having not mastered the language enough to be able to make a translation. We noticed that Andres would not have been much pleased to have him do so. After the business of the Council had closed, we partook of a common meal with them, and then retired to our lodgings to write letters to Bethlehem.

Saturday, 7th.—In the morning we visited Hattelios, and handed him the letter, which he was to deliver in Shomoko. Two Oneidas from Anajot, and one Tuscarora from Sgauatees, who knew Br. David very well, were there. They conversed very much with us, and were very friendly. Toward evening we went to the creek to fish, and caught fine large trout.

Sunday, 8th.—There was much drinking going on, hence we thought it best to absent ourselves, and went into the forest to hunt.

Monday, 9th.—Andres left again, and we wished him a safe and pleasant journey home.

Tuesday, 10th, and Wednesday, 11th.—We stayed at home, wrote, and attended to various matters.

Thursday, 12th.—There was much drinking and noisy carousing going on. Toward evening we withdrew into the woods, built a fire, and spent the night there.

Friday, 13th.—In the morning we visited Otschinachiatha, who had just returned from Oswego. He reported that many traders were there, and that they asked whether there were any white people in Onondago, to which he had replied in the affirmative. They wanted to know why we did not come down and visit them? He told us that they had no good news from Onontio; his Indians were fighting against the Indians on the Ohio. We were forced to flee into the woods, as the Indians drank very hard. Spent a happy evening together.

Saturday, 14th.—We remained in the forest at our fire, and thought often of our Brethren in Bethlehem. In our lodgings all were drunk, keeping up a terrible noise.

Sunday, 15th.—We returned to our lodgings and found them deserted, as our hosts had gone to the woods in search of roots. Their and our own stock of food was completely exhausted, and there was no means, anywhere, of replenishing it. Hence the Indians eat mostly roots and herbs at present, which, however, they are obliged to boil from 24 to 30 hours, as they are poisonous. In the town there was much drinking going on.

Monday, 16th.—We decided to go into New York State, in order to get the things we had left there last autumn, and also to see if it were possible to get some provisions. Not knowing how to undertake the journey, we went to the house of Otschinachiatha, but did not find him at home. He had gone to the lake, to await the return of his sons from the war. The old woman, whom we found, got us to remain till he came, saying that he might have something to tell us. She gave us some corn, and we stayed.

Tuesday, 17th.—In the morning we visited Otschinachiatha, who had just returned. We told him of our plan of visiting Tioga, as for some days we had had nothing to eat. He did not object, and asked if we had any food for our journey, and took us to his sister's house. He told them to give us something to eat, and prepare some food for our journey, which they did at once. Three of Otschinachiatha's sons had returned from the war. When he told one that Br. Henry had come in the place of Br. Rundt, he asked if he had not yet received an Indian name. They debated for some time together, and then the chief said he should be named Ochschugore; a chief of the Onondagos had borne that name, and Br. David, too, belonged to the Onondagos. As we were now provided with food for our journey, we took leave of them and started, spending the night in the woods.

Wednesday, 18th.—It was as cold to-night as if it was autumn, and having no blankets we felt very chilly and uncomfortable, because yesterday we had perspired very freely on our way. During the morning we soon reached a town of the Tuscaroras. With the exception of a few women, all the people had gone fishing, as their stock of food was entirely gone. We went on our way, but soon felt so miserable because of the cold we had taken last night, that we could hardly go on. In the afternoon we reached Tiochrungwe, where there are still a few huts of Tuscaroras. We concluded to stay there, as we felt too sick to go on. An Indian, who had recently returned from the war, asked where we came from. When he learned that we lived in Onondago, and that one of us was named Ganousseracheri, he was charged to give us a letter; and thus, to our great joy, we received a letter from Br. Grube, just as if we had found it on our way. Had we not spent the night there, perhaps we might not have received it, as the Indian did not yet know us. The people in the town were very friendly, and showed us many kind attentions.

Thursday, 19th.—In the morning we went on our way, and soon reached Sganatees, a town of the Tuscaroras. Here we went to the house of Chief Sequalissere, with whom we were acquainted, and remained there till evening as we felt very tired. Here we found several Nanticokes, who had come up from Zeniinge. They were very glad to see us and seemed much surprised to meet us so unexpectedly. Toward evening they went on toward Anajot, and we went with them, as it was not far off, and spent the night there. We were most kindly received and entertained. The Nanticokes held a council with them this evening, and we were present and listened.

Friday, 20th.—We again started on our way. We felt rather better, and with food we might have been quite comfortable, but we had only a little corn meal boiled in water, and a very scanty supply of that. We went on as well as we could, but were quite often obliged to sit down, being greatly overcome with weakness. Toward evening we came to quite a large creek, where we at once began to fish, and as there were many fishes there, we stayed over night and caught enough for the next day.

Saturday, 21st.—We started early and reached Tigach-quet at noon, a creek which is the line of land which has been claimed. We boiled fish and corn meal, and caught several fishes in the creek. We then went on, but with great difficulty, as our strength was almost gone. In the evening we came to a hut where we spent the night.

Sunday, 22d.—In the evening we came to Kasch's. He began to swear dreadfully as soon as he saw us, and said: Why did we wander around in the woods, and not live like other Christians? For we would derive no benefit, but be obliged to live like cattle among the Indians, and spend a miserable life. He said that death already looked from out our eyes. We replied that we had been sick on this journey, and been so completely tired that we could hardly proceed.

Monday, 23d.—We went on to the village, which is 8 miles farther on, to see if we could get some corn and flour. In the whole village, however, we could scarcely obtain as much as a horse could carry, the Indians having hardly enough for themselves. The people in the village soon recognized us, and wondered if we were from Bethlehem. A drunken schoolmaster, and several others wanted to dispute with us, but when they saw that we had no wish to carry on any conversation with them, they said that we thought them beneath us. The schoolmaster asked if we had a passport; admitted, however, that he had no right to demand it. We replied that we were furnished with one, and he was very eager to see it, though he had not the courage to ask for it. In the evening we again went to Kasch. On the way we met two clergymen from the village, who had also visited him.

Tuesday, 24th.—Br. David hastened into the village to look for some corn, but could get nothing but a few bushels of peas, with which he returned in the evening. Many Oneidas came in the evening, who knew us well. Two of the chiefs told Br. David that they wished to speak to us, and he said they should nave a chance of doing so to-morrow. Br. David had helped Kasch to harvest.

Wednesday, 25th.—In the morning the two chiefs sent for Br. David. They brought forward the matter of land on the Tschochniade in Pennsylvania, and desired David to write a letter to Conrad Weiser. They would tell him what to write, and a Tuscarora would travel there and bring him the letter, as they feared he might forget to mention the matter. Br. David refused, and said we would have nothing to do with such affairs, and that he was unwilling to lend a hand to anything of that sort; adding, that if they had any message to send to Weiser, they should do it by means of a belt, which was a much better and surer way than by letter. When they saw that Br. David would not consent, they said they would ask the clergymen in the village to write. They complained bitterly about the whites; they could get no food from them, and they treated the Indians as badly as if they were dogs. They also told us that some of them had been baptized and married by the village clergyman.

Two traveling Nanticokes stopped with Kasch. They complained of great hunger and said: Oh, that we were now in Bethlehem! The Brethren there would certainly give us enough to eat. A woman, hearing their complaints, gave them a piece of bread. A man living near by, came and took leave of us, invited to call on him if we came that way again and said he wished to converse with us on spiritual matters. He regretted our not having lodged with him, so that he might have an opportunity to do so. He felt timid before Kasch, who is rough and coarse. The man is a day laborer, and does not own a plantation. He gave us some flour and meat, as we could get nothing. To-day we went into the field with Kasch and helped him to harvest, as he had asked us. He wished Br. Henry to teach him the Pennsylvania way of harvesting, as he preferred it to theirs.

Thursday, 26th.—We went into the woods to find a tree suitable for a bark canoe, but found none, as such trees are already very scarce in this vicinity, and it is so late in the season that there is not much bark to be had.

Friday, 27th.—At last we found one, but not of the right kind. We took it, however, as we could find none better.

Saturday, 28th.—While we were working on our canoe an Oneida came to us, and saw that we were very awkward about our work. He at once called two of his comrades; they took our work to pieces, and in two hours' time they had finished the boat. We were very glad indeed, as we could doubtless have worked the whole day, and even then with poor success. In this way we had the opportunity to learn how to build that kind of canoe. The Indians were from Anajot, and were well acquainted with Ganous-seracheri.

Sunday, 29th.—In our canoe we sailed down to the cabin of Kasch, packed up our things, and started off toward evening. Kasch's son brought our luggage with horses to the water. He and Kasch had become attached to us during our stay with them. They urgently invited us to stop with them if we came that way again. We sailed but a few miles up the river and camped in the woods.

Monday, 30th.—We went on up the river. Its course was westerly, not counting the curves. It was easy sailing, in quiet smooth water, with hardly any current. We met five boats with traders, which came from Oswego. They were very rough people, who wondered what we were doing among the Indians. In the evening we sang hymns together around our camp fire.

Tuesday, 31st.—We sailed up the creek, passing two forks. The creek grew very narrow, and was so filled with wood that often we hardly knew how to advance. We again met five canoes with traders; they were quite civil and modest. Br. Henry shot several ducks, and in the evening, when we wished to encamp, we found five raccoons on a tree, and caught them, so that we were abundantly supplied with meat.

Wednesday, August 1st.—In the morning we came to a place from which we had to go four miles across the country, to another creek that flowed westward. We found several white people, who remain there, in order to take over the messengers on horses, who go up and down to Oswego. Because we could not dispense with our bark canoe, or let it fall to pieces, we took it on our shoulders, and carried it over into the next creek. These two creeks are but two miles apart, but yet the distance is four miles to where they become navigable, as the one flows to the

east and the other to the west.   There is no mountain
between them and the country is very level.

We met Cayugas who had come up the creek.   Their
canoes had been very much injured, because, as they said,
the water was very shallow; they told us we would have
difficulty in proceeding, because of this.   We returned to
the cabins and spent the night there.   Two boats, with
traders from Cayuga, came across the portage.   The traders were very friendly and modest; soon learned that we
were Moravians.   One of them, an Englishman, had gone
through Bethlehem six or seven years ago, and said he
would like to visit the place again.   They were much surprised at our having dared to try so perilous a trip in a
bark canoe, and, as they told us, to cross such a wild lake
without knowing the way.   They described the way very
clearly, and warned us not to go too far into the lake, but
to keep, as much as possible, along the shore.   There are
Oneidas living here who know Ganousseracheri well.   We
at once saw that they felt more kindly toward us than to
all the traders who were there, and this we observed everywhere.   They entertained us very kindly with food, though
they gave nothing to the others, who had to travel down so
as to get some on the following day.

Thursday, 2d.—In the morning a man brought our
luggage across the portage on horseback.   It rained very
hard, so we stayed till afternoon, mending our canoe which
had been badly torn.   We then went down the creek, which
is not wider than the mill trench in Bethlehem; quite deep
in many places, however, but so shallow in others, that we
had to lift our bark canoe with much care.   After having
gone some miles we came into quite a large creek, called
Wood Kill.   It is so filled with wood and trees, that in a
bark canoe the utmost care is necessary, in order not to
wreck.

Friday, 3d.—We sailed slowly down the stream, not
being able to go on swiftly, because of the needed care for
our canoe.   The creek flows west, but very crookedly; it
remains always of the same size, no creeks flowing into it.
Toward evening we met two boats coming up from Oswego.
The people were very modest and friendly.   At first they
took us to be French; when they heard that we were Germans they spoke to us, asked whence we came and where

we were going. They described our route. We went on, and struck so hard with our canoe that it was almost shattered. We had to land and spend the night on shore.

Saturday, 4th.—The mending of our canoe kept us busy until noon. Two boats came up the creek. In one of them was an Indian from Onondago, who talked to us. When our canoe was again in order, we went on and reached Oneida Lake in good time in the afternoon. As the traders had described it, it is eight Germans miles long and eight English miles wide. Though there was no strong wind the lake was very rough. We went a short distance out, but had to return very soon, as the waves ran too high for our frail craft, and we spent the night there.

Sunday, 5th.—In the morning, at break of day, we sailed out into the lake, now quite calm. Looking ahead we could see no land, and we could almost imagine ourselves sailing into the sea. The lake flows from east to west. We had to cross a bay from six to seven miles wide, in order to reach the nearest land. It grew very dark and windy. Soon a high wind arose, and the lake became as rough as the sea and looked very white. We went into shore, and had to carry our canoe to the land, in order not to have it dashed to pieces by the waves. The wind kept up all day, so that we had to stay here.

Monday, 6th.—The wind had abated, and the lake was calm and pleasant for sailing. We started at daybreak and went straight on, till at last, at noon, we saw an opening where the lake emptied, into which we sailed. A short distance down the river we met quite a number of Onondagos fishing. They were much pleased to have us come to them so unexpectedly. They had a fish-weir there which quite closed the river. Chief Hatachsocu, to whom the fishery belongs, at once came to us and made an opening, so that we could proceed. We stopped with them and they told us of the war. They gave us some dried eels, and we gave them some flour. We went on and came to a fishery where we met Onondagos. Toward evening we reached a fishery where we met Chief Gajagaja, who talked with us about the war. He complained of hunger, and said he could catch nothing in his fish-weir. We gave him of our provisions, went for some distance and stopped for the night.

Tuesday, 7th.—We went on and soon reached the Seneca

River, which flows toward Oswego, and again had to sail against the current. At noon we reached another fishery, where there were also Onondagos, who were very friendly and gave us eels. In the afternoon we again had to mend our canoe, after which we went on, but because of a heavy thunder storm toward evening, we had to build a hut and encamp. Because of the mosquitoes, however, we could not sleep all night.

Wednesday, 8th.—We started early and soon reached Onondago Lake, but before we sailed into it we had again to mend our canoe, which has been so often patched that there was scarcely a whole place on it. We crossed the lake with quite a strong wind, and toward evening arrived in the town. Our hosts were pleased to have us return. Indians of this family had come from Canada, and lodged in our house.

Thursday, 9th.—In the morning we went to the lake to get all our things, and returned at noon.

Friday, 10th.—We had many visits from drunken Indians. They were all very polite and friendly, and welcomed us after our journey.

Saturday, 11th.—We spent a quiet day.

Sunday, 12th.—At noon there was a great noise of weeping and lamenting going on in our house, because the wife of our host had died. In the evening, at sunset, a large company of old women wept and bewailed the one who had died.

Monday, 13th.—In the evening the wife of Otschina-chiatha came and brought us eels, and asked us to come to her husband. When we visited him, he told us what a sad event had taken place in his family. He asked us to make a coffin for the dead woman, which we did. He had much to say to us; he also asked us why we had not visited him in his fishery. We promised to do so if we knew the way. The whole day long we heard nothing but wailing and howling; all ornaments were laid aside and torn rags put on on. At noon food was brought to the dead one, and they partook of it in common. A part of it was given to us.

Tuesday, 14th.—We visited Otschinachiatha. On our way there we met a messenger, who had been sent for us. Otschinachiatha gave us, in the name of all the chiefs, a string of wampum, which was the answer to our message,

viz., a permission to stay in Onondago, for just at this
time the French need not be feared. He therefore proposed
our going with him to the fishery at Tionctong, and helping
him make a canoe. We told him that we would be pleased to
do so, especially as there were few men at home, all having
gone to the fishery. Chief Sequalisserie had sent word to
us to go with him to the hunt, but as we had already promised Otschinachiatha we had to decline.

Wednesday, 15th.—We went to the fishing place with
two Indians, and arrived there in the evening.

Thursday, 16th.—In the morning eels were distributed,
which are here in great numbers. They shared them equally
with us, and during our whole stay they gave us quite as
many as any of the others. Toward evening Otschinachiatha came here by water. As his cabin was too small, he
built an addition to his lodgings for us.

Friday, 17th.—We went with him into the woods to
find a tree for a canoe. At last he led us to a place near the
river, where there were two stones which, he said, had once
been an Indian who had been petrified, and these were his
head and body. They offered sacrifices to him, so that they
might catch many fish, and we found tobacco lying there
that they had sacrificed. In the evening he talked much to
us, asked about Tgirhitontie, wanting to know when he
would return from across the great water, and what he
was doing in Europe. Br. David told him that he had gone
to see Br. Johanan. Our Brethren there held a great council, and would have much to consider and decide on. When
this council was ended he would return. Br. David told
much about the Brethren, and he listened very attentively.
Otschinachiatha told us of the Indian Ochschugore, whose
name Br. Henry now bears. He had lived at this place and
began this fishery, and also discovered the salt in Lake
Onondago.

Saturday, 18th.—We worked at the canoe. We were
invited to a feast at noon, to Chief Zagana, who is also here
fishing; they did nothing but eat. In the evening Otschinachiatha told me much of Br. Tgirhitontie and his journey
to Oswego, when he had made his acquaintance.

Sunday, 19th, 20th, and 21st.—We worked at our canoe.

Wednesday, 22d.—Otschinachiatha talked much to us
and asked us various questions about Bethlehem. He seemed

anxious to visit the place. He asked when we meant to return home. We told him we did not know yet, but in two months' time we would be able to tell him.

Thursday, 23d.—News came that our host, Ganatsch-iagaje has returned from the war with his company, and that our house was so full, that we would not be able to find room there on our return. On that account, Otschinachi-atha told us, that when we came into the town we should tell him our wishes concerning our lodgings, and he would care for us.

Saturday, 25th.—We finished the canoe and launched it. They were much pleased and said there never had been a canoe of that kind in this vicinity.

Sunday, 26th.—Preparations were made to return to the town. Otschinachiatha asked Br. David if the report, current among the Indians, that Ganousseracheri was a minister, was correct. Br. David told him that he was no minister. We went into the woods alone and washed our clothes in the river.

Monday, 27th.—We broke up camp with the Indians and sailed down the river, meeting Chief Gaschwechtioni at the fishery on the way. We left our boats and greeted him. In the evening, when we had camped, Otschináchiatha explained to Br. David how the province is divided, viz., into generations. It is plain to be seen that they have much order in all their affairs. For instance, each one has his own place where he is allowed to fish, and no one is permitted to encroach on his part. A chief is appointed to each fishing place, and he has his people, who belong to him. Thus it is also with the young people. Every chief has his own people under him, who must render him obedience in matters concerning the whole. Finally he spoke of our late Br. Cammerhoff, and David had to tell him how he had fared on his journey to the land of the Senecas. Thus he conversed till late at night.

Tuesday, 28th.—About noon we entered the lake, where we met a canoe, which brought the news that Mr. Johnson was on his way to make a treaty with the Six Nations. We entered the town in the evening. On our way we met an old woman, who gave us bread, and told us that our lodgings were filled with Indians, and that we would scarcely be able to enter. However, we went there first, and welcomed our hosts, who had returned from the war and were very friendly. They made room for us, and did all in their power to please us.

Wednesday, 29th.—We had spent a comfortable night and dreamed of Bethlehem. In our house they prepared a drinking festival, in honor of the newly arrived warriors. A great many people were invited. We went off by ourselves, and on returning we found the house so filled with people that we could not get in. They had just begun drinking. We watched them a short time, and then considered what direction we had best take. Our hostess advised us to go to Tiojatachso, to visit our host, who had returned from the war, as he would not come here soon, because his wife had died here. We followed this advice and went there. On the way we camped in a pretty spot, and partook of some tea and a loaf of Indian bread. Afterward we went to the town and welcomed our host, whom we found very sad on account of the death of his wife. Br. David talked with him and told him of the Brethren.

Thursday, 30th.—In the afternoon we went home, for we learned that to-morrow the drunken revels would begin here, and we wished to get away before they commenced. At home we found all in a dreadful state, and had little rest through the night.

Friday, 31st.—In the morning we went into the woods, where at such times we find our safest lodgings.

Saturday, September 1st.—In the morning we revisited our lodgings, but the situation was not very promising, so we returned to the woods. Br. Henry, who was not well, bled himself and felt better. We dreamed constantly of Bethlehem. We opened the text for our comfort: "Can a mother forget her child?" In the evening we returned to our lodgings. The storm was over.

Tuesday 4th, and Wednesday, 5th.—Great numbers from all the Nations came to be present at the treaty which is to be made here.

Thursday, 6th.—Mr. Johnson came into the lake with three boats. In the evening the Six Nations held a general dance.

Friday, 7th.—We visited Otschinachiatha, who told us much. He again assured us that we need not fear the French, and that we could stay here in safety.

Saturday, 8th.—The treaty was held. We went there also. A place was prepared in the lower part of the town, where they met. All the people went to the lake to meet Johnson and led him forward. We greeted him and he greeted us in passing. Many Indians of all Nations, who knew us, came and shook hands with us, and greeted us very kindly. When all the ceremonies were ended, the treaty began and lasted till evening. After it, Mr. Johnson came and asked us how long we had been here, and how long we meant to stay; whether we were pleased with the place, and what we thought of the Indians? Did we find them approachable? For, he said, we would be obliged to learn their language, in order to promote the cause of religion among the Indians. We told him that as yet we would express no opinion. We were pleased with the place, but first of all must know the language. He took leave of us and returned to the lake with his people.

Sunday, 9th.—We went to the lake, as almost all the people had gone there to close the treaty. No refreshments were offered to-day. We talked much with the Indians about various Nations, who showed themselves very friendly toward us. Henry, from Canajoharie, with whom David had formerly been prisoner, had been there, but he had not recognized him, and David did not make himself known. He asked us whether we had a pass from the Governor, and wished us to show it to Johnson. David told him it was time enough to do so when Johnson demanded it. As yet he had not asked for it. Three Oneida chiefs talked to us a long time, and expressed their displeasure at our being in Onondago, instead of with them at Anajot, saying we could learn the language much more quickly there than here. They gave this as a reason: Ganousseracheri had understood their language best at first, and should have gone on with it; but, instead he settled in Onondago, and had thus become half an Onondago and half an Oneida. David told them that if we went on in this language we would get just as much benefit. They would not grant this, however, but insisted on our living with them. We remained till toward evening, and then returned to the town.

Monday, 10th.—We stayed at home. They began their carousings in the town.

Monday, 11th.—We saw that after the treaty they would again begin their drunken revels; hence we built ourselves a cabin, so that in case of need we might have a shelter. The nights have already grown too cold for us to spend them in the open air. We had scarcely finished our work when the whole drove came up from the lake. Johnson had made them a present of some rum. In the evening we retired to our hut and expected to be alone, but our hosts came also, as they could not stay in the house any longer, because of the drunken Indians, who were very dreadful. During the whole night such a dreadful noise was kept up in the town, that it seemed as if evil spirits were let loose. They almost killed each other; some burned themselves and others were beaten to cripples. Oh, what a sad sight it is, to have to see them thus, as if led to the slaughter.

Wednesday, 12th.—We spent the whole day with our hosts in our hut, and kept ourselves hid from the drunken Indians.

Thursday, 13th, and *Friday, 14th.*—They went on with their drunken carousings, so that we had to remain concealed in our huts.

Saturday, 15th.—In the evening we returned to our quarters. The storm had abated.

Sunday, 16.—All was quiet, for all had gone into the woods in search of roots, Frenchmen having come to buy them. We went into the woods to-day, and were much in spirit with our friends at home.

Monday, 17th.—We had to remain at home alone, as all the inmates of our house left. The warriors set off for Canada, so that our house became quite empty.

Tuesday, 18th.—We visited Otschinachiatha, who related much. He told us that in the spring the Nanticokes would move to Anajot; they had only night's lodgings in Zeniinge. It appears, however, that they are not satisfied that the Oneidas should do this, as they have not asked their advice. After much talk Otschinachiatha asked if Br. Tgirhitontie would soon return to this country. He said they hoped soon to hear what feelings he held toward the Six Nations.

Wednesday, 19th.—We visited Chief Sequalisserie. He and his people were friendly.

Thursday, 20th.—Otschinachiatha sent for us in the

morning. He gave us a basket filled with eatables. He
told us that they would like to have a blacksmith here, for
their axes and guns needed mending badly, and they had no
one who could do it, but had to go a long way to some white
people. Mr. Johnson had promised to send them a smith
more than a year ago, but he had not kept his word. They
meant to make another attempt, and present a petition,
asking for a smith, to the Governor, and in case he did not
grant it, they would apply to Br. Tgirhitontie, and see if he
would listen to their appeal. [I omit a conversation on the
baptized French Indians.] Finally Otschinachiatha begged
us to mend the bridge across the creek. Most of them had
their plantations over there, and when the women carried
their corn across, they were always in danger of falling into
the water. We promised to do it.

Friday, 21st.—We visited Otschinachiatha, and spoke to
him about our being here, as he had often asked us if we
expected to stay here throughout the winter. We made a
proposal to him about the building of a house, as he had
already told us in the spring that he wished us to build him
a small house beside his, but he seemed to have given up
the idea. We told him we would do it now, and he should
permit us to live in it in the winter, for ours was too bad
for us to use it then. We begged him to consider the
matter and give us a speedy answer, so that we might
decide on something, as winter was at the door, and if we
wished to build a house we must soon set about it. He
promised to do so.

Saturday, 22d.—We repaired the bridge for the Indians,
who called out many a "Niarwo." The whole town rejoiced
to have a good bridge, especially the old people. They
brought us plenty of food. Otschinachiatha told us that
now there would be more quiet in their land than heretofore, because, in Oswego, rum had been forbidden to be
sold to the Indians.

Monday, 24th.—Otschinachiatha's mother asked us to
cut her a block for stamping, which we did. She gave us
corn and pumpkins.

Wednesday, 26th.—We visited Gaschwechtioni, Head
Chief and Speaker in Ganassateco's place. He was very
friendly and had much to say. He asked us to make him
a canoe near here, as he greatly needed it for fishing. We

could not refuse him, having made one for Chief Otschin-achiatha. On this we went with him into the woods to look for a tree and promised to make him a canoe, for which he was very glad.

Thursday, 27th.—We went into the woods with him, to make the canoe. He was our cook and gave us plenty to eat. In leaving the woods we met Chief Sequallissere at work. He was very glad and grateful that we had built the bridge for them; said we had done a good work, at which the whole city would rejoice.

Friday, 28th.—When we were at work, Gaschwechtioni told us among the rest, that Onontio was not quite satisfied at our being here, for he had asked them if they did not know that the French Fathers had been in Onondago before the English, and for this reason they had the first right to the land. For, he added, the French meant to take posses-sion of the land here. Gaschwechtioni answered him that the English were their brothers, and that they had never had wars or quarrels with them. With the French, on the contrary, they had carried on severe wars, and had been greatly weakened by them. Besides, he said, they preferred the English, especially Br. Onas, to the French. David asked him whether French priests had already been in the Cayuga and Seneca lands. He replied, nowhere except here. This was one of the reasons why they had been so doubtful about our staying here this whole summer, because they fear the French, who carry the sword in their hands.

Saturday, 29th, and *Sunday, 30th.*—We were at work with Gaschwechtioni. He told us much Indian history, and related how the first Indians had come into the land. He said it must have been more than 1,000 years since they were in this country, and that the first Indian had come down from Heaven, and that the second person, namely, the woman, had been taken from his side, which shows that they still have some faint idea of the creation, only they have mixed heathen fables with it. This account, he said, had been handed down to them by their ancestors, from very remote ages, before any whites had been in the country, and they, in turn, told it to their children, so that it might not be forgotten. He also told us that the Six Nations were a very bad people, for they eat human flesh, but only in war time. They had done so with the French.

Tuesday, October 2d.—Otschinachiatha told us all sorts of stories about the war. They had received news that the Governor of Virginia had sent troops to Ohio, to conquer the French there.

Thursday, 4th.—We visited Otschinachiatha. He looked very sad, for his wife had been sick for some time and her case seems serious. He talked much with us. He told us amongst the rest, that he would not change his opinion about our staying here this winter. He said he thought it most advisable for us to return home, as they had been in fear of the French all through the summer, and they did not know what turn matters would take. Neither he nor they could know what might happen. God alone knew. Besides, he added, we might get into great straits for want of provisions. This was his opinion, and he thought we would do better to return early in spring. Hence we were obliged to decide on returning home for the present.

Saturday, 6th.—We visited in the town and came to the house of a Frenchman, a white man, who was quite old. He had been taken prisoner by the Six Nations, and had been brought here and now lived among them, like an Indian. He was much pleased that we visited him.

Monday, 8th.—After visiting in the town, in the evening we called on Otschinachiatha. His wife was rather better, for which he felt very glad, saying that perhaps God in Heaven would again give him his wife. She, too, was very friendly and spoke to us. She bade her husband say that she already had assigned a plantation to us, if we wished to plant something for next spring, so that we might not suffer hunger again. We told Otschinachiatha that we meant to start very soon. An Indian from our house would soon set off for Zeniinge, to go on the chase, and because of this good opportunity we would go with him, our boat being there.

Tuesday, 9th.—We went to the lake to boil salt. Some French traders were there. We spent a happy day.

Wednesday, 10th.—We returned to the town. Our Indian told us to make all preparations for the journey, as he expected to start in a few days.

Thursday, 11th.—We visited Otschinachiatha, and told him our plan of starting in a few days with the Indian. He had much to say to us. They hoped, when we returned, to hear how Br. Tgirhitontie felt toward Aquanoschioni, for they did not yet know whether he thought good or evil of them. Br. David told him that he could assure them that Br. Tgirhitontie and the Brethren had no evil intentions toward them, for they loved them, and if they knew the Brethren they would say the same, for this is the truth. He spoke very frankly to us, and we could hear and see that they are glad to have us, especially when they know the opinion of the Brethren, and hear how they are disposed toward them. On the whole they are very friendly to us here, and in our intercourse with them we have become well acquainted. The chief of the town, Ganoschgoto, visited us. He had much to say, and asked why it was that we were so different from all other white people or traders. He had never seen any like us. David told him it was because we were people who hated evil, because we knew that our God and Creator took no pleasure in it, and we loved Him so sincerely that we neither could nor would do it, etc. For this reason we and our Brethren were different from other people who called themselves Christians, but whose hearts were wicked, etc.

Friday, 12th.—Br. David again asked Otschinachiatha whether we should tell Br. Tgirhitontie that they wished to hear his disposition toward them. He said: Yes; say to him: Brother! Think no evil in your heart toward us, for we, Aquanoschioni, do not like to hear evil tidings. We know, indeed, that you are our Brother, and the bond connects us closely, but we do not yet know the intentions and thoughts of our hearts, therefore, we pray you, let us hear only good and kind words from you. We then visited Chief Gaschwechtioni and told him that we meant to start. He asked when we would return. We told him in the spring if nothing happened, and he seemed pleased. He gave us tobacco for the journey. In the evening Ganoschgoto visited us again and gave us corn. Several others did the same, and showed themselves very kind to us in leaving.

Saturday, 13th.—In the morning, after we had taken leave, we left with an Indian and a woman from our house, and in the evening arrived at the end of the Onondago Creek.

Sunday, 14th.—In the morning we soon reached the

Susquehanna lake, Onokariske, went down along the outlet of the lake some distance, and camped in a hunting lodge.

Monday, 15th.—Our Indian went out hunting. Meantime we went to look for a tree fit for a canoe, but could find none in the whole neighborhood.

Tuesday, 16.—We went some distance down the creek to the first fork.

Wednesday, 17th.—Finished a canoe and sailed,

Thursday, 18th.—down the creek. On the way we passed many beaver lodges. The Indians robbed one, but caught only one beaver.

Friday, 19th.—We sailed on and met many deer in the creek; the Indian missed his aim. In the afternoon he went hunting, but without success.

Saturday, 20th.—In the evening we reached Zeniinge. We spent the night with the Onondagos; they knew us well.

Sunday, 21st.—We went over to the Nanticokes, who were much rejoiced to see us, and who had long expected us. Patrick at once offered us his house, to which we went. We visited some others in the town, among the rest the old Chief Cossey, who was very glad to see us. We brought them some corn from Onondago. It is very scarce here, and they were grateful for it. Patrick also told that a year from next spring they meant to visit Bethlehem again, and that some Oneidas and Tuscaroras would go with them.

Monday, 22d, and *Tuesday, 23d.*—We remained in the Nanticokes' town. The old Chief Cossey invited us, and told us that the words which the Brethren in Bethlehem had spoken to them, had been made to all the Oneidas and Tuscaroras, and had been most kindly received. They had said that they were good words, and they also wished to know the Brethren in Bethlehem. They complained much of their having no blacksmith. Patrick said he thought the one in Shomoko had a hard time, as there was so much drinking going on there; with them he would be more comfortable, and would have a quieter time. He said they had made known to all the traders, that they were forbidden to bring any rum into the town, or they would break the casks to pieces. All were very busy harvesting. Though they planted very late, they have planted more than 40 acres of corn. They prepared food for us for our journey, and provided abundantly. In the evening they held a festival, to which we were invited. Their ceremonies, however, did not please us, and we did not go a second time.

Wednesday, 24th.—We bid farewell. Old Chief Cossey said he wished we lived here with them, for he would like to have us always near him; we lived too far from them; perhaps he would see no Brethren in a long time. We then sailed down the stream, soon passed the fourth fork and Tschochnot, a Cayuga town, came to the Cayugas in the evening, who were on the hunt, and had camped there. They asked us to stay over night with them, as it would be the last. They had our canoe, which they had brought up in the spring, and we now took it along. One of them had shot a deer, and he gave us venison for our journey.

Thursday, 25th. We went on and spent the night near Tioga.

Friday, 26th.—Because it stormed and rained we had to keep quiet; it grew very cold. From an Indian, who came down from Zeniinge, we learned that on the day we left Zeniinge, the war cry had come from Onondago, and that the Indians were gathering in the towns.

Saturday, 27th.—We passed Tioga, and in the evening reached A-un-ta-ung, where some Cayugas live. Here we met Logan from Shomoko, who wished to return with us, and on that account we staid there over night.

Sunday, 28th.—Logan started with us, as also another Indian from there, with his whole family in his canoe. Toward evening they went hunting, and so we encamped early.

Monday, 29th.—In the morning the Susquehanna had risen very much, and all our canoes were carried off, though we had drawn them far into the land. We soon succeeded in capturing ours, but that of the Indian had been driven far away. We therefore had to take his wife and children into our canoe, till we found the other.

Tuesday, 30th.—We passed Onochsae, camped for the night in Stogecho or Tenkhanick. It had snowed the whole afternoon and almost all night, and was very cold.

Wednesday, 31st.—In the afternoon we reached Hazirok, where we halted, but found hardly any one at home. We sailed on, and had night's lodging with an old Delaware.

Thursday, November 1st.—At daybreak the old Delaware went through the incantations prescribed to him by the sorcerer at Onochsae, so that all might be well with him. In the morning we reached the Shawanes town in Wajomik. We entered, but found only a few women at home. They gave us to eat and we went on, spending the night near Wamphallobank.

Friday, 2d. We passed Neskapeke. A little farther on we saw some new huts, the inhabitants of which, as the Indians said, had come from Gnadenhutten. We stopped, but found none of them at home; learned, however, that Salome, from Gnadenhutten, lived there. In the evening we came to Labach Peter, and remained over night with him.

Saturday, 3d.—We sailed on, stopping on the way with Blackfish, the brother of Abraham in Gnadenhutten. He told us that he had lately been in Bethlehem, and was very friendly. In the evening we reached Shomoko, to our and our Brethren's great joy.

Wednesday, 7th.—We again started, via Neskapeke, for Gnadenhutten. The water was very high, but we were so fortunate as to meet Indians everywhere between Shomoko and Neskapeke, who helped our boats across, and at the other creeks we cut down trees in order to cross, and thus we arrived,

Saturday, 10th.—Safe and sound in Gnadenhutten.

Monday, 12th.—We arrived in Bethlehem, to our great joy, in time to celebrate, with our dear Brethren, the festival of the Chief Eldership, to confess our faults and shortcomings with the congregation, and to express to the Lord our heartfelt gratitude for our merciful preservation, amid all journeyings and manifold dangers of every kind.

REV. W. M. BEAUCHAMP'S NOTES ON JOURNAL
OF 1753.

May 8. The Nanticokes were preparing to leave, the Five Nations having ordered them to go to Otsiningo, some miles north of the site of Binghamton, where some Onondagas had settled.

24. Indian trails were not always well defined, Indian moccasins making but a slight impression. Horses and heavy boots made them plainer.

27. Th trail from Owego went up Owego and Catatonk Creeks, one path going to Cayuga and the other to Onondaga.

29. Tschachnot was Chugnutt or Choconut. Anohoch-grage is now Oquago and had a very much mixed population. The Fork was at Binghamton, once termed Chenango Point.

31. Zeniinge and Otsiningo are the same, equivalent to Chenango. The Nanticokes camped on the west bank.

June 2. They chose a better site three miles down the stream.

3. The division of land was common, as well as the united work.

4. Chenango Fork was Anajota, the Chenango indirectly leading to Old Oneida, which was a day's journey from Oneida Lake, though Otsego Lake may be meant. Tiohujodha is now the Tioughnioga, a variant of Tioga.

5. The fourth stream was Schio, now Otselic River.

6. The fifth was Onogariske, like Morgan's O-nan-no-gi-is-ka, (shag bark hickory), the west branch of the Tioughnioga. They went up the east branch.

7. Lake Ganiatareske (on the way to the long lake) was in Preble, and Zeisberger remembered Lake Oserigooch, in Tully.

8. They went through Christian Hollow and Cardiff, near Onondaga Creek, which they called Swenochschoa, the part now termed Swenoga, (a hollow, or cutting through a deep gulf).

29. Andres Hattelios was Andrew Montour or Sattelihu.

July 16. Out of the Indian country eastward, they would be in New York.

20. They stopped at Oriskany Creek.

21. Tiatachquet seems Sadequoit or Sauquoit Creek.

25. Tschochniade is Juniata.

Aug. 1. They crossed the portage at Rome to Wood Creek.

6. There was a fishery at Brewerton, the remains of the fish weir being mistaken by J. V. H. Clark for a mole belonging to the old colonial fort. The second fishery was at Caughdenoy, and the third at Schroeppel's Bridge.

7. The fishery on the Seneca is known as the Gaskon, (a fall) and is between Three Rivers and Belgium.

13. Burials had changed from the sitting to the horizontal posture, and rude coffins were used.

14. The fishery at Jack's Reefs had its Indian name from Cross Lake, and was an early resort.

17. I do not know of these venerated stones and they may have dissappeared. The canoe seems to have been a dug-out, of a pattern locally new.

27. Kaghswuhtiooni (belt of wampum laid down) or Red Head, had the fishery at Baldwinsville. The idea that the Indians had no personal property is opposed to all facts.

Sept. 8. Johnson gives an account of this treaty, Kaghswuhtiooni being speaker.

9. Henry is King Hendrick of Canajoharie.

22. The first account of a bridge at Onondaga. Zeisberger made a foot bridge later.

24. The block for stamping seems for a corn mortar.

Oct. 6. White captives were often adopted.

27. This was the celebrated Logan, who was a Cayuga by mother right.

Nov. 12. Their journey ended at Bethlehem.

DIARY OF A JOURNEY TO ONONDAGA, RESIDENCE THERE, AND RETURN FROM THENCE, BY THE MORAVIAN BRETHREN, CHARLES FREDERICK AND DAVID ZEISBERGER, FROM JUNE 9, 1754 TO JUNE 4, 1755.

They left Bethlehem June 9, and reached New York three days later. June 15 they sailed for Albany and landed there four days later.

June 19. "'As yet no Indians had arrived. There was much excitement in the town, several Indians having been murdered by negroes, and we hear that several of the miscreants have been hanged."

Sat. 22. "We went out to look at the Indian lodges, when David espied Conrad Weiser, who was much surprised to meet us. . . . He wondered whether we had just come from Onondago. We answered him, " No," and that we had come hither to see how it would fare with the Indians. Toward evening several Indians arrived.

Sun. 23. " David busied himself in looking about for any Onondagoes who might have come in, and presently two appeared at our door who knew him, and we invited them in. One of them was a friend of the Brethren, and the other had been the host of the Brethren on several occasions. David inquired about the state of affairs in their country, and we were informed that peace and plenty reigned there, and that we would find this time propitious for going there. They called on us during the following two days, and David spoke long with them about our going into their country, therefore on the

" 27th we left the town at 8 a. m. We would have preferred to wait until all the Indians had arrived, but it seemed to involve a great loss of time. . . . We had scarcely passed the place where the Indians were lodged, when a negro in a wagon overtook us, and told us that an Indian had been looking for two persons whom he professed to know. Assisted by Conrad Weiser, they hunted up our late stopping place, and, to their disappointment, found that we had already left." They rode on, and " in the afternoon we reached Schenectady; on the road we saw many Indians on foot, with their old men, women and children on wagons. To the public house where we put up, came also the old chief Henrick, who was on his way to Albany, where they had been greatly longing for his presence."

Next day they sent their goods by water beyond Little Falls, and the following day reached the last house east of that place, where they staid over night and part of the next day. At the next place they had religious disputes and abuse. There was more of this trouble farther on, but Wednesday evening, July 3d, they were in Kasch's house. Next day they began making a canoe, which was finished on the ninth, and they resumed their journey on the 13th, sleeping in the forest that night. They made the portage on the 15th, reaching Oneida Lake on the 17th. A high wind delayed them there. "Toward evening several bateaux for Oswego passed us, loaded with fire-arms, and we were pleasantly greeted. They soon went on, as the waters had quieted down considerably. We delayed our start till next day, as the lake is usually quieter in the morning.

18th. Before sunrise we were on our way, enjoyed calm weather all day, and were able to make several miles up the river on the other side of the lake.

19. We passed a bateau coming from the country of the Senecas.

Sat 20. About noon we crossed the Salt Lake. There were several Indians there engaged in fishing, who made us a present of an eel, which was very acceptable. As one of them was about going to the town, we asked him to secure help to move our goods into the house which we were to occupy. Our arrival promised to be a welcome one, for food was becoming very scarce in the town.

Sun. 21. We entered Onondago in the afternoon, and in a short time were visited by nine chiefs, who were desirous to know what we had to say. David told them the words of Tgirhitonti:

1st. It is not *land* that we are after.

2d. That, unlike the ministers who travel through these wilds occasionally, we came to learn their language, and as soon as we were sufficiently advanced we wished to bring them the words of the Creator.

To all of this no objections were raised. Thereupon David gave them a string of wampum, which was promptly accepted.

Monday, July 22. We called on the family of the chief whom we had met in Albany, and, on his return later in the day, we talked with the chief himself.

Wed. July 24. The chiefs met in our house, and held long consultations over many belts and strings of wampum, especially on one which had been sent by the Nanticokes, about excessive drinking among the Indians, and representations, both verbal and in writing were made, praying them to take measures tending to stem this tide of evil. Thereupon council was dismissed. Toward evening they again met, and brought with them 8 or 9 women. The women usually bring in the supplies of rum, therefore they should be interested listeners also.

The arguments of the Nanticokes were as follows: It is quite evident that there are now so few Indians, where they had been so numerous formerly. The cause of this

falling off is their use of too much rum. Let the Indians
try to do without rum for but four years even, and they
will be astonished at the increase of population, and at the
decrease of diseases and early death. All this is the result
of rum drinking, which is also the primary cause of famine
among them, caused by their not planting their crops at the
proper time.

Their arguments were also accentuated by a letter,
written on wood with black paint, in which one stroke
represents God; a second a city; a third the Devil; a fourth
hell, etc., etc., showing that it is of no use for a man to do
his drinking in secret, hiding his liquor in the woods or
some such place, and to say to some good friend: " Come
with me to such or such a place; there I have some rum and
we will have a spree."

He that dwells above sees everything and will punish
these. Nor dare any one say: " When we come to die
everything is at an end." No! those that have been drunkards will be sent to the Devil, and what will *he* do with
them? He will torment them. In what way? He has a
great kettle of boiling water, and will say to such an Indian:
" Come here! You were fond of drinking; now you shall
have a great plenty." He will throw the Indian into the
kettle, where he wil be cooking without dying. Occasionally he will be given a little rest for catching his breath;
then he will be boiled again, etc." The council, however,
could not agree on the subject, and now, as before, there is
no end to drinking.

Fri., July 26. We went to the lake to get salt, of which
there is a scarcity here.

Sat., July 27. We returned home, and fell to writing
and studying the languages as hard as possible.

Thurs., Aug. 1. We visited a chief, who had invited us
to his house, for the sake of former acquaintance with
David.

Tues., Aug. 6. We called on another chief, who questioned us eagerly about Tgirhitonti; if he would not soon
visit here. We told him he was too busy with work.

Thurs. Aug. 8. To-day David talked with an Indian
living in our house, who said that when he was in Canada,
2 years ago, he had been greeted on his arrival there by a
minister, who asked him to allow himself to be baptized,

and to take as wife a baptized Indian woman, which would be a very nice thing to do. He told the minister that at present he had no desire to do so, but might agree to it at a later time. He told David that he saw nothing better in the baptized Indians than in the others of that region. This gave David opportunity to tell him that to be baptized and to be called a Christian is not enough; for the heart of man is by nature wicked, and if he does not become acquainted with his Creator, all the rest will do him no good.

Fri. 9. David finished a little log hut, for the bear's cub belonging to our hostess.

Wed. 14. We visited the French Indian, who asked our aid in making a canoe. David made a foot bridge over the creek near our house.

Thurs. 15. A woman from Canada came to our lodge. She was attended by 2 bateaux, for the purpose of buying the well known root.

Mon. 19. The Indians were very boisterous to-day, about 40 of them, and were drinking heavily. Toward evening our host got into a quarrel with a woman, and it came to blows. We were compelled to interfere and keep them apart, for which the woman next morning thanked us. Later the crowd again collected by our house, and we found it advisable to find a sleeping place in the forest, which we did.

Tues. 20. We went into the woods, and made some boards for an Indian.

21-22. These 2 days were spent by the Indians in carousing.

24. The entire council was in session to-day, as also on

Sun. 25th. Toward evening two of the chiefs came to our house, and asked us to tell Tgirhitonti that our doings and intentions were now known to them, and they gave David a string of wampum.

Tuesday, August 27. The Speaker of the Council called on us to-day, and told us that the Governor of Virginia had fought a battle, and intended to give another. It seems the Indians are displeased thereat. He also asked us whether Tgirhitonti was as great a man as the Governor at Philadelphia. We assured him he was not.

Sat. 31. To-day our friend, the chief, told us what had been said about us in Council. The chiefs who were strangers to us, asked what we were doing here, and whether we did any work? They had been answered: "Yes; that we had been busily employed and would probably continue so, if we could find work to do; that otherwise we were not as other white people coming among the Indians, going from one house to another gossiping, but that in visiting we were quiet, and would listen to what the Indians had to say, and that we were trying to learn their language.

We think that the Indians have become favorably inclined toward us. This particular chief has twice before told us that when he was with *Kasch,* the latter had warned him about us, saying that though we had come ostensibly for the purpose of learning the language, that our ultimate purpose was something else, which we would not divulge. David said, " What does Kasch know about our intentions? Our business is no affair of his." The chief said no more about the matter.

Sun. Sept. 1st. We went to the other village to let some blood for a sick man.

Tues. 3. We were aroused during the night by our people, because a messenger had come from Albany, bringing letters said to be intended for Oswego. They brought news that the French Indians had plundered a town above Albany, and had made threats against the latter town also. The chiefs asked us to remain at home to-day, so that David could read a letter for them. The council met in the afternoon, but the letter was not read, as it had been sealed; so it was sent on to Oswego, together with a string of wampum.

Thurs. 5. We went into the woods to collect some of the roots. Our house being full of traders, we hoped to earn a little something by doing so, especially as it began to look serious for our maintenance during the winter, because of scarcity of food. After we had finished our shelter in the forest, we discussed the advantage of building a house for ourselves, for use during the winter. We laid the matter before the Lord in prayer, and felt advised to propose the plan to the chiefs and await an answer.

Sun. 8. Returning, as we approached our house, we heard the sound of revelry, and found many drunken Indians in the village, our house being full of them. Our friend was there also, and in the presence of all greeted us with a kiss. A woman present was very ill, and things looked very wretched here.

Mon. 9. We hear that the traders are about leaving, so we went down to the lake with what root we had dug, but disposed of it with difficulty, getting for it no more than a traveler's kettle, an article we badly needed.

Thurs. 12. Our host, with 14 others, starts for Canada to-day. Our hostess was very much dejected because the traders had persuaded her daughter to go with them to Canada.

Fri. 13. Her son left for Oswego to-day, to tell the chiefs to bring back his sister.

Sat. 14. David did some blood letting in town. Last night there was a heavy frost, and to-day it is cold, hence we are anxious to know whether our building a house will meet with the approval of the chiefs, which we hope to learn on their return from Oswego.

Mon. 16. Was passed in visiting in town and in writing.

Fri. 20. The above mentioned chief returned to-day and we called on him at once, but could get nothing definite out of him, he being partly under the influence of rum, though very friendly.

Mon. 23. We again visited this chief, and David said to him: " Brother, we are come to tell you that we intend staying here over the winter. We want to do so because it is a long journey to our home, and on our travels we get little chance to learn your language. It would please us if you were to tell all the chiefs of our wishes. We will not begin to build a house till they all know of it, so that if other Indians should come and say: " Why do you build here?" we may continue our work undisturbed. The chief promised to do this and bring us our answer.

Tues. 24. David was called to the chief's house to let blood for him, when the chief said that the Indian whose business it was to inform us was absent now, but it signifies nothing; that we had better go ahead with building. In the afternoon we went to the other town to do some blood letting. There is much building going on there, as many are moving thither from the other village.

Wed. 25. Began work on our new house.......Several, seeing it, were astonished at our building.

Mon. 30. It was very noisy with drunken men in our house, and we spent the night in the woods.

Tues. Oct. 1. Our good friend, the above named chief, Otschinochiatha, (in Albany called Bundt) invited us to his house to partake of bear's meat with him. He said that the Governor of Virginia was about to declare war with them because a white man had been slain by an Indian there. He asked, "What did David think of it?" David said that he thought it very unlikely, because the English are not fond of warfare. The chief said that a council would soon be called, and if war seemed immediate by that time he would inform us, so that we could leave for home.

We had often looked around for a suitable place for our house; at last, at the desire of our host, we concluded to build against one end of his house.

Fri. 11. David visited the Speaker of Council, who spoke to him about the singing in the Low Dutch Church at Albany, imitated it, and asked if we did the same in our Church. David said that God looks upon the heart alone, that all ceremonies are of no avail, etc. He thereupon invited David to a feast, something very general here, as now one and now another gives a feast. David is often asked why he did not bring a smith with him, instead of another man. David replied that he did not know a smith was wanted. N. B. There had been a smith here from Albany last winter, and he intended coming here again, as we are told, but late in the season. In the evening Otschinochiatha came to us in the woods, bringing each of us a tobacco pipe.

Sat. 12. We debated on our trip to the town, as we could not very soon complete our house, and the season is too late to go by boat on the river, from danger of freezing in. David made arrangements with our hostess and her son, to supply us with food through the winter.

Wed. 16. We bade farewell to Otschinochiatha, who, with his family, goes to Canada a hunting. He said to David, " If drunken Indians come and ask, ' Why do you build here?' tell them that I have allowed you. If the blacksmith or any trader asks this, tell them that Bundt had given his permission. If they become violent and wish to drive you away by force, I shall depend on your remaining here till I return. I shall always remember that my brothers are in Onondago."

Mon. 21. We began building to-day. The speaker and several members of the Council looked on and admired the location as being very good for a smithy, and said that David ought to learn the trade.

Monday, November 10th. Got our house under roof and lodged therein at once, on account of the many drunken Indians. Dimensions: 13½ by 12½ feet inside; the walls of hewn logs, roofed with shingles, for we could get no bark at this time of the year. Moreover, it is the smallest but the best house in Onondago.

The oldest daughter returned home to-day with her husband, whom we had never seen. In the evening he held a conversation with us. "Why are you building a house here?" "Because we wish to remain over winter and learn the language." "Who allowed you to build?" "Otschinochiatha." "Then he should have supplied you with corn also, because if you are here my children will suffer from lack of food." And he had much to palaver besides, saying that our hostess was not well pleased at our being here. We hear that a black smith and two traders have arrived.

Tues. 11. To-day we spoke with our hostess, urging her to tell us plainly whether she objected to our living here. She cast all the blame on her children. We said that we intended going down to the town in a few days, to buy a few things for the winter. In the afternoon we went 5 miles to secure 5 salmon, which an Indian caught yesterday.

Sunday, 17. We went to the town, and by evening were again with Kasch, intending to leave next day. But we were detained, partly by bad weather; also because we could not secure enough provisions to last 3 days. The woman of the house was not at home, and the son was not empowered to deal out provisions; nor did we have much money, which was perhaps the chief reason.

The young man, not an ignorant fellow either, told us during the evening, that the minister of that place, having seen the two brethren the last time, had asked him who they were. The young man told him they were "Herrnhutters." "Indeed," said the minister, "That is the name of a place in Germany." He was originally from Hanau. We asked, "Did he not say anything farther about them?

for he must know about them." "No," was the answer,
but that he had often declared in the pulpit, "it matters not
whether you call yourselves Reformed or Lutheran; all
depends on a change of heart."

It is quite possible that such declarations have fore-
stalled the enmity which is often shown toward us, for,
with the exception of a very few, they treat us kindly. He
said farther that any one who called would be furnished
with lodging, if only he did not meddle with their religious
beliefs. We told him that this was not our practice; that
we would gladly leave every one to his own opinions; only
that whenever we found any who did not know his Creator
and Redeemer, and showed any wish to be saved, we would
willingly point him to the Saviour of the world, who died
for us, and whose blood washes away all guilt, be he white,
black or brown. We also told him about Herrnhut, and
that its people were from all parts of the world, though all
of one mind. He seemed to listen with much interest.

Tues. 19. Leaving here to-day we had a deep snow-fall,
and it was fortunate that we had no great distance to travel.

Fri. 22. Toward evening we reached Onondago.

Tues. December 3. Now at last we regard ourselves as
in order. It would be better if we had more provisions.
In fact we have none on hand, and depending on the Indians
for food is very precarious, as they have not much themselves. We earn a little sometimes by grinding axes, sharp-
ening tools, felling trees, etc.

Thurs. 5. David went to the other village, to do some
blood letting.

Wed. 11. We went to the lake to make salt. On the
way David shot a duck, so we got some meat. Toward
evening came the Speaker of the Council, Chief Kaschwechtioni, and said that his wife had sent him to invite us to
go with them on a hunting expedition. There David might
shoot a deer, which would give us a supply of meat, for
here at home we could get nothing. We told them that
we were not prepared to go with them, having neither a
stock of provisions nor bullets. He said: "We have
enough! I will share with you." As we needed salt badly
David went away with him, leaving me here to do the work,
intending to return for me in 2 or 3 days.

Thurs. 12. David left early this morning.

Fri. 13. I reached home this evening and told our people of David's going on the chase with the chief, and of his intended return in a few days. Meanwhile my daily occupation was collecting firewood, of which we had not yet been able to lay in a sufficient stock.

Dec. 21st. As I was quite alone I had plenty of time to mediate on the Saviour's birth, heartily wishing that I could celebrate the day with the dear congregation at home.

Wed. Dec. 25. I passed Christmas day in solitary devotions, in hymn reading from the " Saron's buchlein," and especially enjoying the sainted " Christel's " hymns on the nativity of our Lord.

Mon. Dec. 30. Thought much of David to-day, as he stays away so long, and as a deep snow has fallen, he probably will not return very soon. Our hostess also longs for his return, hoping he will bring some meat with him. She often says that she doesn't like a lean soup, and I have learned the same by experience. Thus far she has managed to utilize old deer or fish entrails, or sometimes *very* old blood, so that were it not for extreme hunger one would rather run away from it than eat thereof. I often wish for just one piece of bread. How we would enjoy it, even if it were *Cassava.*

Tues. 31. In spirit I spent the day with the dear home Church, recalled the blessed watch-meeting of last year, which I attended at the Linsey House, (London, Eng.) and entreated the Lord for forgiveness of all my sins and short-comings, best known to Him and to myself.

1755.

Thurs. Jan. 2. This evening David returned, to his and my great joy. He had wished to turn back long ago, but they would not have it so, as they wanted to secure some game first; they did not get a single deer in all this time. He brought with him, however, 2 pieces of old venison with which they had supplied him. David had frequent opportunities of talking with them, especially with an old chief, a bright old man, who on one occasion asked him: " What do you think of the baptized Indians of Canada? I have seen some of them at my house recently, and I think they behave worse than our own Indians."

David: " Don't you think that their minister points out

the right way to them?"   Ans.: "Yes, he may tell them,. but they do what they please."   "For him to tell them to sing and pray, and go to Church is not enough; they must be taught to know their Creator."

At another time he asked David about Europe, about the voyage across the ocean, and about Bethlehem; whether it was a fine place, where there is plenty of bread.   He was told that they baked large loaves there.   Ind.: " And here you are in the great forest, when you might have all these comforts at home!"   David: " Yes, but we love the Indians, and therefore are here willingly."   " That is kind of you!" was the answer.

Mon. 6. This is our annual " Heidenfest" day, and David and I enjoyed a happy love feast together, and partook of the Holy Communion afterward.   We talked much about Europe, Bethlehem and the various missions, acknowledging with gratitude what the Lord has accomplished among the aborigines, wishing heartily that the time would soon come when *these* Indians would be prompted to inquire about the Lord and Saviour.

Wed. 8. Our host returned from Canada, bringing with him his daughter, mentioned above.   The Indian from that region, who had come with him, visited us, and said that he had been told that we were suffering from want of food. Why did not Kaschwechtioni, the Speaker, provide us with the needful food while he was still here?   We told him that it had been too late in the season to go for provisions.

Thurs. 9. Our host called on us, saying that it was very good that we had built a house here.   "You are here to learn the language; which is very good, because when once we want to visit your country, we may meet with somebody with whom we can converse.   Therefore you ought to plant corn and beans, that you may have food."   They evidently think that we ought to settle here permanently, and he even asked us when we intended paying a visit to our home!

Thurs. 16.   David bled some patients in town.

Sat. 25.   David finished making a door for some one, and in pay got a little corn.

Thurs. 30.   We were much bothered to-day by drunken Indians.   One came in with no clothing, and when about to leave he picked up a blanket or spread from our bed, wrapped it about him, and said he must go.   David told him he must leave the cover here. He became violent and wanted to take a shirt also. We called in another Indian, on which the drunken fellow calmed down and soon left the house. We told the new comer that if such a thing were to happen again, we would bind him hand and foot, till he had slept off his drunken fit. This Indian came next day and said that he was about to drink rum, and that if he should come here and vex us, we should bind him; for which he would thank us after he was sober again.

Tues. Feb. 11. We visited the blacksmith, as also the two traders. They were very pleasant to us.

Sat. 15. We called on a chief called Icohaquanti, a good " Englishman;" he was kind to us and hoped we would often visit him. Our hostess' son came in to-day. During the winter he had shot 20 deer, but he brought no venison home. He had not taken proper care of his game, and worms had spoiled it.

Mon. 17. An old Indian woman brought us a little corn, as pay for medicine which we had given her grandchild.

Tues. Feb. 18. An old woman invited us to her house, to see her son who had just arrived. He asked us to estimate what we would charge to build him a storehouse.

Feb. 21. He inspected our house and declared that he wanted one like this. We made him a bid for building one, at a low price, as he himself admitted. He left us, saying that he would consult with his friends about the matter.

Sun. 23. The traders called on us and expressed surprise at our settling down here, all alone. Later in the day we went into town.

Wed. 26. Our host and his wife came in to live with us for a few days, as their house is too cold. There are but a few living in it.

Thurs. March 6. We built a little hut for an old woman, who intends boiling maple sugar.

Fri. 7. We got our axe from the smith, who would take no pay for his work.

Sat. 8. David captured a Fish Otter, which was very welcome, not only for the meat, but the skin, being quite valuable, would go toward buying food, of which we have little.

Thurs. 13. A noisy day because of drunkenness. Some

remained in our house all night, an old chief lying on the floor near the fire.

Mon. 16. Began building a house 2 miles from here, for an aged couple, for sugar boiling, and they intend living in it next winter. So we made it of wood and rather large. We worked at it about a month, and got our daily pay in the shape of water soup, which was very acceptable to us.

Mon. April 9. We went to town and made two troughs for storing maple sap.

11-14. During these days we finished the house on which we had been working. We debated on remaining here longer or returning home. We at last determined on the latter, but thought best to confer with our friend, Otschinochiatha. We will go to the village, with the first opportunity, and get provisions, as our hostess has but little corn left.

Mon. 17. An old chief, a little the worse for drink, came in and asked for tobacco, with which we could not serve him. He was vexed, and demanded, "Who sent you here?" David: "You are a chief and don't know that! You surely must know better." At last he said: "Yes, I know that Tgirhitonti sent you here to learn the language, and when you can speak it you intend to bring us the word of God." David: "'Is not that good and proper?" "Let it be!" he said, "To-day I am drunk. To-morrow, when I am sober, I will call again." "Do so."

Wed. 19. An Indian came for us, that we might know when our friend would return home, as he had sent a string of wampum to the chiefs. But the messenger was so drunk that we could get nothing out of him as to our friend's whereabouts.

Fri. 21. We went down to the village, overland, for provisions..

Mon. 24. The hostess' son went into the forest with David to make a canoe. They had soon selected a tree, which, however, as also a second one which they felled, did not answer the purpose. The third was hardly in good condition for peeling so early in the season. Our food supply is now dwindled to 4 spoonfuls of flour a day.

Wed. 26. We carried the canoe down to the creek and rowed down stream. It rained, was cold, and we were hungry besides. Toward evening we came to the river, and near the mouth of the creek we found 2 bateaux about going up the creek. We asked for something to eat, got a piece of bread and a drink, which refreshed us very much.

Thurs. 27. We passed 4 bateaux; among the men was the baker of the town, whom we knew and who gave us some bread. In the afternoon we reached Kasch's place. They were more cordial than ever before and he received us kindly. We found also that he would supply us with immediate necessaries, and that, too, for a few skins which we had brought, though prices of goods are high on account of rumors of war.

28. To-day Kasch asked what religious doctrine we upheld. Ans.: "Lutheran." Kasch: "What do they believe in Bethlehem?" We told him that the belief there was that Christ came into the world, suffered and died for all men, and that through his blood is obtained remission of sins. He admitted that this is the right doctrine.

29. David and our Indian companion went into the village to make some purchases. He took the Indian with him because he (David) was a stranger to the people of the town.

30. Early next morning we were to leave, and we cast up our accounts and found we were in debt 4 shillings. We told him we could do no better this time. " Well," said he, " go, and God be with you. You will come again." A bateau went in our company, and the men told us much about the war.

May 1. Our canoe was injured by striking a snag. The goods got a wetting and we hurried on shore to dry them, to prevent more serious injury.

2. Next day we repaired the boat and reached the port age by 4 o'clock. There were boats ahead of us, waiting to be carried overland, so we had to wait until next morning. Having no money, we fully intended to carry our boat and goods ourselves, for the 4 miles overland. Hunger was plaguing us besides, and, as several Indians offered to carry our things for a little corn, we consented, chiefly at the request of our host's son, our companion, though rather unwillingly, and thus got over by next day..

3. On our way down the " Holzkille " we stove another hole in our canoe. We stopped it up, landed, and stowed our goods in the dry.

4. Reached the lake, found it windy, and were obliged to wait, as did also six bateaux which came in later. Before sundown they set off and we with them, and rowed till 2 a. m., when we ran ashore, as the wind again became too strong. We rested 4 hours and again started off with a strong wind on our backs, and we finished the voyage before the rest of the party, though they were supplied with sails.

10. By afternoon we had crossed the Salt Lake. The Indian left us here, but his sister came before evening, in order that she might get off early in the morning, as they are now planting.

11. David went to the town, whither he carried some of our provisions. Soon after came the son of another Indian, and they took away nearly all the rest. David returned, and by evening we were both at home again.

Word was sent us that a letter had reached the town, and as the chiefs were about to meet David should come also and read it. It was given to the Indians by the traders, who said they should open it; then they would see what was inside. The whole town was full of it, and when David entered the room and got it into his hand, he said: " This letter belongs to me! It is written by Brother Tgirhitonti." They were at first unwilling to believe David. He read that Bro. Spangenberg was anxious to know of our welfare, since he had not heard from us all this time. The Indians declared that there must be more than that in the letter, which David would not read to them. They asked us whether Tgirhitonti did not ask us to return to Bethlehem? and if there was nothing in it about the war?

David assured them that there was not, as we were men of peace and not interested in war. Meanwhile we were overjoyed to learn of the welfare of our Brethren at home, and that all was going on well. It was fortunate that the letter reached us before leaving this place.

12. Several Nanticokes visited us to-day, among them being John White. He said, " Tell Brother Joseph [Spangenberg] that I intend coming to Bethlehem next spring." He praised Bethlehem highly on account of the good eating he got there. He was glad to hear of the welfare of Bro. Spangenberg; he also said that if he had to stay here long he would starve. We gave him of our food, for which he

seemed very thankful. In the evening there came to our house the Tuscarora who had visited us once before, in company with a woman. He called up David, whom he addressed in English as " My friend." David did not recognize him, as it was dark, and said, "I don't know you; come to-morrow to see us." Ind.: "Why! Don't you remember me? I call you my friend, and I must see you. Don't be afraid of me, for I called you *friend*."

Whereupon he burst in the door and entered. He was followed soon after by the old Nanticoke chief. They were both quite drunk. They spent the whole night in our house, as they could not find the way to their homes. They were very noisy, and seemed anxious to get up a fight. David then told them to get out, as they did not treat us as a brother or friend should. The Tuscarora said: "When you get into my town I shall fight you." These savages were ashamed of their behavior afterward, and did not call on us to say farewell, as did John White and another Indian.

May 13. We went to the lake to boil salt to supply us on our journey, and returned next day. Mr. Talck, of Albany, came here and reported that much corn had been bought up for the Six Nations, because the famine among them was great, and that it could be gotten in the town.

May 16. Our friend Otschinochiatha returned to-day. He was not in when we called to see him.

17. We went a second time to see him. He said he had been told that we had left, but saw his mistake at once on his return, when he saw that there was fire in our house.

18. We paid him a farewell visit. He said: " You have been here a long time, and have had opportunity to get acquainted with our chiefs and they with you, while I have been away the greater part of the time. Greet Tgirhitonti from me, and tell him that I know only *good* about him, and that I am well disposed toward him." We left this place directly after this interview. On the way the wife of one of the chiefs said to David: " Will we not see you again." " Oh yes! " said David, " You will probably see us again."

19. We went to the creek to make a canoe, in which we intend going down the stream. Our hostess' son came also to hunt in the vicinity, but helped at the canoe instead.

20. Felled a tree and carried the bark to the creek.

21. Finished the canoe to-day.

23. We went back to get our things, which we had hidden in the forest, and reached our hut by the creek next day.

25. We started off in the canoe, slept next night in the boat, and were at the river at noon of the 26th, and by evening reached the home of old Cossi, whom the Nanticokes have chosen as their king, and after him his son, as the father is very aged. We slept in his house and bought of him a little corn and beans.

May 28. Passing by an island we saw a wild animal, and, taking it for a deer, David tried to shoot it, but his gun missed fire twice. We then saw it was a wolf, which turned about and went his way. In the afternoon we passed by the Delawares, who rummaged through our goods but found no store goods among them. This party had, shortly before, robbed the traders of two bags of flour, and hoped to secure some from us.

May 31. We made inquiry about our Brethren, who had moved up here to Wyoming from Gnadenhuetten, and were told that Bro. Post was in this neighborhood, only 2 miles away. We made haste and by evening reached his place, and found him disabled by an axe-cut on his leg. We spent all of next day with him. He has finished planting, and wants to build himself a house. He must first, however, obtain consent from the Six Nations, some of whom he expects to see in a few days. Our former Gnadenhuetten friends visited us to-day, and we find that, besides these, there are many Indians about here who are anxious to have the Gospel brought to them.

June 1. We left Wyoming in company with several others, overland for Gnadenhuetten.

3. Early this morning, when about half way between Wyoming and Gnadenhuetten, we met our dear Brother, Dr. Matthew Otto of Bethlehem, in company with another Brother. We enjoyed together a happy love feast, and parted with many expressions of love. He told us much of what had happened in our long absence. We again started off; the Indians of our party delaying a while, because one of their number had shot a deer. By evening we quietly entered Gnadenhuetten to the surprise and delight of our Brethren.

The Lord be praised and thanked, for all the benefits which we have, this past year, received from His bounteous hand, and especially for love, grace and protection which He has vouchsafed us.

And to our dear friends we say: " Take us and welcome us anew into your ranks, for we are your fellow members, children and sinners."

Charles Frederick and David Zeisberger.
Bethlehem, Pa., June 11th, 1755.

NOTES ON THE JOURNAL OF 1754-55.

BY REV. W. M. BEAUCHAMP.

This journal has frequent intervals of several days, as well as abrupt changes from one place to another, without reference to the way between. Some of these will be pointed out. The chronology is also faulty, the day of the month and week not always agreeing, and events plainly happening on successive days being dated a week apart. One item of interest, not found in the journel, is contained in the Bethlehem Diary, Aug. 2, 1755. They celebrated the birthdays of two of the Brethren. "Bro. Joseph (Spangenberg) tendered his hearty congratulations to the two Brethren, in a poem for each Brother.

" During discourse which followed, two points were brought out, showing with what esteem Bro. David Zeisberger (who was also present) is held at Onondago. 1. When, for example, the children on the street would say: ' That is an Assaroni," (because he is white,) the elders will correct them: 'Aquanouschioni! not Assaroni.' Since he and Charles Frederick have built them their own house, the Council has given into these Brethren's care their entire archives, a whole pile of belts.

" Query: Where now are these archives, since you have left there? Ans: Our people (as one says, our family to which we belong) have moved into our house and the archives are still there."

De Schweinitz tells of this as though Zeisberger became the official wampum keeper, which was not the case.

Charles Frederick was born in Holstein, Oct. 4, 1715,

was a missionary among the Indians and negroes, and died in Surinam, Jan. 24, 1761.

June 22. Sheds were provided for Indians who visited Albany for trade or treaties, and these were at the public expense. Conrad Weiser was there with the Pennsylvania commissioners in 1754.

27. Henrich was the old Mohawk chief known as King Hendrick, afterward killed in the battle of Lake George.

July 18. They went *down,* not up Oneida River.

20. The Salt Lake, as on old maps, was Onondaga Lake.

21. Tgirhitonti was Spangenberg. The Moravians have no wampum now.

24. Women had a recognized place in some councils. The Nanticokes' arguments sound much like the preaching of Ganeodiyo, or Handsome Lake, half a century later.

Aug. 9. Indians sometimes kept tame bears, or shut them up to fatten for food. An instance is described among the Mohawks in 1634.

14. The foot bridge was of considerable size, though of course rude.

15. I recall no other instance of a woman going about so well equipped as a trader. She wanted ginseng, the well known root.

19. A fight with a woman seems below a chief's dignity, but Iroquois women had reserved rights.

Sept. 1. The other village was Tueyahdasso.

8. Otschinochiatha was rather given to kissing, and Kirkland described his affectionate greeting. He lived to be a very old man, but another took his office in 1764.

Oct. 1. Sometimes their house seems away from the rest, but here very near.

11. A smith was of great importance and here had political importance.

12. " The town " was German Flats, the nearest market for supplies.

Nov. 10. This is the first account of a house of hewn logs and shingles in Onondaga, of which the dimensions are given. The houses of the mission of St. Mary of Ganentaha were evidently of logs, and the French brought planks for their attempted fort and chapel at Onondaga in 1711. These were destroyed.

17. No incidents appear of the way " to the town."

Dec. 5. The Indians were even fonder of "blood letting" than the whites of that day.

11. Kaghswughtioni (Belt of wampum) or Red Head, had been a French partisan but was now Johnson's warm friend, and died in 1756. It is curious that the invitation to this hunting party came from his wife.

Dec. 25. " Christel's Hymns " were written by Christian Renatus Zinzendorf, son of the Count.

30. Indian villages were always liable to famine, and almost anything was enten. Cassava is the manioc root, freed of its poison, being then starchy and edible. Its best form is tapioca.

Feb. 15. "A good Englishman " favored the English.

23. Their house was not properly " in the town," and the chief's may not have been.

March 16. Indian houses were then much scattered, but this was probably in the valley two miles away. Another error in the day of the week begins here, and the later dates are much confused. The " water soup " was maple sap partly boiled.

April 9. Indians commonly had bark sap troughs, but these seem hewed out of logs.

21. They started again for German Flats, the son of their hostess going with them to Oriskany Creek.

26. This creek was near and beyond Old Oneida, and they made a bark canoe, paddling down to the Mohawk. The bateaux may have gone up the creek toward Oneida.

27. Kasch's was some miles west of German Flats and north of the river, the most westerly house of all. Frank's was a little below on the south side.

May 3. " Holzkille," literally Wood Creek.

4. Oneida Lake was often passed in the night because of strong winds in the day, the north shore being preferable.

10. A manifest blunder in dates makes the passage of Onondaga Lake six days after that of Oneida, while it was evidently but a day or two later.

11. Canoes rarely went up Onondaga Creek, because of fallen trees.

19. When they left Onondaga they went up the valley, but say nothing of this, passing the Tully lakes, and building a bark canoe on the outlet of Big Lake in Preble.

25. It is not clear just what they meant by the river here. The Nanticokes were some miles north of Binghamton. Old Cossi died a year or two later.

28. The Delawares were then very troublesome, and these may have been below Tioga.

31. Gnadenhuetten is now Lehightown, Pa. C. Frederick Post was then at Wyoming and was long prominent in Indian affairs. He was thrice married, two of his wives being Indian women.

Message to Cayuga, 30 April, 1766, carried by Bro. David Zeisberger and the Indian Brethren, Anton, Johannes, Abraham and Jacob. Translated by Augustus H. Leibert, from Mss. in Moravian Archives, Bethlehem, Pa., 1904.

Journey to Cajuga, Spring of 1766

I summarize the speeches in this and make other omissions, but retain most notes of the journey.

April 23. We started from Mechwihilusing—some of us on foot and some of us by water, alternating; thus we could take with us provisions enough for our entire journey.

April 24. We reach Schechschiquanunk, a small Indian village, where we were kindly received.

April 25. We passed Tioga, where, however, no one lives at present.

April 26. We came to Oweke, an outpost of Cajugas, where they keep a chief as watchman on the Susquehanna. We were welcomed and quartered in their visitors' " Logis," which has been erected for such purposes. Bro. David here met Andrew Montour, who with several Indians was on his way to Ohio, where he expects to join Mr. Crogan on a trip to the Mississippi. . . . .

April 27. We again started, this time afoot, as the path now leaves the Susquehanna. As the streams were swollen we had much trouble in crossing the creek.

April 28. To-day, as well as yesterday, we had to wade through the water the greater part of the time, because the swamp which we had to cross was filled with water, and it was raining besides; so there was not a dry stitch on us. There were so many fallen tree trunks in the way that we worked hard to get through. We reached Cajuga Lake to-day.

April 29. We traveled along the lake and at night lodged with a Tuteler. . . . .

April 30. We arrived at Cajuga. . . . We went immediately to the house of the Chief, Togahaju, where we were pleasantly received, and places shown us where we should lodge. Mats were spread out for us on which to recline. This resting place was, as usual, very hard. Something was soon brought us to eat, and after we had finished the repast the chief came up to us, and greeted us all with a shake of the hand, and addressed the four Brethren. " . . .

Greetings were exchanged and the Council would be convened next day, which was done. Sir William Johnson had wished to buy the Susquehanna lands up to Owego, but they " had told him they must reserve this land for their Cousins, the Delawares; that they could not throw them out. They had, however, granted them the land from the settlement to the Wajomick mountain, and even to the east side of the mountain. The sources of the Delaware are the boundary to the north, and some distance below Shamoko the line runs across the Susquehanna, so that Wajomik is not included. . . . . After they were assembled, we were placed on one side of the fire, which was in the centre, immediately opposite them. There were six chiefs present, who constituted the Council. Near us, at our side, there was another fire, where were seated the hearers, who were all warriors, so that the house was entirely filled."

Togahaju opened the Council with the usual ceremonies. Johannes then spoke with five strings and two belts of wampum. The path had been cleared and cleansed as well as Wihilusing, whence they came. Anton followed, with a belt of ten rows. The Indians there differed from others, and wished for a separate town. Johannes then spoke with a large belt:

" Uncle! You made known to us last year that you wanted to remove us from Wihilusing and place us at the upper end of this lake. Now, however, it is our desire that you would permit us to remain at Wihilusing. We have already built us houses, and the place which you cleansed for us a year ago is agreeable, and we like to live there, as we can live there quietly and undisturbed."

The Delaware interpreter here proved incompetent, and Bro. David had to take his place. Togahaju asked him: "Is it not your idea that you do not wish to live so near the Tutelers?" Answer: Not only the Tutelers are meant, but also other towns." David then addressed the Council by its proper name: "Brother Sanunawaentowa! (which is the title of the Chief, the Great Pipe of Peace)." His people "desired only good things, and you love that which is good."

The Cayugas asked how many Indian Brethren were at Wihilusing. "Answer: There were about 150 men, women and children; at which they were astonished and pleased." Any who wished to serve God, they would "gladly receive and dearly love; to which they shouted in a loud Niawo, (that is to say, we rejoice at this). . . . The matter now hung on this, that the Chief take back his word, which the Six Nations seldom do. Without this the project could not go forward, as he had given a belt. He, however, found a way out of the difficulty. He replied: I do not recall that I ever said that you should make night quarters at Ganiataragechiat, (that is, the upper end of the lake). (Which meant as much as to say that you should live there one year; then remove further to another place). This never came into my mind." This was also the truth, for he did not really say it, but it came from a Delaware chief, who had told it to our Indians. Johannes asked whether he wished to take his belt back again? He answered: Yes. Johannes quickly returned him his belt, without much questioning, and with this ended the matter."

Togahaju then spoke, "after he had opened his council-bag or sack, which he had brought with him, taken out such strings and belts as he needed, and placed every thing in order." He used four strings and four belts, as it was an important affair. This was the Cayuga edict:

"Up to this time you have had no abiding place, but now I will take you and seat you permanently. You can therefore remain there, and the land shall be yours; and as your number is many and may probably increase, so I have still further thought of you. We will, therefore, give you all the land from Wihilusing up to some distance beyond Tioga, (which is by land a good two days' journey). There you may build, plant, hunt, fish, and make use of the place as you wish; it shall be yours. And I am happy to hear that you will not turn your faces anywhere except to my fire; and you do well thereby."

They parted with mutual good wishes.

"*May 2.* Very early in the morning we left Cayuga and traveled a long distance to the end of the lake, where there is a Delaware Indian village. Here we were kindly received and stayed over night. About 3 or 4 miles from here is a Tuteler town, whose chief, who is a Cayuga Indian, sent word to Bro. David to visit him, but the others of the party were in a hurry to get home, and so Bro. David could not go to him.

"*May 3.* We traversed the bad swamp, and on

"*May 4.* reached Oweka, all of us almost exhausted. We did not tarry here, but started off directly by water, and as the Susquehanna was very high and the water swift, we made over 50 miles this day, reaching Schechshequanunck, where friends of the Brethren are living, to whom, at their request, Bro. David preached a sermon, and on the *5th of May* we reached Mechwihilusing."

REV. W. M. BEAUCHAMP'S NOTES ON THE CAYUGA JOURNAL.

The first arrangement appears in Annals of Friedenshuetten, when the messengers returned from Cayuga, June 27, 1765:

"The chief then said: "Hearing that you were come to Wyalusing, I sent for you. The place is not a good one— it is stained with blood. I will appoint you a better locality near us, at the upper end of Cayuga Lake." On our Brethren observing that they wished their teacher to go with them, he asked: "Who he was and where he lived?" "One whom you know well," they replied, "for he has lived among you, and speaks your language." "It is well," said the chief, "for as to your belief no one shall interfere."

The aforesaid locality pleases our Indians, but there is no game there." Wihilusing was not called Friedenshuetten till June, 1766.

July 21, the Moravians spoke to an old Cayuga chief " about the proposed migration of our Indians to Cayuga Lake. He agreed that it was no good place, because of the absence of all game, and they were accustomed to eat meat. Up the branch of the Tioga would be a better locality, as game was there in plenty."

David Zeisberger certainly wrote the journal of the spring of 1766, but this was not his custom.

April 26. Oweke is Owego. This is the first mention of such a watchman on the Susquehanna, and his office seems much like Shikellimy's. He came to Friedenshuetten in June, 1768, to investigate some matters. The strangers' house has been mentioned by others, but was not common. Andrew was Madame Montour's son. Croghan went west the year before, to confer with Pontiac and others, and this year Pontiac met Johnson at Oswego.

28. The route from Owego to Ithaca would be nearly that of the D., L. & W. railroad, but in lower land.

29. Tuteler is better known as Tutelo. A small people adopted by the Six Nations.

30. Togahaju was long a prominent Cayuga chief, and signed the boundary line treaty of 1768, his mark being a great pipe. Indians were quite particular about shaking hands. The Six Nations were uncles to the Delawares, but addressed them as cousins.

May 1. In Council the Cayugas are addressed as the Great Pipe.

2. In the Annals of Friedenshuetten it is noted, July 21, 1765, that " The whole nation of the Tutelars passed here to-day," going to Cayuga Lake.

JOURNEY TO ONONDAGA AND CAYUGA, BY DAVID
ZIESBERGER AND GOTTLOB SENSEMANN,
OCTOBER, 1766.

A report having come to Friedenshuetten a few months ago, which seemed as though the Onondagas were not per-

fectly satisfied that the Chief in Cajuga had turned over
this land to our Indians; it appeared to them as though
he had only done this on his own account, without the
Consent of the Six Nations; therefore to become clear as
to the truth of the matter, and to renew old friendship, it
was decided by the Oeconomats—Conferenz at Bethlehem,
that a journey thither should be made. We started therefore on *30 Sept.* with the blessings of the Congregation at
Bethlehem, arriving on the *9th of October* at Friedenshuetten, after a tiresome and difficult journey, on account of
the swollen streams on the way, at Brother and Sister
Schmick's, and after we had partaken of the holy communion with them and their brown Brethren, we proceeded
on our journey.

October 14th. We set out from Friedenshuetten in a
canoe, in company with four Nantikoks, who were returning from Philadelphia and were journeying homeward.
Bro. Sensemann, who was not accustomed to traveling in
a canoe, fell into the strongest current of the Susquehanna,
from which nothing serious resulted, only his being
drenched through and through. In the evening we arrived at Wisachk, an uninhabited hamlet.

October 15th. At noon we arrived at Schechschiquanunk. Bro. David spoke with Johannes' son, whose wife is
at Friedenshuetten, telling him that we would like him to
take her away from there. This town, during the last summer, has greatly increased, and there are five Indians among
them who receive the Brethren very kindly, and are glad
to hear of the Saviour. To-day we went a short distance
beyond Tiaoga, and in the evening we were overtaken by
Chief Newallike, who had come down the Susquehanna and
remained with us over night. There was a severe storm
raging during the entire night, and the above named chief
lost his canoe, the wind having torn it from its moorings,
and the strong current sweeping it along down the river, so
that he had to continue his journey next day on foot.

October 16th. As one of the Nantikoks was out hunting and shot two bears, we made only a short day's journey.
They shared the meat very liberally with us.

October 17. We passed Oweke and two wolves chased
a deer toward us, which we shot. They, however, escaped.

October 18. We passed a Cajuga Town; also Tschoch-

not, a Delaware Town. This part of the country is generally
very well populated by Indians. Our fellow travelers, the
Nantikoks, had intended to reach Zeniinge to-day, but as
they saw that we could not keep up with them in their
travels, and not wishing us to remain behind them, the
Chief came over into our canoe and helped us along. We
then arrived there in the evening, and yet much fatigued,
the Chief receiving us in his house. We were very warmly
welcomed by many friends. They are still living in the
same place where they settled 13 years ago, after leaving
Wijomick.

October 19. Made an early visit to the near by Onondaga town. The people there were very happy once again
to meet Bro. David, and we, among other things, inquired
into the condition of the road leading to Onondaga, as we
meant to go from here to there by land. We learned from
them that the road was not passable, being very much out
of repair. They advised us to go by way of water, which
we also decided to do, in spite of the route being by stream
and very hard work. The Council met at our lodging place,
and we heard the answer of the Governor at Philadelphia
to the Six Nations. Bro. David was asked to read a letter
which they had brought along from Philadelphia, wherein
the whole nation was invited to remove to Philadelphia,
as the climate here was so very cold, and no good hunting
about Zeniinge, and various other reasons. They were also
assured that every thing possible in assistance and help
would be given them (probably the Quakers). We also
looked up our Brother Samuel, who had, several weeks ago,
come here to bring back his wife. He was very glad to
meet Brethren here, and at once offered to go with us to
Onondaga, which pleased us very much, as otherwise we
would have had to take a strange Indian.

In the evening Bro. David had an opportunity to speak
with the Nantikok chief, and to learn about various things;
for example, what intention the Six Nations had of the
partition of their land, and how far each nation's district,
over which it should have authority, should extend, which
it is particularly necessary for us to know, since our Indians
live at Friedenshuetten. The same with regard to Wajomik, which they said could not be inhabited by Indians,

as the place was soiled with blood, until the same had been cleansed by the Six Nations.

He said further, that the white people had settled in this country at the time when they (the Nantikoks) yet lived in Maryland, at which they had been rejoiced, and had made a present of half of the land to the English, who afterward became so numerous that they, who after all were the owners of the land, had to leave, and on that account came to this country. Regardless of this, however, they had always lived in peace with the white people, and never interfered in any war. At last, he said, even though having no preaching nor the word of God, they were at the same time the best among the Indians, for no one could say any evil about them. They were otherwise helpful and friendly toward us, but we could plainly see that they were not favorably disposed toward the Gospel and the work of the Lord; had much to find fault with in our Indians in Friedenshuetten, not being kindly disposed toward them. This you hear and see continually here at Zeniinge on all sides; and they, for the greater part, have been brought up among the white people, and therefore can speak and understand English pretty well. There is still found among them a great deal more witchcraft and heathenish practices than there is among all the other nations.

October 20. We saw that the usual evil of drinking was still prevailing among them. We heard that two barrels of rum had arrived here, so we could make up our minds that here we would have very little rest. We would have liked to take our departure to-day, but as they had hid our canoe for us, and not being able to find it, we had to remain till the next day. We were greatly disturbed by the drunken Indians. Yesterday and to-day there has been a fall of snow, and the temperature very cold.

Brother David had a conversation with an Oneida Indian, who lives in the Onondaga town, who asked him why he did not come here also to preach? Bro. David answered him: Where are there people who have hearts and ears to listen? He replied that there would some turn up, and that he loved to hear from the Word of God, for I am baptized, and I think there are a number here who would like it. Bro. David answered him: If I should preach to you, you must do away with drinking and all other heathenish practices, or else I cannot live among you. It is not enough that you are baptized, but you must also know your Creator, who gave His life for you and purchased you with His blood.

An Indian minister, who had studied in New England, lived here for some time and preached here. In the beginning several came to the preaching once or twice. As after that, however, no one attended again, he gave it up, and some days ago left for his home again. Samuel, who had during the past days been in Anohochquage, where there is an English minister, said that he had twice attended service there, and had at the one seen four, and at the other two Indians. The rest meanwhile were drinking. It is no wonder, then, that the Indians say that baptism amounts to nothing, for they still remain heathenish, as before.

October 21. We, with our Samuel, took up our journey, the Nantikok chief instructing him to take such a road, in which we could proceed without the least difficulty. About a mile beyond the Nantikok Town we passed a small Mohikan Town, and about 10 or 12 miles farther, where the river, which is here about as wide as the Lehigh, again divides, we came to an Onondaga Town.

October 22. On account of heavy rain did not proceed on our journey till noon.

October 23. In the afternoon we came to the last fork of the river. The Indians at Zeniinge advised us to take the fork to the right, and continue about a day's journey, as after that we would have only a short day's journey more, by land to Onondago. After we had gone on several miles we were compelled to return, on account of large trees having fallen across the creek, thus obstructing the way. We therefore had to return as far as the forks, and try if we could not from thence proceed. The whole of the following night and next day we had a heavy fall of snow, and we had to remain here, in a very wild and desolate part of the country, where there was neither road nor path of any kind.

October 25. Prepared early to leave this place by way of land. We might have gone up this stream some miles, as the water had considerably risen, but we did not like to venture, for fear the water might have fallen on our return, and we would again have a hard task to get out. We therefore left our canoe here in the woods, as well as some provisions. We had, however, a very hard day of it, in finding our way through a wild and broken down forest, with no path or road, as quite an amount of snow had fallen. We traveled to-day from the Susquehanna to the end of the lake, and remained there overnight.

October 26. In the morning, after we'had gone on about three or four miles, we came to the Onondago Creek, and as we had plenty of good road we arrived in Onondago toward evening. About half a mile from town we met an Indian, who at once recognized Bro. David, and who at once offered to escort us to town. We arrived at the house which had been formerly occupied by Bro. David, and were very cordially received and welcomed by many, who during the evening came in to see us. We soon heard that the Chief and old people were all at home, but that most of the younger part of them had gone to war against the Cherokees.

October 27. In the morning Bro. David inquired as to the place of the Council House and asked the chiefs to be assembled. After they came together we were also called and brought before them. The Council House now is the house of Otschinochiatha, which is built on a very high and steep hill, from whence the whole town and surrounding country can be overlooked. During our sessions and to our honor, the English flag was raised and floated over the house. We were very kindly received by all of them (about eight chiefs). As they asked by what way we had reached here, Bro. David said that it was now high time that they cleansed the road, as it was almost impossible to reach them, and if they should wait much longer then it would be altogether impossible. Thereupon they answered, first the reason was this, because the road of peace to Pennsylvania had disappeared. Then, however, they said that the deep snow which had fallen last summer in *June,* had caused the breaking down of so many trees and bushes.

After this Bro. David addressed them as follows: Brethren, you Onondagos, it is a great pleasure to me, after the lapse of eleven years to see you again, and to speak personally with you. You may know of it, that I am now living in Friedenshuetten with your cousins; therefore I have found it needful to visit you once again, to smoke a pipe with you, and to inquire and consult with you on various subjects. I have, however, no formal matters to transact with you, (that is, I will not speak through Belts or Strings). But notwithstanding this, everything that I shall say to you will come not only from my mouth, but also from my heart; and I expect the same in like manner from you.

After a short pause, the Speaker, who sat by the side of Bro. David, said that he might now speak. He then continued and said: Brethren, you Onondagos, you have no doubt heard that the Indians, your cousins, who now reside in Friedenshuetten, are those who hitherto had lived in Bethlehem, and whom Brother Onas (the Governor of Pennsylvania) afterward, when the war had broken out, had taken to Philadelphia and had protected them until peace was again restored. That he then had allowed them to return into the Indian country in peace, which then took place during the past spring. After they had arrived in Friendenshuetten they notified the Chief Togahaju, in Cayuga, who sent them word that they themselves should come to him, as he wished to speak with them, and which also then took place. He then made the following proposal: to move to Cajuga Lake. The matter, however, remained unsettled till last spring, when I, with four Indians of Friedenshuetten, went to the above named chief to Cajuga, and there explained our entire wish and spoke our whole heart's desire, that we were a separate people, who could no longer live according to the manners and customs of the Indians, but that we wished to live according to the will and desire of our God and Creator, who had given us the Gospel, by which we directed our ways, and from which we could in no wise depart. Therefore it would be a difficult matter to live with, or even near the Indians who were not of the same mind, as we could not have our services as quiet and undisturbed. We therefore desired of him that we might be allowed to stay in Friedenshuetten. With this representation the Chief granted our request, and gave our Indians the land from Freidenshuetten till near Oweke, above Tiaoga, for their purposes and use; for which we were very thankful. Bro. David would at that time gladly have visited you, but it was impossible. This is, therefore, the chief reason of this visit to them, so as to speak with them about it, and get their idea with regard to our Indians living in Friedenshuetten.

He, therefore, had this question to put to them: whether the matter which the Cajuga Chief at that time transacted and decided, that our Indians in Friedenshuetten should be firmly settled and the land given them, was so understood and agreed to by the whole Council, or whether he had done it only on his own account?

He said, also, that in order that they might be informed of everything, he would tell them besides that there lived among the Indians at Friedenshuetten, beside himself, another Brother and his wife. I was also well enough known among them for many years, and that we Brethren, among the Indians, were not seeking after land, gold, or any similar thing, as we were a separate people, and from other white people quite different. We had a close communion with God; that with Him we spoke although unseen, even as he was now speaking with them, and that it was our desire to have all Indians brought into this same communion with Him; for we could, from experience, show them the way to Him; and as we were a separate people from other Europeans, in the same way our Indians were also different from other Indians; and as we, white people, were composed of different nations, so also were our Indians: as some were Mohikans, Dellawares, Monsies and Nantikoks.

They were astonished and said: What! are there also Nantikoks with you? Brother David answered, Yes; here sits one of them with us; pointing to Samuel. Therefore when we hear of Indians who desire to hear the word of God and the Creator, then we feel it our duty to make known and proclaim this to them, no matter to what nation they belong; and if we should once hear that they wished to hear, the Aquanochschioni, it would be a great pleasure to us, for all Indians who believe on Him are our Brethren. As they had now heard that our Indians were quite different from others, it would thus be good if we had something to tell them. That we were doing it ourselves, though we also knew that a Delaware chief lives at Cajuga Lake. He, however, did not know or understand any of our affairs, and therefore could not speak for us either. We hoped that they would have no objections to this.

Those affairs, however, which were only affairs of the Indians and which did not concern us, these we would gladly leave to him, as he understood them better.

Every thing which Brother David had said was repeated by the Speaker, and he added thereto that the Delaware chief is no believer, neither has he a desire to lead such a life as you; therefore he cannot speak for them, as he does not understand their affairs. Bro. David continued further: Now he would like to ask about a matter. He had always heard that the land along the Susquehanna, below Tiaoga, belonged under the direction of the Chief in Cajuga, and for that reason our Indians had addressed him in regard to the matter; whether this was not the case? Which they at once answered by saying yes.

Brother David then said that now he had ended his remarks. They then asked him various questions, such as: How many Indians were living at Friedenshuetten, and if these were all our Church children? If no other white people except Brother David and Schmick lived there? and if Bro. Schmick was his brother? Here they did not mean a real brother, but whether he was one of the Brethren from Bethlehem. They also asked about Brother T'girhitonty, and whether everything was going on peaceably throughout the land? Whether the Conestoga Indians had all perished, and if none of them were now in existence? Brother David answered that he had heard of one or two of them who had escaped. As it appeared, they were not much affected by this report, for they and the Conestogas were not very good friends, having previously had wars one with the other. At last they asked us how long we expected to stay here with them? Several among them answered this question themselves by saying: Until spring; and Otschinochiata said: I thought you would again build yourself a house, as the old one has gone to decay.

Whereupon Bro. David answered:

You, Onondagos! I am very glad and am rejoiced thereat, that I am still in good remembrance among you and am welcome here. You acknowledge me as an Aquano-schioni, which I also am. Of this I am glad, but all this is not enough for me. But when I can hear that and see among you that you have a desire to become acquainted with God our Creator, who has loved all mankind and you, and that you desire to hear of Him; when this is once your desire, let me know; for I love you and would like to see you become a happy people.

After this there were other matters attended to, about the Governor in Oswego, and after we had finished this we bade them farewell and returned home.

October 28. Visited Otschinochiata, announced to him our visit to Cajuga, and learned whether the roads were passable; of which we were given poor hopes, as Indians who had come from there said that they had a very perilous journey across the creeks, which had been very much swollen. We were somewhat uneasy at the thought of not being able to get to Cajuga; neither knew of any help, and beside this there had been a steady fall of snow for several days, so that we might expect to find a very hard road. He told us that last year a minister, who he thought had come from New England, arrived here, and offered to live with them and preach to them. They had, however, given as an answer that if they should have a desire for it they would let him know, but for the present he might go home again. That the one who had lived for some time in the country of the Senecas had also gone home again, and that the French Fathers in Canada still continued among them. One of the Indians said to Brother David: Is it not true that you would like to see us become believers in God? This would be my greatest joy, replied Bro. David, for then you would be a happy people.

October 29. Resolved at once to go to Cajuga, and trusting in Providence whether we get there or not. Our Brother Samuel staid behind, as he was not very well, which we regretted very much, as we depended much on him for aid and guidance, as an Indian always finds a way to proceed.

October 30. In the morning we were met by a party of Cajugas, who told us that one creek was very dangerous to cross, and warned us to be very careful. We found it just as they had said, for there were only two thin trees, the thickness of a man's leg, thrown over the outlet of a large lake, which had an awful depth, and as we crossed they bent so far down that you would be in water up to your knees, and therefore had to be very careful to keep your balance, so as not to fall into the water. We, however, to our great joy, crossed safely, and in the afternoon arrived in good time in Cajuga. When we were still a mile away from town we passed through several plantations, where stood several huts. In front of one stood an Indian. As we were passing he asked Brother David: Are you not Ganousseracheri? He answered: Yes, I am. Come in, he said; you shall first eat with me; then you can go farther. We entered, and they set before us bread and bear's meat. They were very friendly and were very glad to see Brother David.

They asked whether he was not living in Friedenshuetten? to which he replied: Yes. Thereupon he asked whether it was true, which he had heard, that we did not allow drinking in our town? He said: Yes, this was so. That we did not allow this, and that one did not see or hear any thing of the kind, for we wished to live peaceably and orderly. This pleased them, and they said that for this reason they were living so secluded, as they did not like it either. But, said they, when stranger Indians bring rum to you, what do you do? He answered: If strange Indians come to us and have rum with them, we ask if they wish to stay with us over night, and if they say that they do, we take their rum from them and put it away for safe keeping; and when they take leave of us we hand it back to them; for with us they must not pour out any and drink. They replied that this was very right and proper.

We then went the rest of the way to town, stopping with the Chief Togahaju, whom we found alone, for we had met his people on our way from Onondago. He was very glad to see us, and said to Brother David: I have always believed you would come, for I dreamed about you. Brother David told him that he came from Onondago, where he had had a talk about various things with the chiefs, and that for the same reason he had also come here, asked him to give him the opportunity, as we did not wish to stay long, as in this time of year we were afraid a heavy snow might fall, and we might be snowed in. He said we should have come a month sooner; then we would have had time to stay with him awhile, and be able to look around. He then seated himself beside us, and Brother David told him that he wished to ask him several questions, which he would like answered. He said: What I may know, you shall also know.

Brother David then asked him if he had ever heard any thing that the Onondagos were not satisfied that he had received our Indians and given them land along the Susquehanna? That he [Z.] had heard something of this, and desired to be informed more about it; that he had not asked the Onondagos about it, as he wished to hear and learn it from him. The chief answered: Of the Onondagos I do not know anything; have not heard anything like this from them, and I do not believe there is anything in it. Would not know of any reason either, for when the Six Nations had met for a treaty at Lancaster, after the last war, and had kindled a fire, and said that this should not be extinguished, even should it rain as hard as it could. This fire, therefore, is still burning; and that they had but two fires on the Susquehanna, namely, one at Zeninge, and one at Friedenshuetten, so that when, therefore, the Six Nations traveled by this way, they could smoke their pipe there. He had, therefore, placed our Indians at these places to keep up the fires, and that we had to see to it that they were not extinguished. And in order that we should not think that he did not do this on his own account only, he would let us know that all he had settled and treated with us last spring, he had talked over with the Grand Council at Onondago. The whole assembly had given their consent to it. He thus did not remember of any dissatisfaction having been caused in the Council, nor had he ever heard of any. He knew, however, of two persons who had spoken to him about this in a very inimical way; one of them being an Oneida chief from Anohochquage, and the other an Onondago from Zeninge, who did not, however, have any say in the matter. These two had expressed themselves to him in the following words: We hate these people, for we know them and do not want them in our country. We dislike them, and on their account we also dislike you, as you have accepted them. So much, he said, he did know about the matter.

Brother David further asked him whether he had, during the summer, sent a String of Wampum with a message to Friedenshuetten, and what the latter was? He answered: Yes, he had sent a message to us, which had been caused by the following circumstance, namely: that soon after we had gone home from our visit here last spring, there came one message after the other to him, which said that we intended establishing a storehouse at Friedenshuetten, and another at Tiaoga, making the two places trading posts. At first he did not wish to believe it. However, as so much about it had come to his ears, he thought he had better send a message, and again remind us of the conditions which had then been determined on. Then he also thought that we might not have clearly understood one or the other thing. He had, however, sent us good words in it:

Cousins! I have given you the land, but not for the purpose of allowing the white people to build storehouses thereon. Therefore adjust yourselves to what we have decided with each other. Do not give the traders place among you, and do not permit them to build any houses.

Brother David saw from this, that this message 'had been given us incorrectly. He kept quiet, however, and did not appear to worry; told the Chief that he could be sure that all things which had been told him about us were nothing but lies, and that I could tell him quite different about the matter, for after our return home from our visit here at that time, we found some traders who had just come into our place about the same time. We called them before us, and in his name and that of the Six Nations we told them that they could not come and settle here with us, and that they must clear out and go back home.

We were glad that you had given us the power to order away from our town any traders, for up to that time we could not have done this, as the place was not yet ours. He should firmly believe, therefore, that it was also our wish that Friedenshuetten should not be made a trading post, for these traders we did not wish to have among us, even if he were to allow it; for they brought to the Indians nothing but wickedness and disorder. David had then already told him that should he at any time hear any thing wrong about us, he should not believe it till he should hear it direct from us; and this he wished to recommend to him again; for as there always would be Indians who would be unfriendly to us, and who would invent lies about us, he should pay no attention to them, but tell them at once that they were lies.

Brother David further said: Now he would like to ask a question more: Whether, if our Indians in Friedenshuetten had occasion to confer with him or with the Six Nations, it would be necessary to do it through another chief, or whether they themselves could speak personally with him? He told them that it was not necessary to do it through any one else, but that they could at once address him, as he was the man. Brother David asked further, what relations he had with Newallike? That as far as he knew he was now the Delaware chief. He answered: Yes; he is, but you in Friedenshuetten still have the preference, for we, Aquanoschioni, have our fire there. He then said that when he had received Newallike and his Indians, he had given him night quarters at the upper end of this lake, (that is) he had given him permission to live there a year and to plant there. That during last spring he had offered them another place between Onondago and Cajuga, but that they had asked permission to remain where they were, which he had granted them. He earnestly recommended Brother David to make it very plain to our Indians in Friedenshuetten what was their wish about the white people or traders. That we should not permit them to remain with us, or build any houses, or allow them to bring any rum to us. He did not wish to say that we should not allow any traders to come there. This they might do, but as soon as they had disposed of their wares they should go on further.

In the evening we had many visits from town. They also brought us food, as the Chief was quite alone and had nothing prepared.

October 31. At noon, after we had made all the necessary agreements with the Chief, we again prepared ourselves for our journey. He told us that after the chiefs were again at home, he would refer everything to them that we had agreed on, and that he was very glad that he had had again the opportunity of speking with Brother David, and to learn how matters stood. After we had taken a friendly fareewll, we journeyed with the son of the Chief, who intended to go to the settlement, and arrived

November 1, safely at Onondago, and found that our Samuel had gone to Zeninge.

November 2. In the Council House we received the answer from the Chiefs as follows:

Brother Genousheracheri! The questions which you have asked us we have considered, and will now give you our ideas about them. Had you spoken to us through belts, we would have exchanged one or two belts with you. However, we do not see any necessity therefor, for the matter was finished and decided long ago, and shall remain so and not be changed. We let you know herewith that the matter which the Chief Togahaju, in Cayuga, treated and concluded with you, meets with our and the whole house's consent, and we all know what he has done. We are not only all satisfied therewith, but it pleases us very much that you live in Friedenshuetten, and that you shall have a council fire there, which is intrusted to you, and which is no small matter. We have heard your mind in regard to living among the Indians; you are their teachers, and you do well that you instruct them in good things. They need it, for the Delawares, our Cousins, are very much inclined toward the bad. This could be plainly seen in the late war.

If your Indians, our Cousins, have anything to propose, they shall at all times have liberty to speak personally with us, and bring the matter before us without the aid of another chief, who may not be of the same mind as they. As to your religion and your religious services; we do not wish to find fault with that, but that it will please us if you will continue among the Indians with your instructions.

Here it is well to note, writes Brother David, that it was well that we had brought forward our business without strings or belts of wampum, as there occurred so many special points; for example, the matter of Newallike, the Delaware Chief, and the Chief in Cajuga; and then again with the Chief in Cajuga about the Onondagos, for in this way everything remains in its place, and does not get out any further. Brother David showed his delight and pleasure at the answer, and thanked them therefore.

The Chief Tianoronto, the Speaker, permitted Brother David to look through his documents, among which was his Warrant from Sir William Johnson, appointing him the Chief and Speaker of the Onondago Nation, together with the great Seal.

Brother David then announced his departure, and said that he was very sorry that he could not remain with them any longer, as the time of the year was already so late, and that in this region there was nothing at this time to expect but snow, therefore we must hurry in order not to be snowed in. They asked Brother David whether he expected ever to come here again to visit them? He replied: If it please the Lord and I live, I will see you again; which they were very glad to hear. We then bade them a friendly farewell and went to our lodging place. During the night a party of warriors, of which they were the last and who expect to leave here to-morrow, had their war dance, which lasted till toward morning.

November 3. After we had given farewell to our hosts, as well as to the Chief Aschinochiata, who had always unto this time been our good friend, we bade farewell at different houses, and all expressed their joy that we had visited them. We rested over night in our former quarters at the Susquehanna Lake.

November 4. To-day we had a hard day's journey before us, for which we were greatly concerned, as we did not have a pilot and had to pass alone through these wild woods, which were filled on all sides with fallen trees, and where it is an art to keep in the right direction, as no straight course could be kept, because of having to cross and recross the path.

We were, however, as happy in the evening, when we found our canoe in good condition, as though some one had given us a most valuable present.

November 5. We started off again, having now overcome all the difficulties of the journey, and we passed down the creek very quickly, without much effort. Toward evening we chased a large bear, which had crossed the stream ahead of us. However, we could not overtake him, much as we would have liked to have him. We were, however, made happy later with a raccoon which we shot.

November 6. Noon; we called in at the Onondago Town in the Fork. There were, however, very few at home. In the evening we arrived at Zeninge, and put up again with the Nantikok Chief, where we were welcome.

November 7. Visited Canai Town, across the water. They wished to tell us all kinds of tales about Freidenshuetten, which they had heard. We told them, however, that there was no truth in them. We also spoke with Samuel, who had arrived here from Onondago only a day ahead of us. He resolved to go with us to Friedenshuetten, and to leave his wife here, as she did not wish to go along.

November 8. Toward noon we again proceeded on our way, and passed by Tschochnot and the Cajuga Town. We called at both places, and the Indians were very friendly toward us.

November 2. We passed Oweke, and on the *19th of November,* Scheckschiquannunck, and reached on the *11th* to our joy, our Brethren at Friedenshuetten, from whence we again journey, and by way of Christiansbrunn, arrived on

November 22 in Bethlehem. Many thousand thanks be given our good Lord for His gracious leading and protection, during our whole journey.

REV. W. M. BEAUCHAMP'S NOTES ON JOURNAL OF OCTOBER, 1766.

The journey to Onondaga was occasioned by reports that the Cayugas had exceeded their powers in granting lands to Indians at Friedenshuetten.

Oct. 14.   Friedenshuetten was Wihilusing.

Oct. 17.   Tschochnot is now Choconut.

Oct. 19.   By conquest the Nanticokes became tributary to the Five Nations. Zeninge was Otsiningo. The Nanticokes had a bad moral reputation.

20.   The Indian minister may have been David Fowler or Samson Occum. Samuel Ashpo was at Otsiningo in 1763, and the Rev. Eleazar Moseley at Oquago the same year.

21. This Onondaga town was at Chenango Forks.

23. The last fork was at Cortland.

25. They could have gone up the west branch to Big Lake in Preble. The lake they reached was the large lake in Tully, from the distance traveled and that to Onondaga Creek.

26. North of the lake their road lay through Tully Valley and Christian Hollow, the latter named from a Revolutionary soldier.

27. Otschinochiata, was the Bunt. (Otsinoghiyata). When the Rev. Samuel Kirkland saw him at Onondaga in 1764, he said the venerable old chief spoke like a Demosthenes for over half an hour, and then embraced him and kissed him on each cheek. Kirkland returned the compliment. The Bunt died during the Revolution. The deep snow in June seems to have amused the missionaries. The full Onondaga Council included fourteen chiefs. The Conestogas were the ancient Andastes or Minquas, whom the Iroquois fought so long. There seems a reference to the conference at Oswego in 1766, between Johnson and Pontiac, the noted western chief.

28. I am not sure who this minister was at Onondaga. The Rev. Samuel Kirkland was the one in the Seneca county, and he visited Onondaga in 1764, not on his return.

30. This dangerous creek was the Owasco, (bridge over water) and there must have been a similar bridge at an early day. He does not say so, but they probably first lodged at Skaneateles, and on their return at Owasco Lake.

Nov. 2. This informal mode was proper at this time, as there was no new business, but mere explanations of what had been done. Chief Tianaronto or Teyawarunte was probably mentioned in 1756, was Speaker in 1762 and held that office in 1775. This was Zeisberger's last visit to Onondaga.

3. The Susquehanna Lake was the large lake in Tully.

7. Canai town was that of the Conoys. Samuel was a Nanticoke, but commonly called Conoy Sam. He was with the Moravian Indians in Philadelphia and wished to live with them at Wihilusing, where he was baptized Aug. 19, 1766. There was some hesitation about this because of

the burial customs of the Nanticokes.   He was reinstated as a Nanticoke chief by the Six Nations in 1768.

11.   They stayed at Friedenshuetten till Nov. 15.

ADDITIONAL REVOLUTIONARY SOLDIERS.

Josiah Curtis, son of Zachariah, died in Elbridge in 18—.   He served from Vermont as sergeant in Capt. Nathaniel Smith's company, and moved from East Dorset to Elbridge about 1805, with his wife, Tamson Gale.   They had five children.   He was a farmer, and it is said "he always wore Union blue."

William Goodwin married Amy Stanley, who was born in Goshen, Ct., March 1, 1761.   His third wife was Miss Mills, and by her he had a son Joseph, born in Marcellus, where the father died about 1813.   He was a corporal under Capt. Moses Seymour in 1779.

In memory of | *Elisha Gridley* | died|30th Dec. 1842,| Aged 83 yrs. 9 m's. 6 ds.|

In memory of |*Louis,* Wife of|Elisha Gridley,|Died|Sept. 15, 1847|Aged|83 y'rs. 7 m's &|15 days.|

In Soule cemetery, Sennett, where some Skaneateles people were buried.   He was a Rev. pensioner and served in the Conn. militia.

Samuel Gridley died in Onondaga Valley, April 11, 1824, ae. 73.   He was in Capt. Matthew Smith's Co., Farmington, Co. in '81.

Benjamin Lee, born in Lyme, Ct., Feb. 27, 1740, married Mary Dorr, Aug. 23, '60, ('43-'25).   From Lyme he went to Bethlehem, N. Y., and then to Pompey and Truxton, dying in Truxton, July 2, 1826.   He was in Capt. Eliphalet Holmes' Co., in '76, and under Capt. Isaac Stone at Saratoga.

In|memory of|*Ebenezer Phelps,*|who died|Nov. 1, 1832,| aged 73 years.| I am now ready to be offered.|the time of my departure is come.|

In Memory of |*Mrs. Submit,*|Wife of|Ebenr. Phelps, who|died Aug. 16, 1821, Ae. 59.|
Great God I own thy sentence just|| And nature must decay| I yield my body to the dust | To dwell with fellow clay.|

Yet faith may triumph o'er the grave|And trample on the
   tombs,|
For Jesus, my Redeemer lives,|My God, my Saviour comes.|
This Rev. pensioner served in the Mass. militia, and
was one of the founders of St. Peter's church, Auburn, but
was buried by the rector of St. James' church, Skaneateles.
Some other pioneers in this cemetery may have seen service.

Ephraim Pierce.—The Skaneateles Columbian announced the death of this pensioner, father of Major Samuel
Pierce of Skaneateles, which occurred in Le Ray, N. Y.,
Sept. 24, 1834, in his 90th year. He had lived in Marcellus,
where he bought land on lot 61, near Thorn Hill, June 21,
1815, which he sold April 29, 1829, on his removal to Jeffer-
son county. There he applied for a pension, Nov. 26, 1832,
which was granted a year later. He was born at Concord,
Mass., March 15, 1746, serving in '75, as a private in Massa-
chusetts from Putney, Vt., and later as an ensign. He was
at Bennington and Saratoga, and was discharged March 1,
'78. He left Vermont in 1806. His wives were respec-
tively Mary and Abigail. By the first he had nine children,
from '64 to '91. His first wife died Feb. 4, 1801, and he
soon after married Naby (Abigail) Howe, perhaps in New
Hampshire.

Rufus Rose came to Marcellus in the spring of 1803, and
died there in 1826, ae. 74. He was grandfather of Hon.
Nathan K. Hall, and went first to Lyme, Ct., then to Bennington, Vt., and Hoosick, N. Y., where his wife Catharine
was born. She died in Marcellus in 1813, aged 55 years.
His name appears in Capt. James Chapman's Company,
New London, Ct., in '75, and in the Mass. census of 1790.

Gen. Othniel Taylor, who died in Canandaigua, Aug. 5,
1815, in his 67th year, once lived in Onondaga county
according to the Onondaga Register. He was lieutenant
and adjutant under Col. Thomas Marshall in '77, and held
the same rank and that of captain in the Mass. 10th to '81.
In 1790 he was in Charlemont, Mass.

Capt. Tousley, father of Judge Sylvenus Tousley of Man-
lius, bore the same name as his son, who was born in 1780.
This might carry the father's birth back to 1758, and the
latter's service was in Capt. Stoddard's company, in '75.
The Onondaga Register said he was drowned in Skaneateles

lake, Dec. 20, 1815, but gave no farther account, nor is there any local tradition of this.

Capt. Martin Godard, a Marcellus pioneer, according to Mr. Belus F. North was a lieutenant in the Connecticut militia in 1784-5, and he thought he served in the Revolution, though his name is not in the published rolls. Such an early rank and his subsequent title would indicate such service, and records are imperfect. He came to Marcellus with his nine sons and bought land there Sept. 1, 1805. In his will of Nov. 25, 1807, probated March 2, 1808, all these were named, but the oldest had died between May 25 and Nov. 25, 1807. Dr. Parsons said that four of the sons died of typhus fever that year. It should be the father and three sons, the former probably dying in December. As the third son was born in 1781, his father's birth was probably before 1755. His wife, Abigail, survived him, and his youngest son died Dec. 31, 1875, in Baldwinsville.

In volume for 1914 Jabesh Hall should be Jabesh Clark, as in context. Powel I. Amerman, pensioner in Cayuga county, rests in the De Groff cemetery, town of Owasco, toward Owasco Lake. He died Feb. 25, '41, ae. 78 years, and his wife, Charity, died April 29, 1844, in her 76th year.

INDEX.